IMAGES
of America

LOS LUNAS

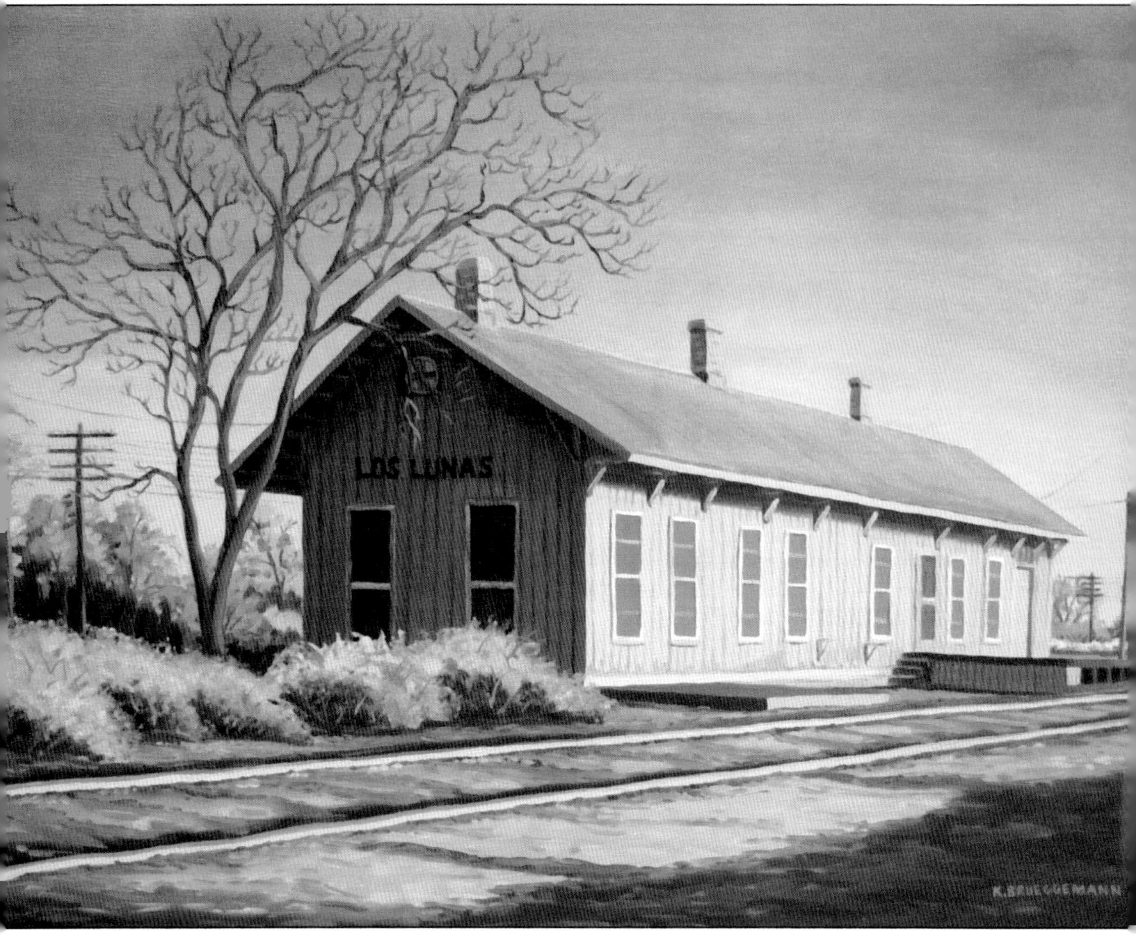

The arrival of the railroad in the village of Los Lunas in 1881 meant that local agricultural products such as grain and wool could reach wider and more profitable markets, and local residents could travel greater distances from the village. The Los Lunas Depot was the center of that activity. (Painting by Karen Brueggemann, courtesy of Los Lunas Museum of Heritage and Arts.)

On the Cover: Farming has always been an important activity in Los Lunas. The Pasqual Sais farm, located on Los Lentes Road, was one of the most successful. Pasqual Sais, on the right, is overseeing the bailing of hay some time around 1915. (Courtesy of the Valencia County Historical Society.)

IMAGES
of America

LOS LUNAS

Baldwin G. Burr

ARCADIA
PUBLISHING

ISBN 978-0-7385-9534-4

Published by Arcadia Publishing
Charleston, South Carolina

Printed in the United States of America

Library of Congress Control Number: 2011945297

For all general information, please contact Arcadia Publishing:
Telephone 843-853-2070
Fax 843-853-0044
E-mail sales@arcadiapublishing.com
For customer service and orders:
Toll-Free 1-888-313-2665

Visit us on the Internet at www.arcadiapublishing.com

This book is dedicated to the memory of James Fernández, longtime Valencia County official, endlessly knowledgeable Los Lunas historian, and the founding coordinator of the Los Lunas Museum of Heritage and Arts.

Contents

ACKNOWLEDGMENTS

Many people helped make this book possible. My sincere thanks go to Dr. Richard Melzer, Dr. Margaret McDonald, Patty Guggino, and John Taylor for their scholarly and critical reading of the text. Laura and Alex Sanchez, Barbara Castillo Arnold, and Louis Huning all read and helpfully commented on portions of the text as well. Of course, any errors or omissions that remain are the responsibility of the author. The staff at the Los Lunas Public Library and Los Lunas Museum of Heritage and Arts was especially helpful throughout this project. I am grateful to Cynthia Shetter, Andrea Chavez, and Ricardo Gonzales at the library and museum for their help proofreading, locating photographs, and obtaining permissions.

I am also grateful to all of those who provided access to historical photographs, including Charles Griego, Barbara Bergère Nau, Buddy Major, Ruth Perea, Robert Vialpando, C.C. Castillo, Brenda Uptain, and Pete and Hortense Torres.

I appreciate the wisdom and guidance provided by the very capable acquisition editors at Arcadia Publishing: Jared Jackson, Stacia Bannerman, Lauren Hummer, and Laura Bruns.

Finally, I would like to acknowledge the unflagging enthusiasm and encouragement I received on this project from my wife, Laura Gilbert Burr.

Introduction

The village of Los Lunas is located along the route of the ancient El Camino Real, the Spanish Royal Road from Mexico City to Santa Fe, New Mexico. In addition, village land shares boundaries with Tiwa Indian lands. Finally, German merchants brought Anglo goods and culture to the village. It is this overlapping influence of different cultures that has made life in the village of Los Lunas interesting, challenging, and richly rewarding for residents throughout its history.

The Luna family, for whom the village is named, was influential in local, state, and federal government affairs. Don Antonio José Luna was active in politics in the earliest days of New Mexico's territorial period. He passed his political interest and influence to his sons Tranquilino and Solomon Luna. Tranquilino was a delegate to the US Congress from the Territory of New Mexico, and Solomon was a member of the Republican National Committee. Don Antonio's daughter Eloisa Luna Otero Bergère was the mother of Nina Otero-Warren, a strong advocate for the rights of women during the 1920s. Nina Otero-Warren was also the first Hispanic woman to run for the US House of Representatives.

Los Lunas was always a rural, agricultural community. The presence of the Rio Grande, which flows through the village, has made the cultivation of crops possible. Field crops such as wheat, corn, and alfalfa are grown, and vegetables, especially green chiles, have long been produced by area farmers. Although field crops dominate local agriculture today, sheep were once the foundation of agricultural wealth and prosperity in Valencia County. The Luna and Otero families combined efforts in the 1850s and drove herds of over 50,000 sheep from New Mexico to California. Profits from the sale of sheep and wool formed the basis of wealth and influence for these families for many years to come.

The Huning and Major families maintained extensive cattle ranching operations in the open grassland around Los Lunas. The Hunings were early merchant pioneers in Los Lunas. In the 1860s, Louis Huning followed his brother Franz from Germany to New Mexico. Joined at various times by brothers Carl and Henry, Louis established a mercantile business that was operated by the Huning family until the 1990s. Louis and his wife, Henrika, were instrumental in establishing another early Los Lunas pioneer merchant, Emiliano Castillo Sr. German immigrants John Becker and Simon Neustadt also established successful businesses in Los Lunas. After first working for Louis Huning in Los Lunas, John Becker moved to Belen and established a mercantile business there.

Transportation has played an important role in the development of the village of Los Lunas. Two elements of transportation in particular have been important. The first was the coming of the railroad to Los Lunas in 1881. The railroad provided a means to reach wider markets for local agricultural products and brought a wider variety of goods to village residents. The railroad also allowed convenient travel to and from Los Lunas. The second important transportation development for Los Lunas was the pre-1937 path of US Route 66. Many local businesses were established in the period from 1927 to 1937 specifically to serve travelers coming through town on Route 66. The presence of the interstate highway on the west side of Los Lunas is spurring the same kind of economic progress that was provided by Route 66 during the 1930s.

The built environment has also contributed to the quality of life in Los Lunas. An indigenous architecture with Spanish and Native American roots has dominated building in and around the village until quite recently. Adobe and *terrone* have been used in residential structures from the most humble to the most splendidly elaborate, as well as public and commercial buildings. Made of adobe, the original Huning Mercantile Company compound has been in constant use from the 1860s to the present day. Newer structures, such as the Los Lunas Transportation Center, pay homage to the architectural styles of the past.

Several Los Lunas members of ranching and merchant families have held public office and have played a large role in local government. The Huning and Castillo families, for instance, have provided six of the mayors of the village of Los Lunas. The mayor and village council members were instrumental in creating and supporting the Los Lunas Museum of Heritage and Arts.

Religion and education have also been strong components of life in the village of Los Lunas. The Catholic Church maintained a presence in the area prior to the Pueblo Revolt of 1680 and is an important part of many residents' lives to this day. Before public schools were provided, the first schools were in the homes of prominent families and then were established by the church.

The weather in Los Lunas has always invited residents outside. Year-round recreational opportunities like horseback riding, picnics in the bosque, hiking along the river, and organized sports continue to be popular today.

One

Founders

When Francisco Coronado entered New Mexico and explored the Rio Grande in 1540, there were already Pueblo Indian settlements in the vicinity of what was to become the village of Los Lunas. In 1680, the Pueblo Revolt drove the Spanish from the area. After Don Diego de Vargas reconquered New Mexico in 1692, Doña Ana Sandoval de Manzanares petitioned the Spanish Crown for a land grant, which came to be known as the San Clemente grant. Felix de la Candelaria inherited the land in 1716, and he sold it to Domingo Luna around 1750. Born in 1808, Antonio José Luna inherited the land from Domingo Luna. It eventually passed to his heirs, including sons Tranquilino and Solomon and daughter Eloisa.

Solomon Luna married Adelaida Otero, and Solomon's sister, Eloisa Luna, married Adelaida's brother Manuel B. Otero, thus uniting two of the most affluent and influential families in the territory of New Mexico. The Luna-Otero families would control ranching, business, and political activity in New Mexico until the 1930s, and the village of Los Lunas would become the center of that activity.

In 1876, the Lunas were instrumental in moving the seat of Valencia County from Tomé to Los Lunas. Don Antonio, Tranquilino, and Solomon all held important elected county offices. In particular, Solomon Luna was a key player in the territory of New Mexico's bid for statehood during the latter part of the 19th century and the early 20th. Strategy sessions were held at Solomon's Los Lunas home. During convention sessions, it was said that a nod or a frown from him could determine whether a particular provision would be included or deleted from the final document.

The village of Los Lunas was incorporated in 1928, and about that same time, US Highway 66, the "Mother Road," was routed through Los Lunas. The unique north–south alignment was active until 1937, when Route 66 bypassed Los Lunas and went east–west through Albuquerque. The road brought national highway traffic through Los Lunas, which led to much local commercial development.

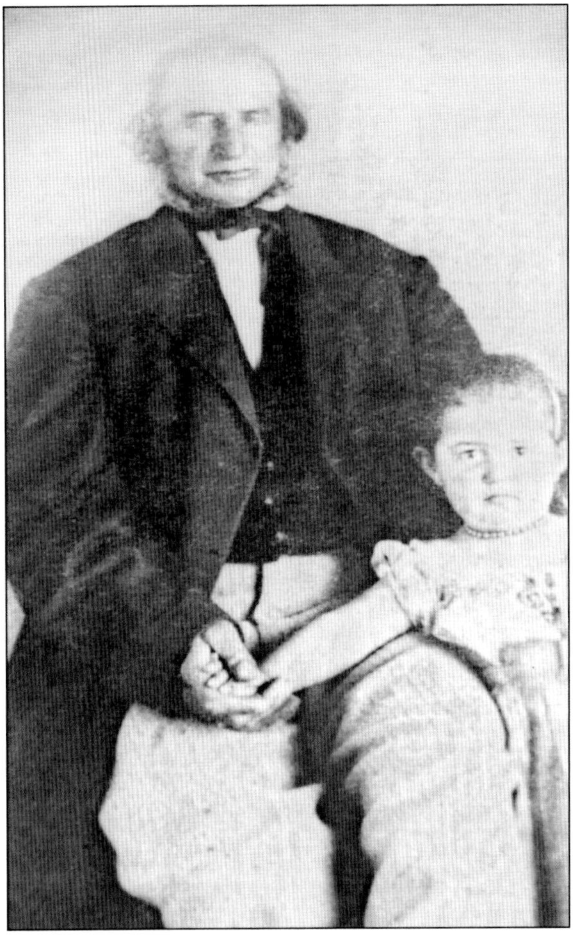

Don Antonio José Luna, shown here with his daughter, Eloisa, is frequently called "the father of Los Lunas." He joined with Don Antonio José Otero from Peralta to drive a herd of over 50,000 sheep from New Mexico to California in 1855. At the time, a single sheep in New Mexico sold for 50¢, while that same sheep brought $15 from hungry California gold miners. Luna and Otero became instant millionaires (in today's dollars), and that trip was the foundation of both families' wealth and political influence for many years to come. (Courtesy of Los Lunas Museum of Heritage and Arts.)

In 1880, the Santa Fe Railroad sought a right-of-way from the Luna family that would have required the destruction of the existing Luna home. The railroad offered Luna $13,000 with which he could construct a new home in return for the right-of-way. Pictured here is the Luna Mansion from the east side as originally completed in 1881. Unfortunately, Luna died before he could occupy his new home. (Courtesy of Barbara Bergère Nau.)

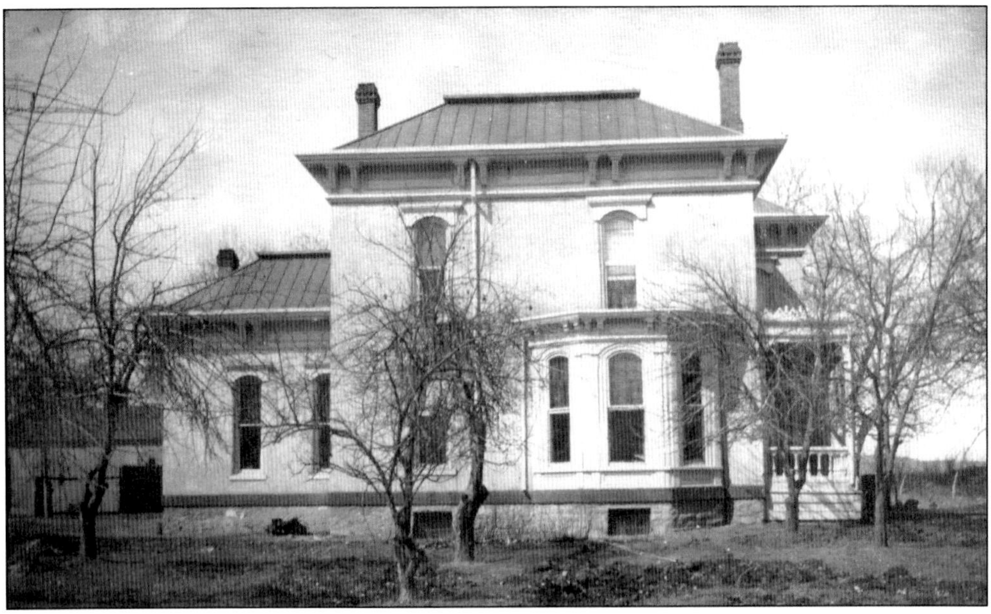

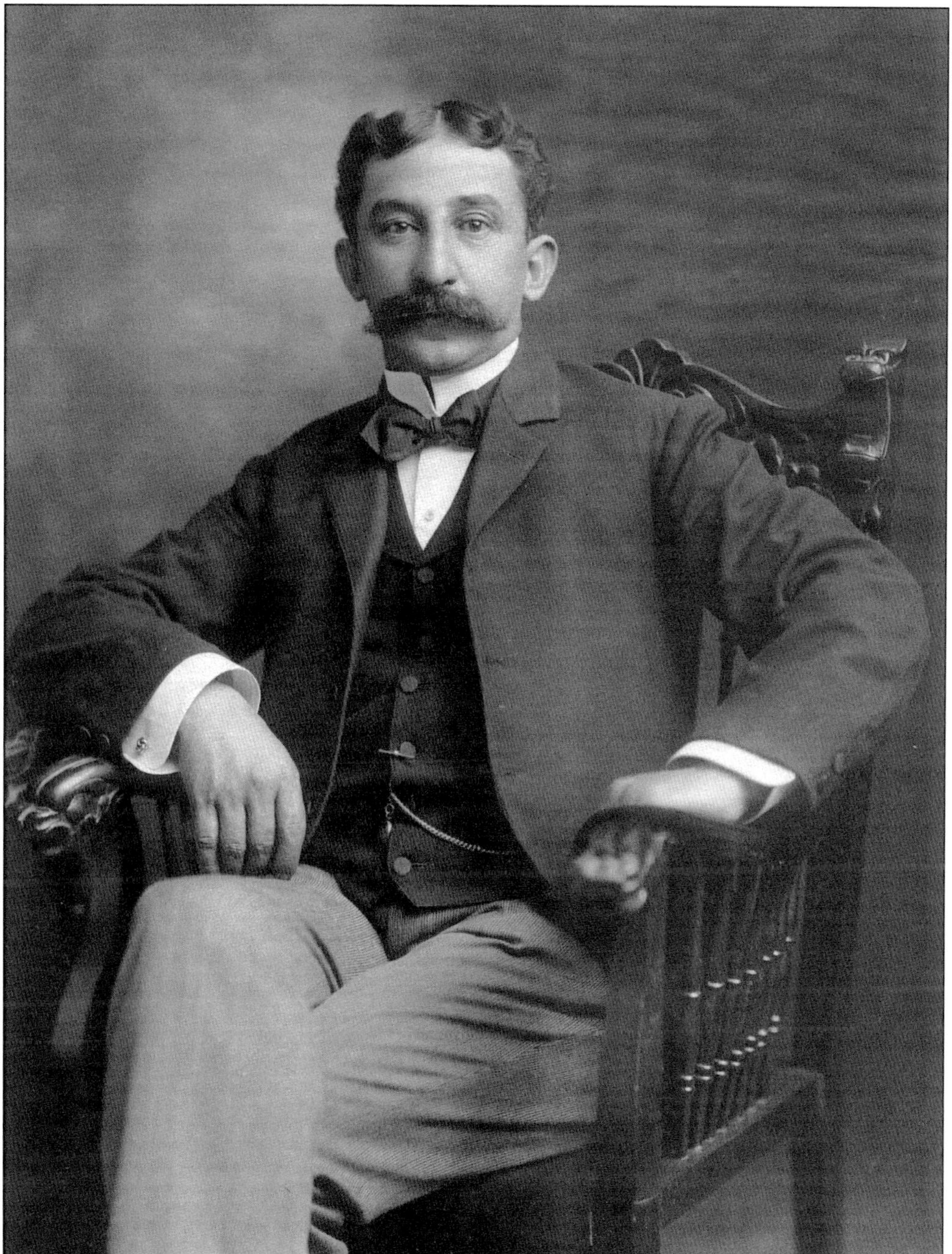

The son of Don Antonio José Luna and Isabel Baca Luna, Solomon Luna was born in Los Lunas on October 18, 1858. He was educated by private tutors and at St. Louis University. After college, he returned to Los Lunas to join his father raising sheep. In addition, he held many public offices, including probate clerk (1885), county sheriff (1892), and county treasurer (1894). In 1896, he was chosen as a member of the Republican National Committee to represent the New Mexico Territory. In 1881, Solomon Luna married Adelaida Otero. (Courtesy of the Valencia County Historical Society.)

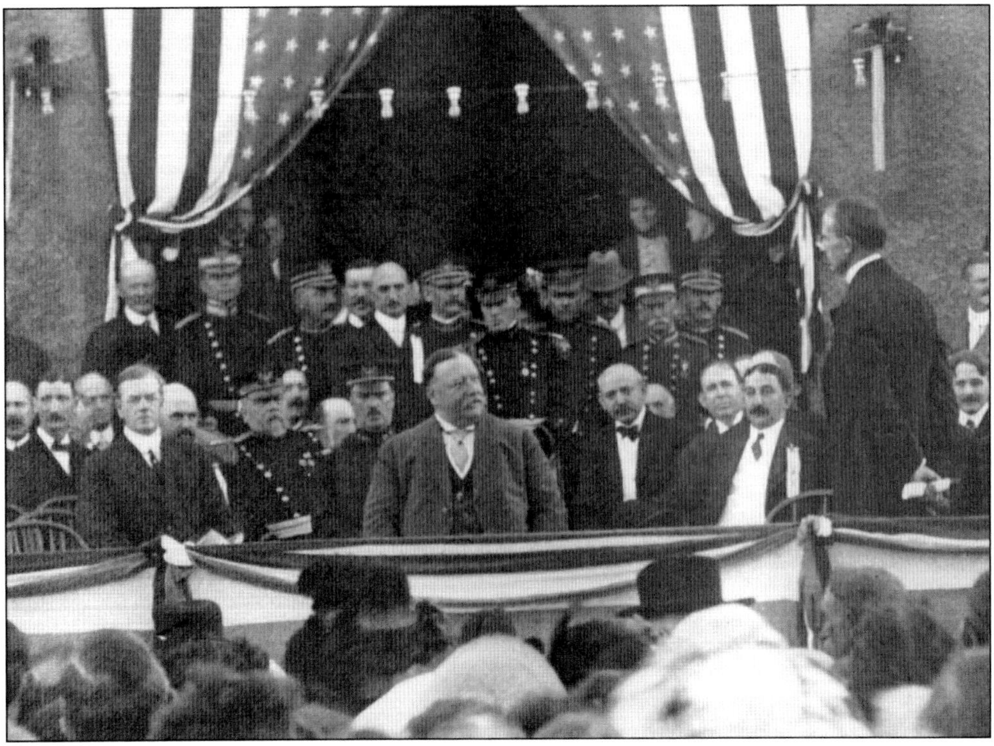

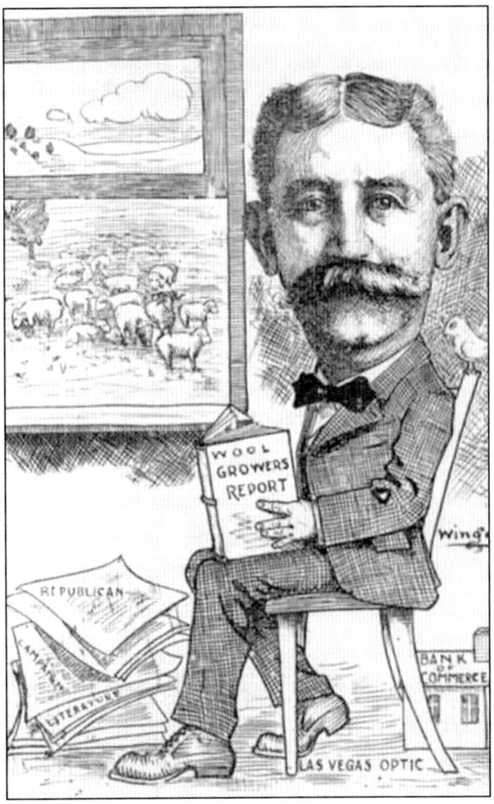

Solomon Luna, seated beside President Taft at the Alvarado Hotel in Albuquerque in 1909, was a powerful advocate for New Mexico statehood. As a delegate to the 1910 constitutional convention, he played a major role in the development of the New Mexico constitution. Anticipating the influx of Anglo citizens into New Mexico following statehood and the possibility that the rights of Hispanics might be jeopardized, he crafted provisions that made future amendment of the state constitution extremely difficult. (Courtesy of the Albuquerque Museum.)

This political cartoon from the 1906 Las Vegas *Optic* illustrates the range of Solomon Luna's interests and influences. The sheep and the "wool growers report" refer to his ranching activities. One of the papers, labeled "literature," notes his education at St. Louis University. The bank to refers Luna's membership on the board of directors of the Albuquerque Bank of Commerce. The papers labeled "Republican" and "campaign" acknowledge his power in state politics. (Courtesy of Office of New Mexico State Historian.)

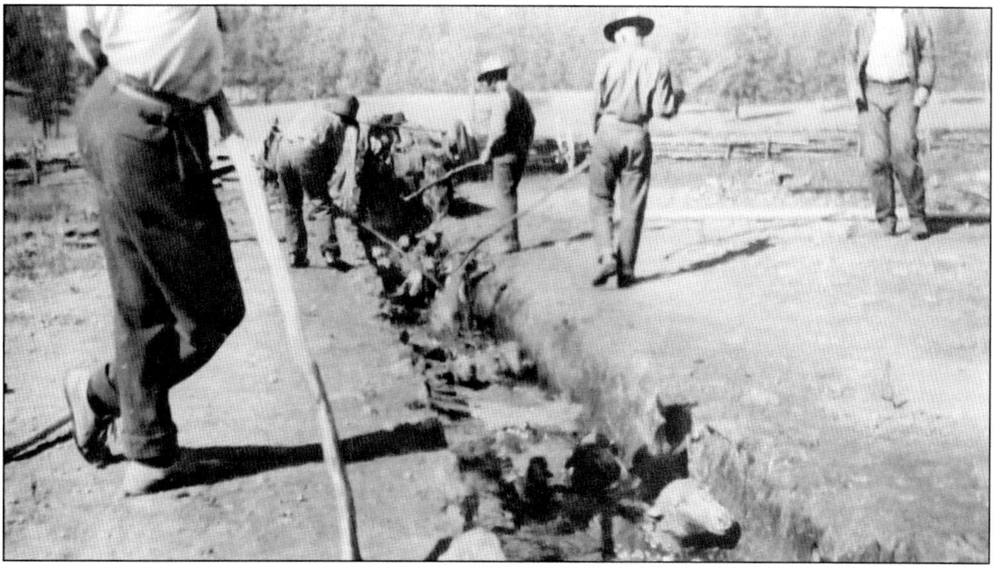

On the morning of August 30, 1912, the body of Solomon Luna was found face down in a sheep-dipping tank on the ranch of Montague Stevens at Horse Springs, New Mexico. New Mexico had been a state for just eight months. Solomon Luna stumbled into the trench and drowned in the early hours of the morning. Although many rumors and suspicions surfaced, Luna's death was ultimately ruled an accident. Thus the life of one of the most enlightened and powerful politicians in New Mexican history tragically ended. Upon his death, Luna's ranching interests and political influence passed to his nephew Eduardo Otero, son of Manuel B. Otero and Eloisa Luna. Eduardo married Josephita Manderfield Armijo, and they moved into the Luna Mansion in 1912. Eduardo is shown here with his favorite horse, Prince. (Both, courtesy of Barbara Bergère Nau.)

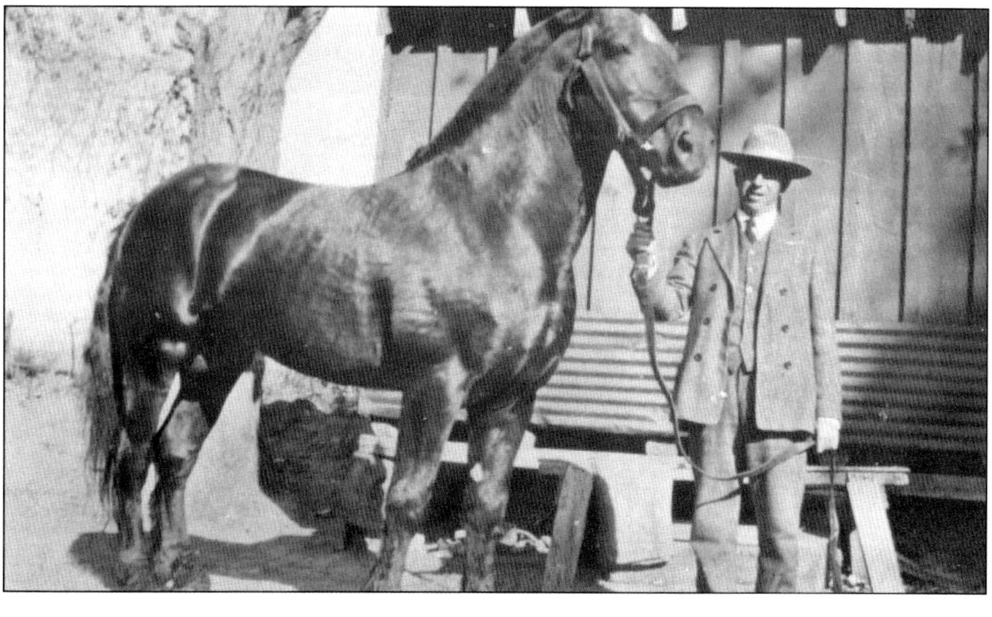

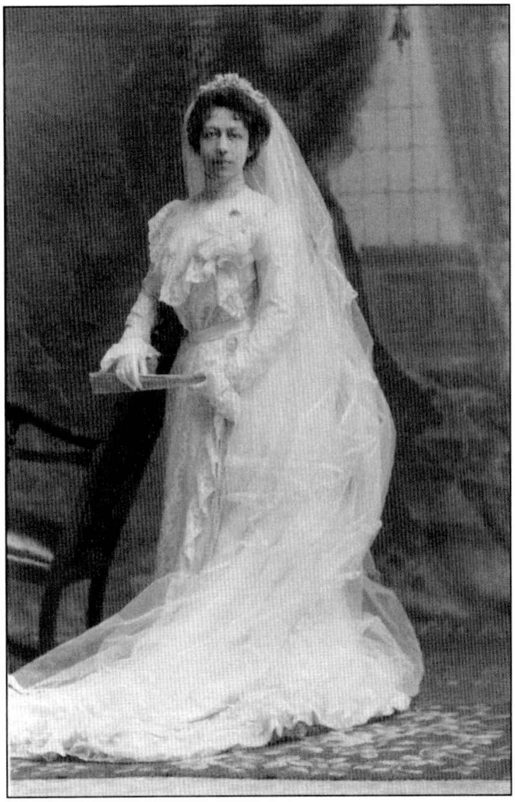

Josephita Manderfield Armijo is pictured here on her wedding day. Her father, William Manderfield, was the publisher of the *Santa Fe New Mexican*, a newspaper that was characterized as "lively, political, and opinionated." (Courtesy of Los Lunas Museum of Heritage and Arts.)

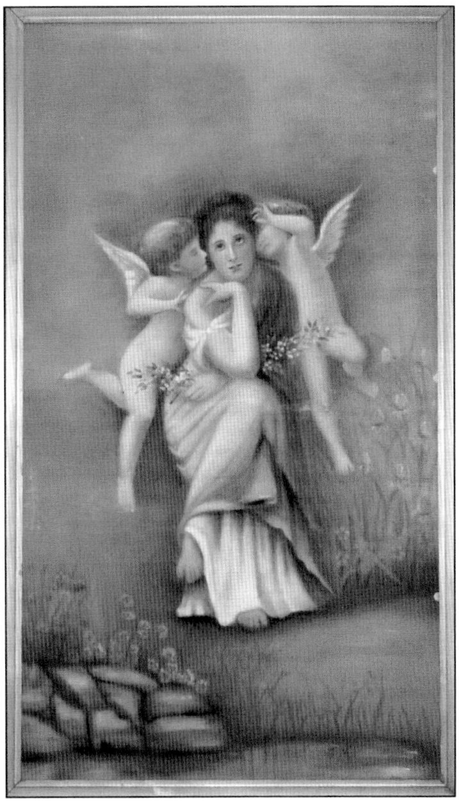

Along with her sisters, Cyrilla and Eugenia, Josephita Manderfield Otero had a strong aesthetic sensibility. She undertook a major renovation and redecoration of the family home, now called the Luna Mansion. Also an accomplished artist, she painted this classic Victorian work some time between 1915 and 1920. It still hangs at the Luna Mansion. (Author's collection.)

Josephita Manderfield's first husband was George Washington Armijo, the grandson of Col. J. Francisco Chaves, the powerful president of the New Mexico Territorial Senate. Armijo served as a sergeant in the Rough Riders during the Spanish-American War and was Col. Theodore Roosevelt's aide. President Roosevelt was godfather to George and Josephita's son Theodore "Teddy" Roosevelt Manderfield Armijo Otero. Teddy is shown here in his military school uniform. (Courtesy of Barbara Bergère Nau.)

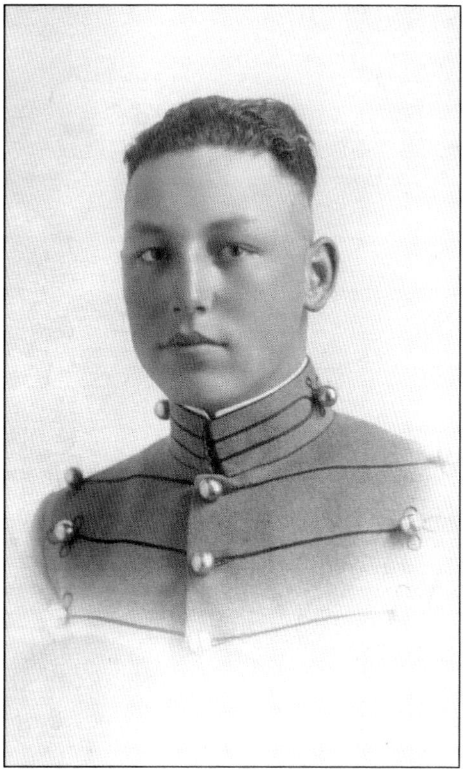

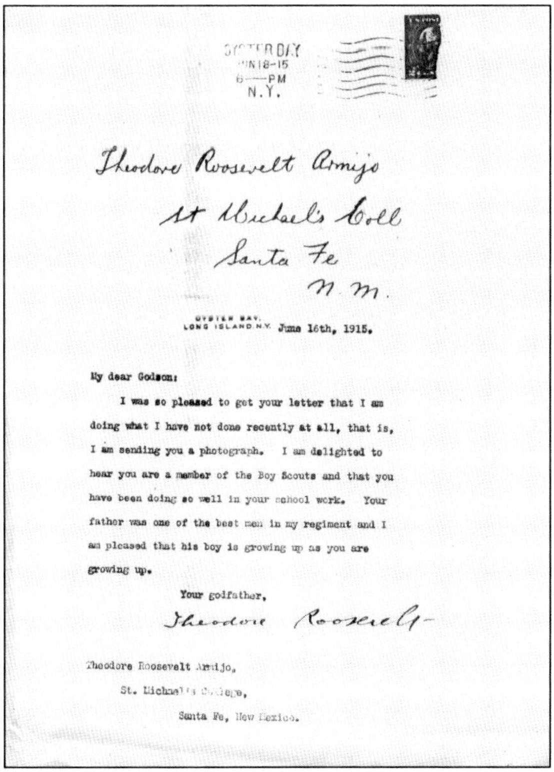

OYSTER BAY
JUN 18-15
6-PM
N.Y.

Theodore Roosevelt Armijo
St Michael's Coll
Santa Fe
N. M.

OYSTER BAY,
LONG ISLAND N.Y. June 16th, 1915.

My dear Godson:

I was so pleased to get your letter that I am doing what I have not done recently at all, that is, I am sending you a photograph. I am delighted to hear you are a member of the Boy Scouts and that you have been doing so well in your school work. Your father was one of the best men in my regiment and I am pleased that his boy is growing up as you are growing up.

Your godfather,

Theodore Roosevelt

Theodore Roosevelt Armijo,
St. Michael's College,
Santa Fe, New Mexico.

Pres. Theodore Roosevelt wrote this letter in 1915 to his godson Teddy. The president traveled to New Mexico in 1903 for Teddy's christening. (Courtesy of Barbara Bergère Nau.)

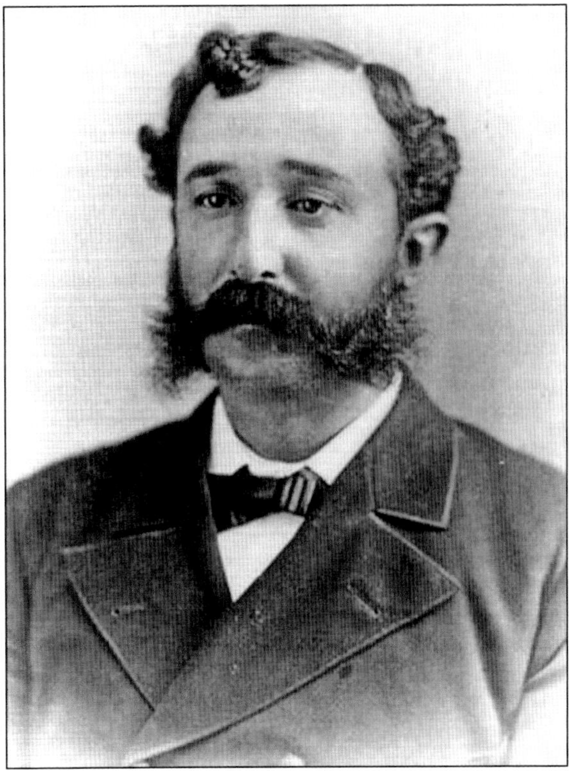

Nicknamed "El Guapo," or handsome one, Tranquilino was born on June 29, 1847, and died on November 29, 1892. He served as sheriff of Valencia County and was elected to the US Congress in 1880 as the congressional delegate from the Territory of New Mexico. He married Amalia Jaramillo y Romero and had one son, Maximiliano. (Courtesy of the US Congress.)

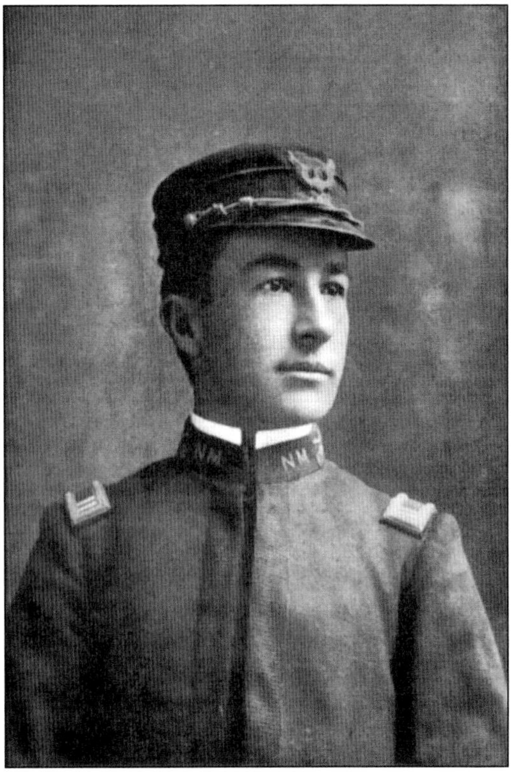

Born in 1870, Tranquilino's son, Maximiliano Luna, served as Valencia County sheriff for two years and was also elected as Valencia County probate clerk. After heroic service as a volunteer captain with the Rough Riders, Maximiliano returned to New Mexico. He was soon commissioned a lieutenant in the Regular Army and was sent to the Philippine Islands. He drowned while crossing a river in the Philippines in 1899. (Courtesy of the Luna Mansion.)

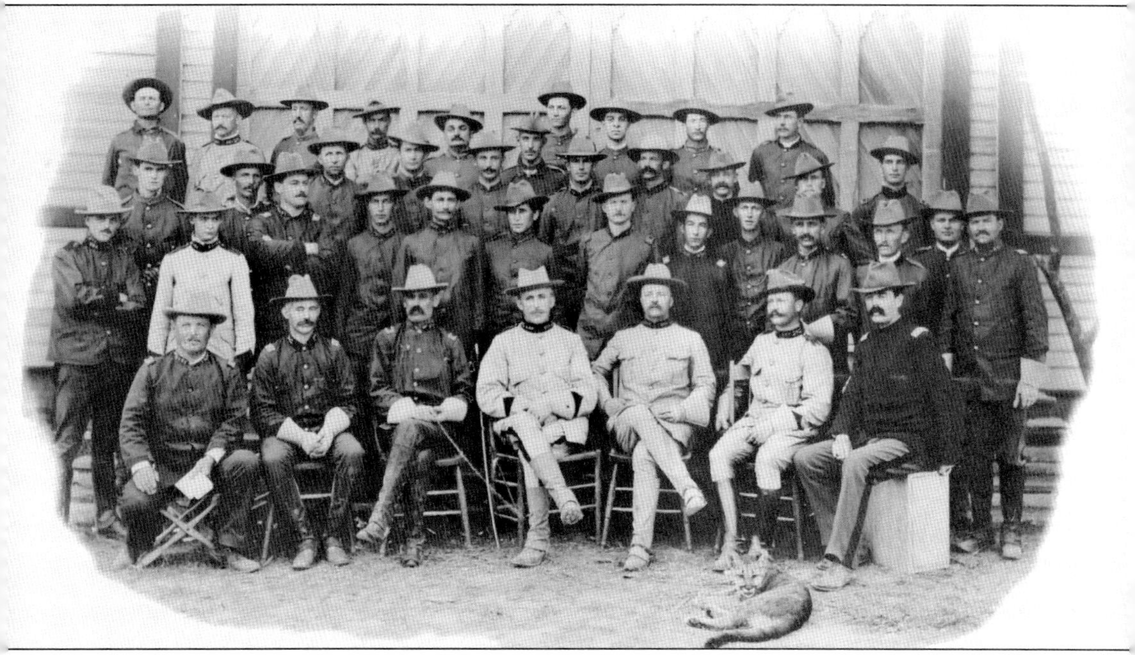

Col. Theodore Roosevelt is shown here (first row, third from right) with the officers of the Rough Riders in 1898. Maximiliano Luna (second row, sixth from right) is directly behind Colonel Roosevelt's shoulder. The service of notable Hispanic soldiers like Maximiliano Luna in the Spanish-American War went a long way toward assuring the rest of the country of the loyalty of residents of New Mexico to the federal government. The Rough Riders' mascot, a puma, was named Josephine. (Courtesy Museum of New Mexico, Negative No. 152651.)

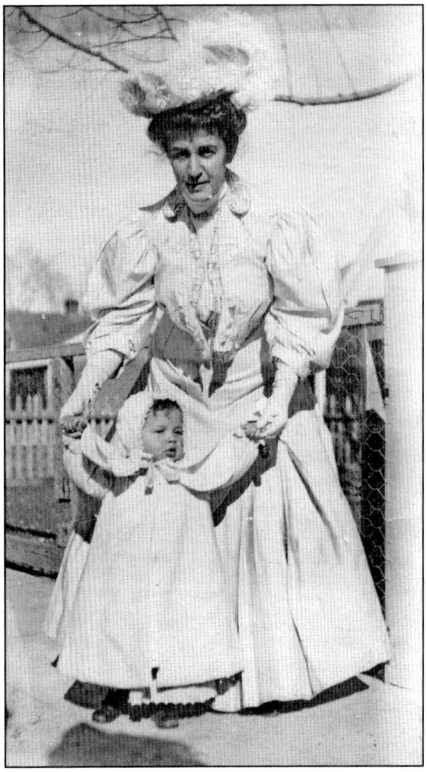

The youngest child of Antonio José Luna and Isabel Baca Luna, Eloisa Luna was born on March 1, 1864. She had three brothers, Jesús Maria, Tranquilino, and Solomon, all distinguished leaders in territorial New Mexico business and political affairs. Eloisa was educated by private tutors and at a finishing school in New York City. She married Manuel B. Otero in 1879. They had three children: Eduardo, Manuel, and Adelina Isabel Emilia "Nina." Eloisa's husband was killed over a land dispute in the summer of 1883. In 1886, after an appropriate mourning period, she married Alfred M. Bergère. Together they had nine children. Pictured below around 1906 are A.M. Bergère and Eloisa Luna Otero Bergère with 11 of their 12 children. Nina Otero-Warren is shown in the back row on the right, holding baby Charles Joseph Bergère. (Both, courtesy of Barbara Bergère Nau.)

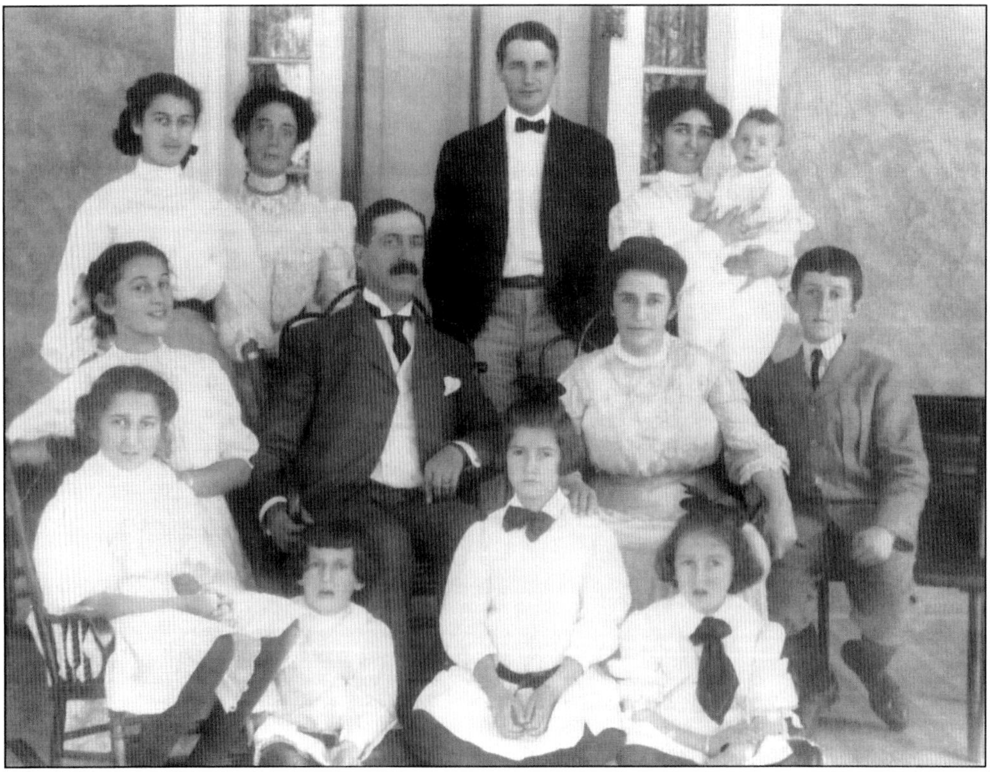

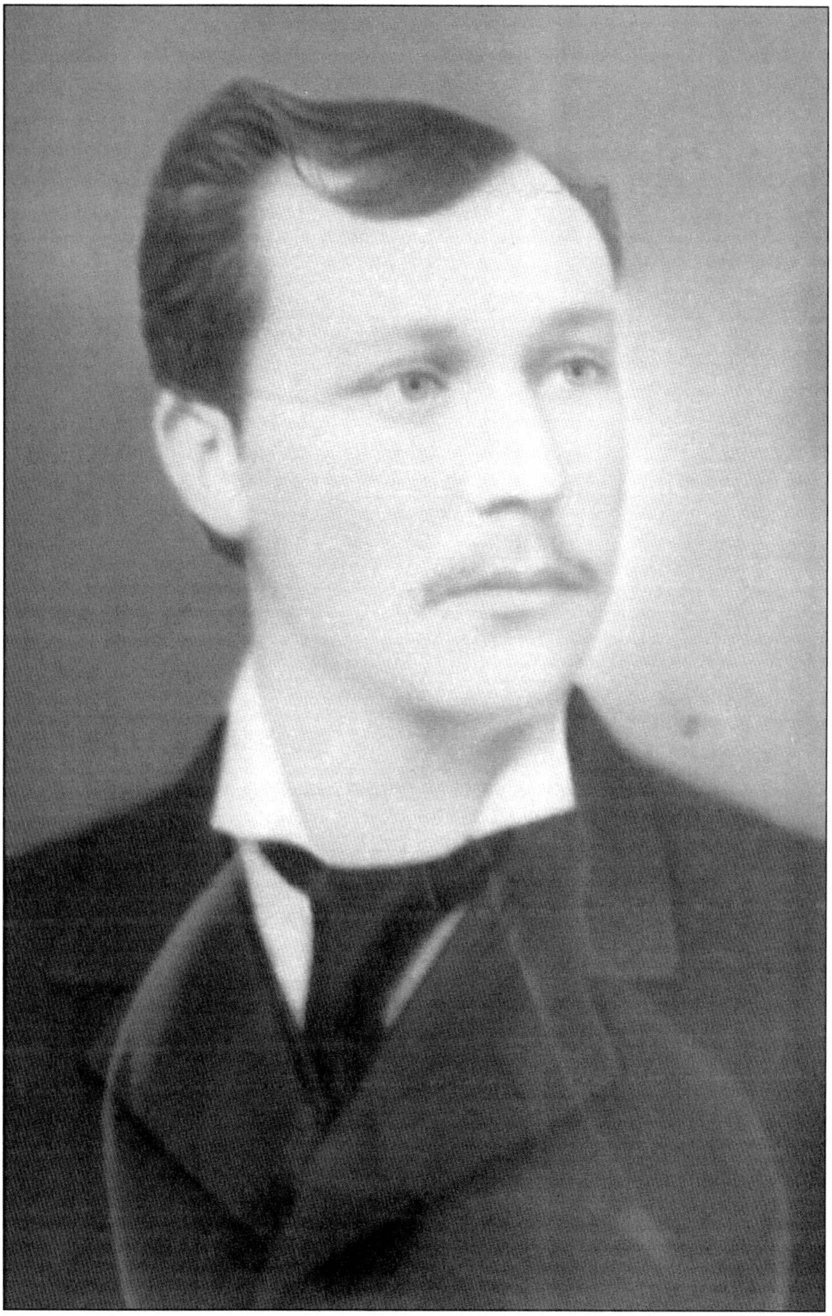

Manuel B. Otero, the son of Manuel Antonio Otero and Dolores Chaves from Belen, was educated in Europe and was fluent in many languages. His uncle Antonio José Chaves was appointed to the first New Mexico Territorial Supreme Court by Gen. Stephen Watts Kearny in 1846. Manuel B. Otero was involved in a dispute over ownership of the Bartolome Baca Land Grant near Estancia in Torrance County with Joel and James Whitney, wealthy Boston businessmen who claimed to have purchased the grant from the heirs of Gervacio Nolan. The dispute escalated, and a shootout occurred during which Manuel B. Otero was killed. His brother-in-law Dr. E.C. Henriques was wounded. (Courtesy of Los Lunas Museum of Heritage and Arts.)

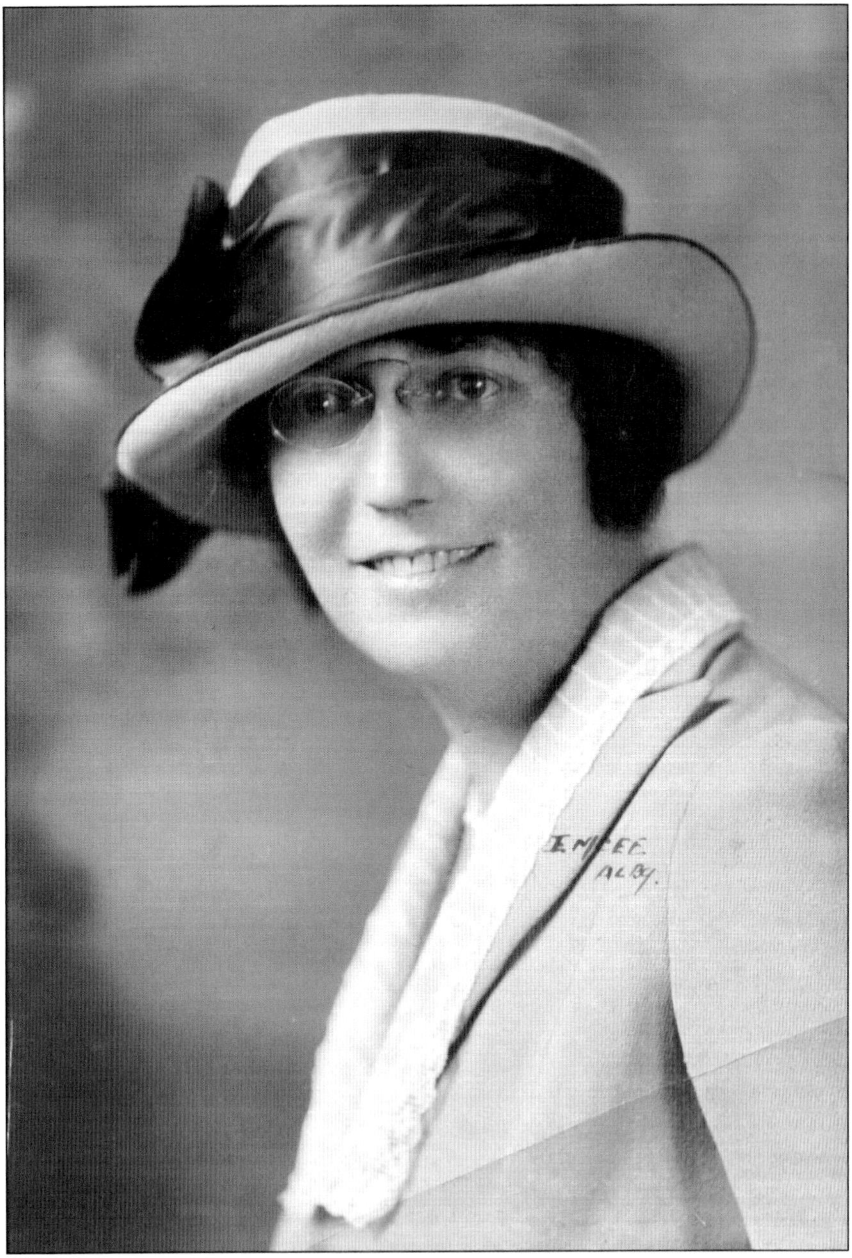

Nina Otero, the daughter of Manuel B. Otero and Eloisa Luna, led a life full of accomplishments as a suffragette, educator, politician, homesteader, writer, and entrepreneur. She was married briefly to a US Cavalry officer, Rawson Warren, and they lived at Fort Defiance, Arizona, but she was not happy as an army wife. She divorced Warren, although she kept his name the rest of her life. She was a leader in the quest for the vote for women, both in New Mexico and nationally. Following in her uncle Solomon's political footsteps, Nina was chair of the women's division of the Republican state committee for New Mexico. In 1918, she defeated a male opponent in the run for Santa Fe school superintendent. In 1922, she was the first woman from New Mexico to run for Congress and carried 80 percent of the Hispanic districts in a losing effort. (Courtesy of Barbara Bergère Nau.)

During the 1930s, Nina Otero-Warren served in several federal agencies. She was also an active participant in the Santa Fe Fiesta. She is shown here in her fiesta dress. In 1936, she published her book, *Old Spain in Our Southwest.* In the late 1940s, she founded the Los Dos Realty and Insurance Agency in Santa Fe. She died on January 3, 1965. (Courtesy of Barbara Bergère Nau.)

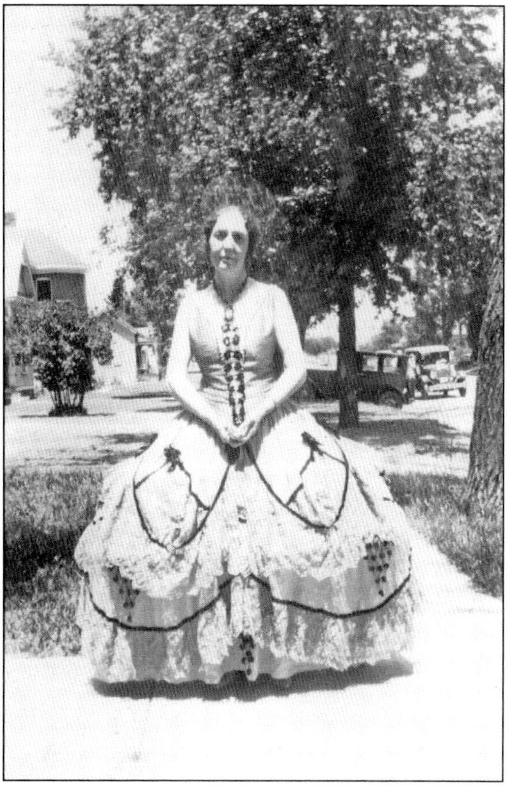

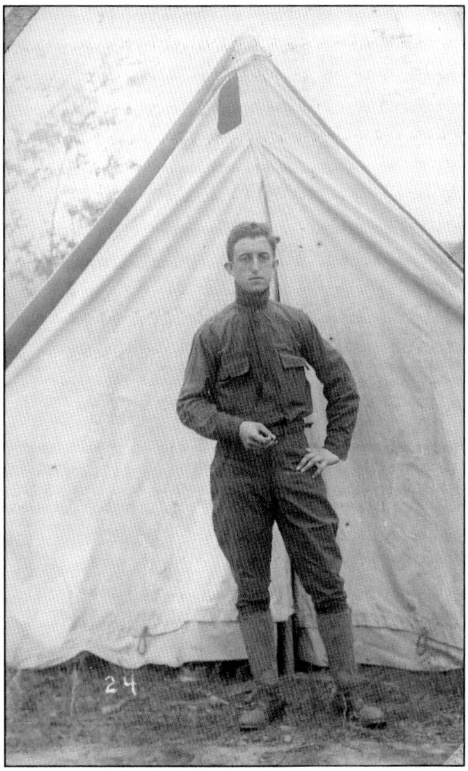

Antonio José Luna Bergère, the son of Eloisa Luna Bergère and Alfred M. Bergère, served as a first lieutenant of the US Army in France during World War I. (Courtesy of Barbara Bergère Nau.)

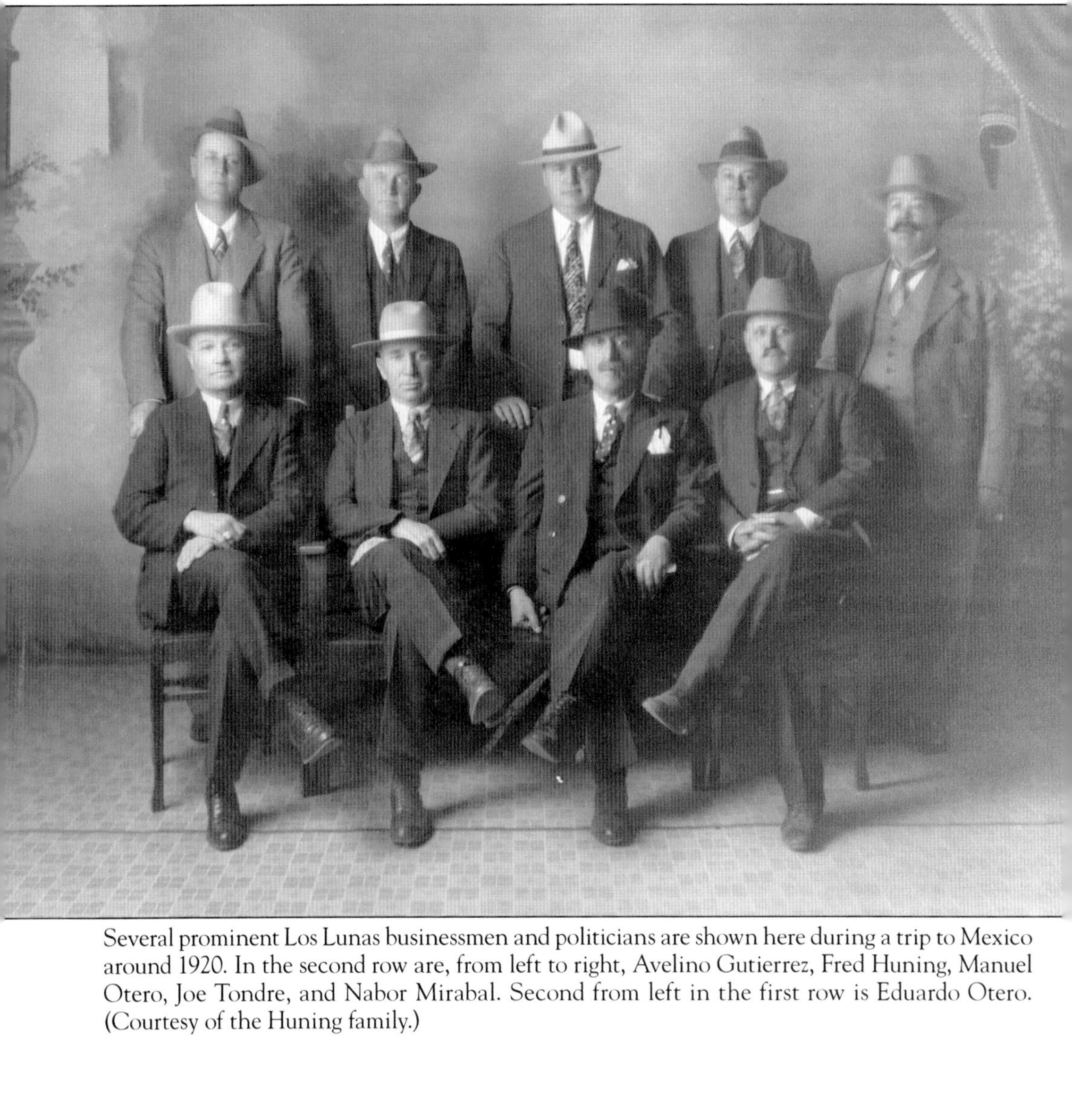

Several prominent Los Lunas businessmen and politicians are shown here during a trip to Mexico around 1920. In the second row are, from left to right, Avelino Gutierrez, Fred Huning, Manuel Otero, Joe Tondre, and Nabor Mirabal. Second from left in the first row is Eduardo Otero. (Courtesy of the Huning family.)

Two

Ranching and Agriculture

The Luna and Otero family fortunes were founded on vast herds of sheep. Solomon Luna's holdings at one time numbered more than a million head of sheep. Luna's nephew Eduardo Otero, who expanded the family sheep business, inherited his herds. The coming of the railroad to New Mexico in 1881 made it easy to transport wool and other agricultural products to eastern and southern US markets.

Cattle ranching was also an important economic activity in the Los Lunas area, and the Luna-Otero, Huning, and Major families maintained extensive cattle operations. The Huning Land and Cattle Company is still in business today.

The Rio Grande provided water for irrigation, making agriculture a dominant aspect of the Los Lunas and Valencia County economies. The Sais, Sichler, and Tondre families established successful farms, raising corn, wheat, alfalfa, and chiles and, in the case of the Tondre family, an extensive winemaking operation. During the Great Depression, farm families were relocated from Oklahoma. They traveled via Taos Junction, New Mexico, to Los Pinos, to the northeast of Los Lunas (now called Bosque Farms), as part of a major government resettlement project. Although they were largely unsuccessful at crop farming, a switch to dairy farms took advantage of a market for dairy products in central New Mexico.

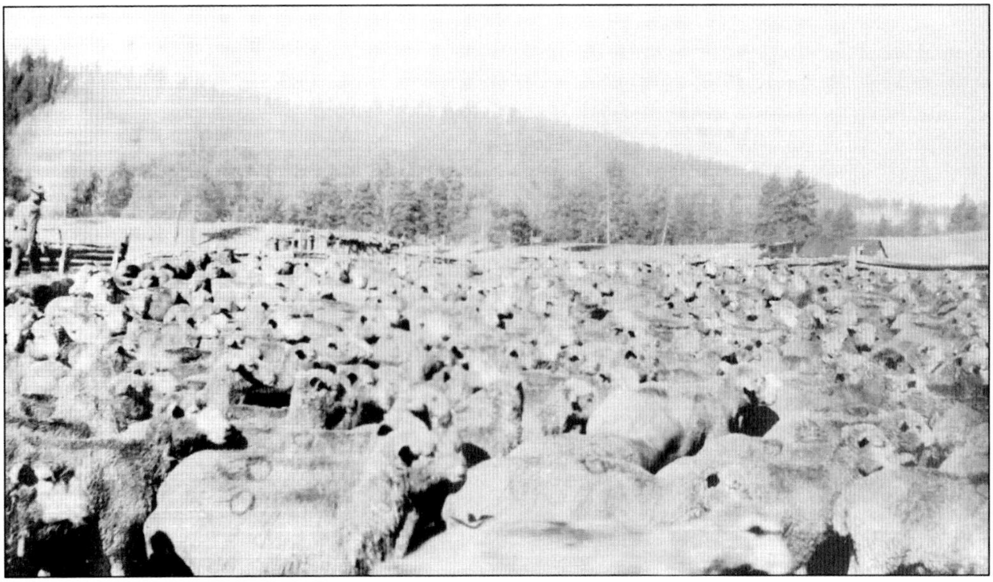

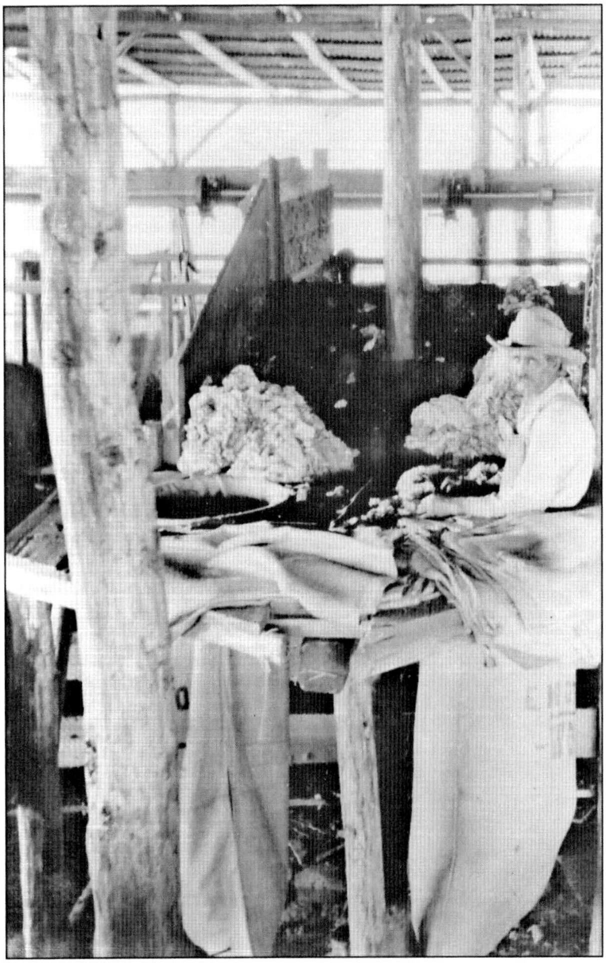

In 1598, sheep were introduced to New Mexico by the Spanish conquistador Don Juan de Oñate. The herds grew, and by the mid-19th century, Luna and Otero, two of the largest sheep ranchers in the United States, had a combined herd of over 50,000. Eventually, sheep in New Mexico numbered over a million. (Courtesy of Barbara Bergère Nau.)

In the background, a horizontal board supports the drive mechanism for steam-powered sheep shears. The sheared wool was tossed upward from the shearing pen onto the slanted boards, where it would slide down toward the bagging chutes. When they were full, the bags would be tied off, and a new bag would be suspended from the chutes. (Courtesy of Barbara Bergère Nau.)

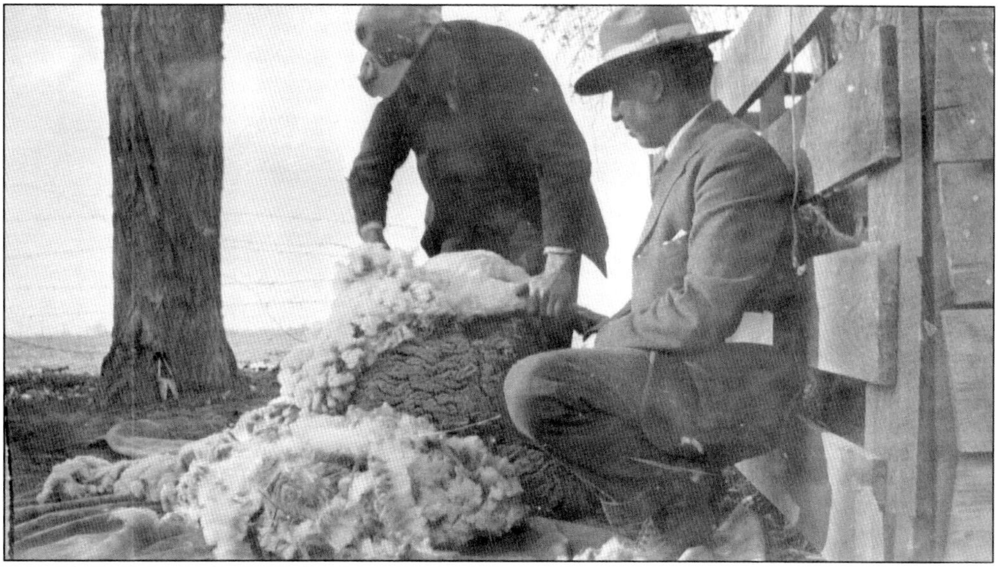

Eduardo Otero watches as a shepherd shears a sheep using hand shears. Another pair of shears is leaning against the tree in the background. Hand shearing was the practice in remote areas where steam power was not available to run belt-driven shears. (Courtesy of Barbara Bergère Nau.)

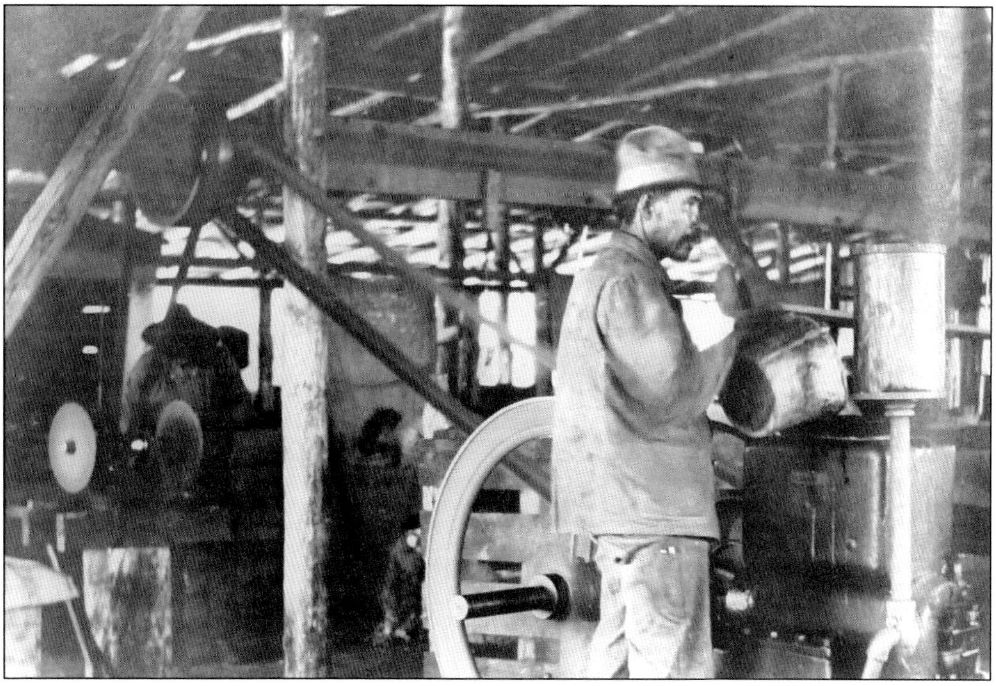

A worker is pictured adding water to the boiler of a steam engine used to power the belt-driven shears on Eduardo Otero's sheep ranch. The belt, attached to the large flywheel, drove the overhead mechanism powering each individual set of shears. The smaller flywheel in the background is attached to a grindstone, where another worker can be seen sharpening a pair of shears. (Courtesy of Barbara Bergère Nau.)

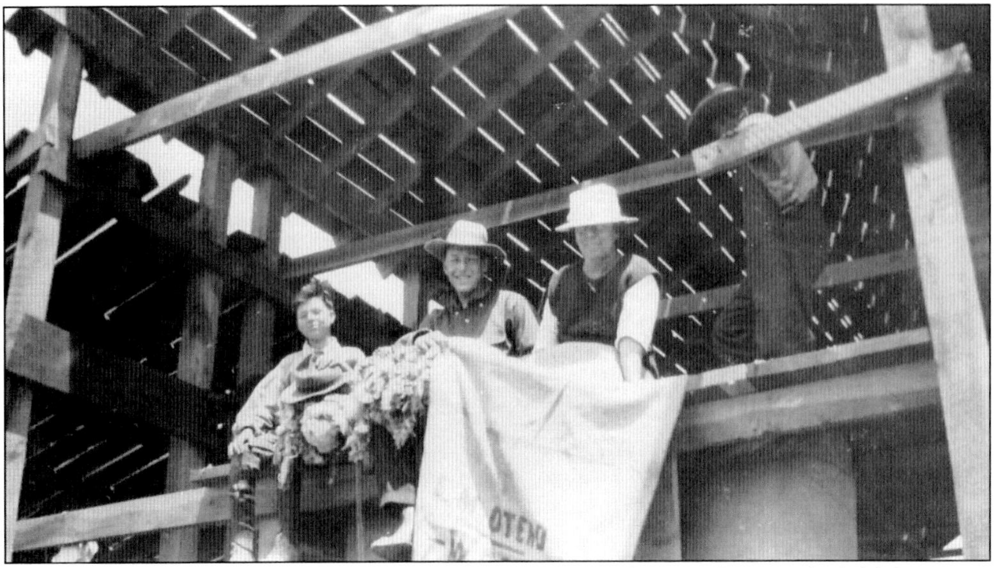

Theodore Roosevelt Manderfield Otero (center) and his mother, Josefita Manderfield Otero, are shown on a raised platform inside the sheep-shearing shed located on Otero land near Los Lunas. Sheared wool was moved by a steam-driven conveyor belt up to the platform, where it was packed into the hanging bags. Filled bags of wool were then transported by wagon to the railroad depot in Los Lunas for shipment to eastern markets. (Courtesy of Barbara Bergère Nau.)

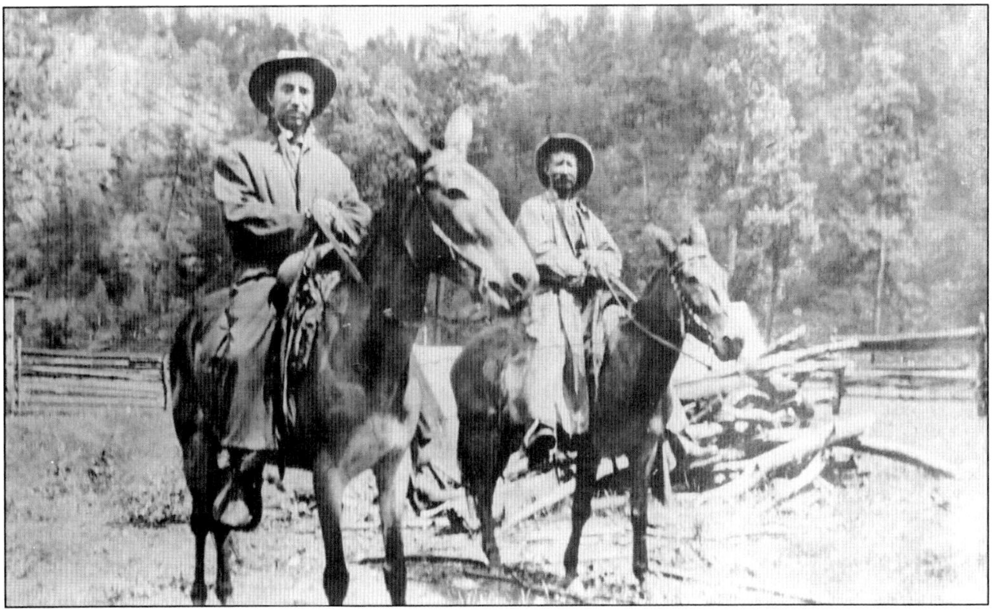

Eduardo Otero, son of Manuel B. Otero and Eloisa Luna, is pictured on the left at a sheep camp with his top shepherd, Jesús Archuleta. Upon the death of his uncle, Eduardo inherited the Luna family's political interests and power. Eduardo Otero and the Republican party continued to rule Valencia County until Franklin Delano Roosevelt's New Deal in the 1930s brought Valencia County, and the rest of the nation, under Democratic influence. (Courtesy of Barbara Bergère Nau.)

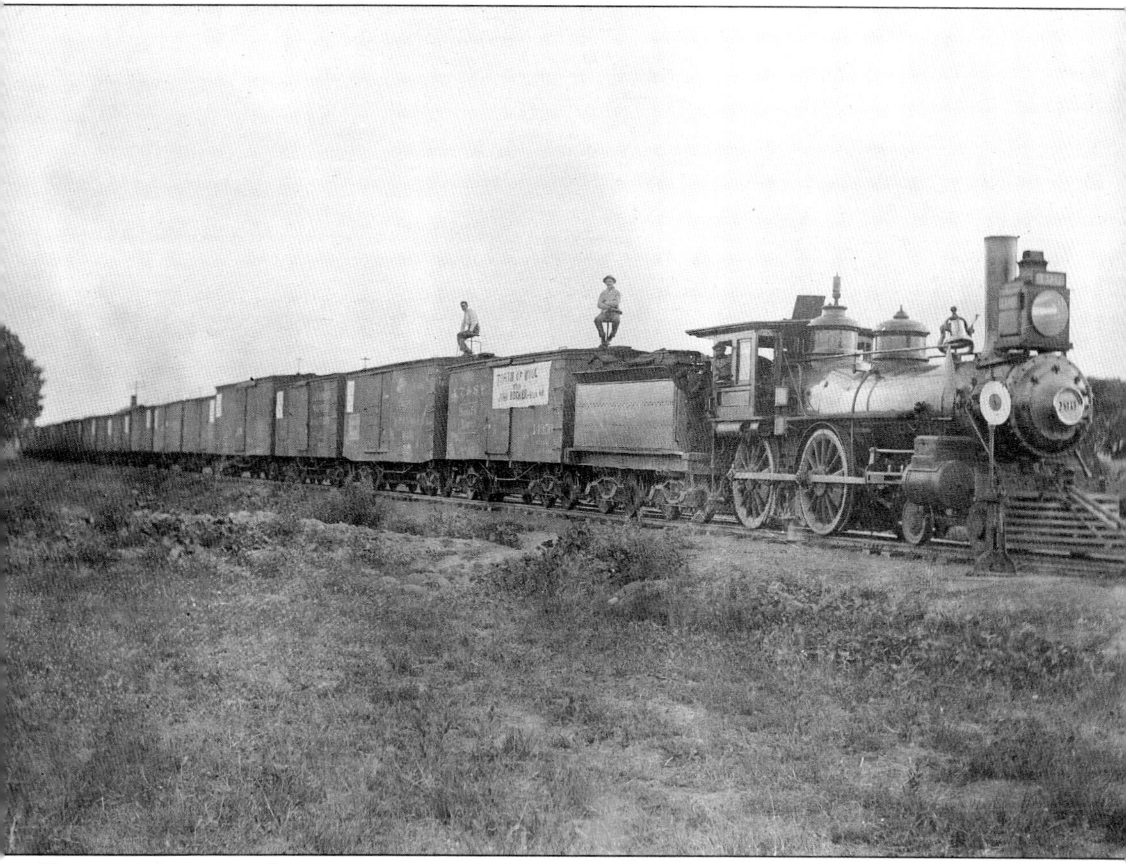

Sheep ranching was also a major economic activity in the area around Los Lunas. This train consists of 30 boxcars belonging to John Becker. Filled with wool, the boxcars were shipped to eastern markets in 1896. John Becker first worked for the Huning brothers at their store in Los Lunas. He was sent by the Hunings to manage their Belen branch store. He was quite successful in this endeavor, and soon he was supported by prominent Belen merchant Felipe Chaves in opening a store of his own in Belen. (Courtesy of the Valencia County Historical Society.)

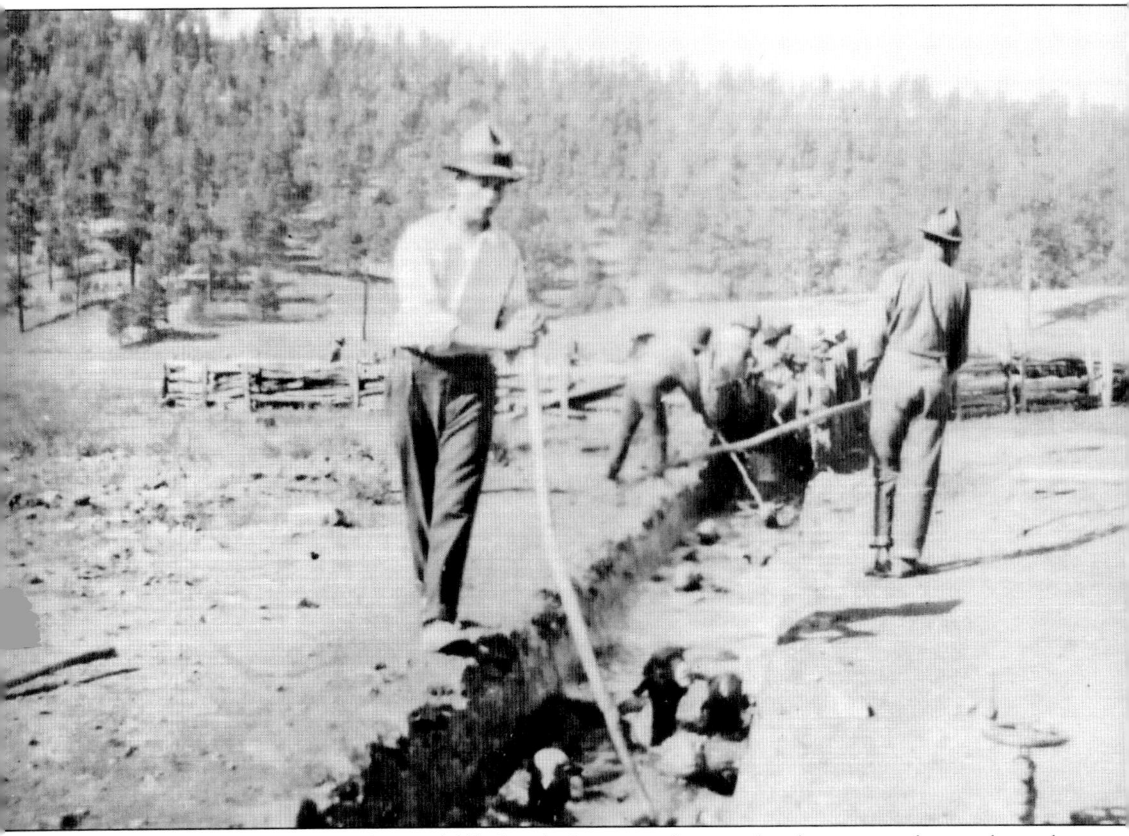

Once a trench had been dug and filled with dipping solution, the sheep were driven through it. The solution, which protected the sheep from external parasites like mites, ticks, lice, and flies, soaked into their wool as they passed through the trench. The sheep that exited the opposite end of the trench were left to air-dry so that the residual solution would protect their skin and wool. (Courtesy of Barbara Bergère Nau.)

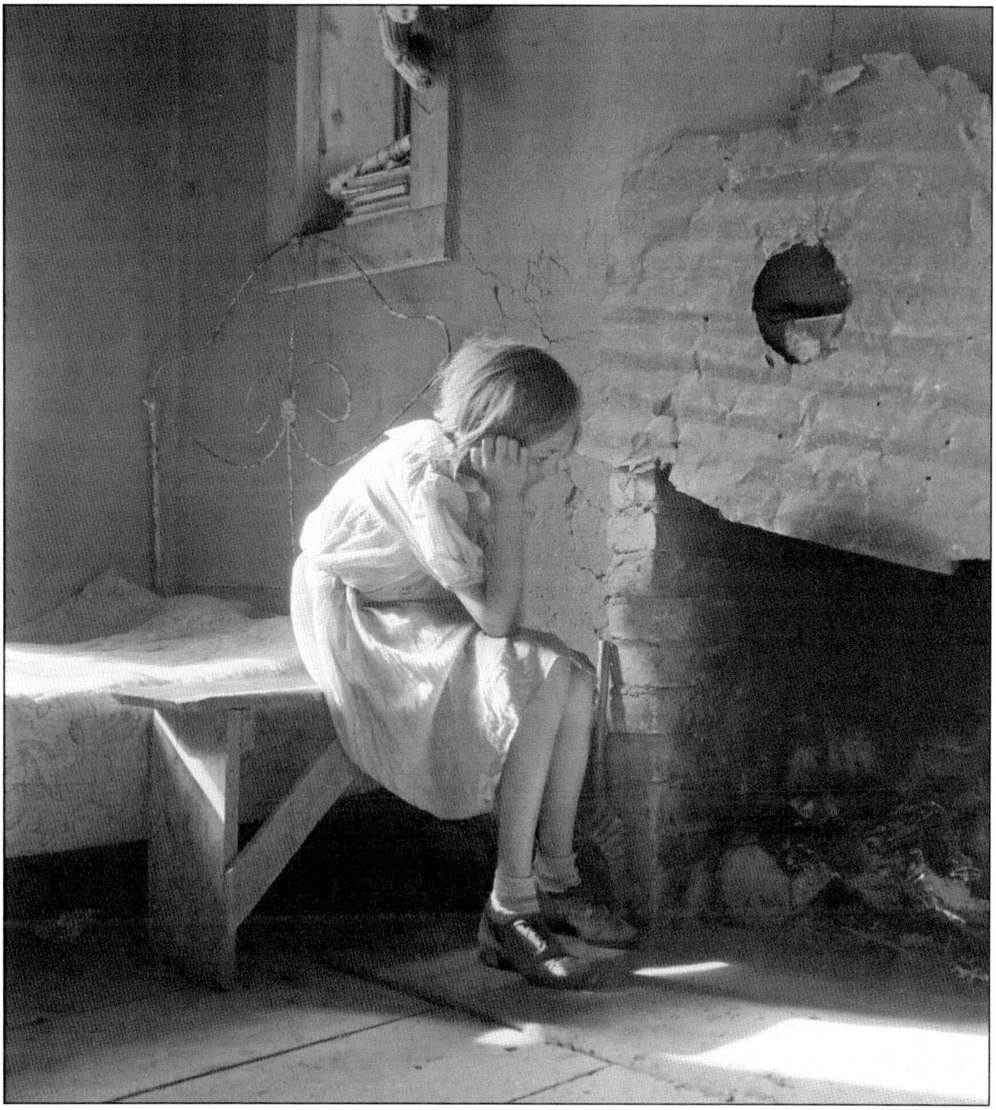

In 1906, Eduardo Otero obtained the land that eventually became Bosque Farms from Francisca Connelly. In the 1920s, he sold the land in small parcels but had to repossess them when Depression-era buyers were unable to make payments. In 1934, Otero sold 2,420 acres to the New Mexico Rural Rehabilitation Corporation, which in turn was taken over by the New Deal Federal Resettlement Administration in 1935. Initially, 42 families from Taos Junction, New Mexico, along with 17 families from eastern New Mexico, were resettled to homesteads in Bosque Farms. Each homestead consisted of 40 to 80 acres, and each family paid $140 per acre with a 40-year mortgage. The federal Works Progress Administration (WPA) paid for the drainage and irrigation of ditches, the clearing of cottonwood trees, the construction of adobe houses, and the creation and maintenance of roads. Pictured here is the daughter of one of the original Bosque Farms families. (Photograph by Dorothea Lange, courtesy of the US Department of Agriculture, Farm Security Administration.)

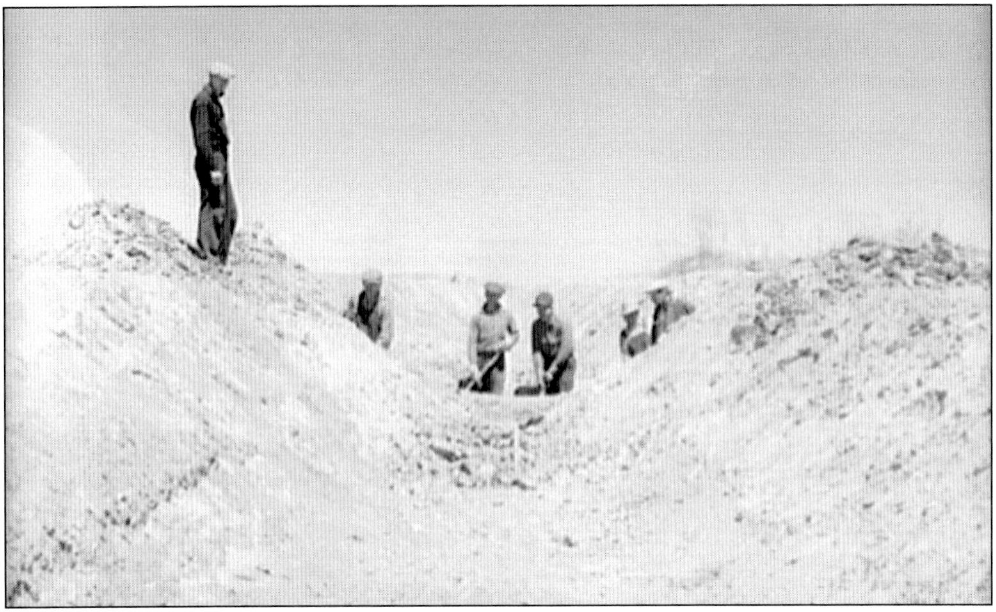

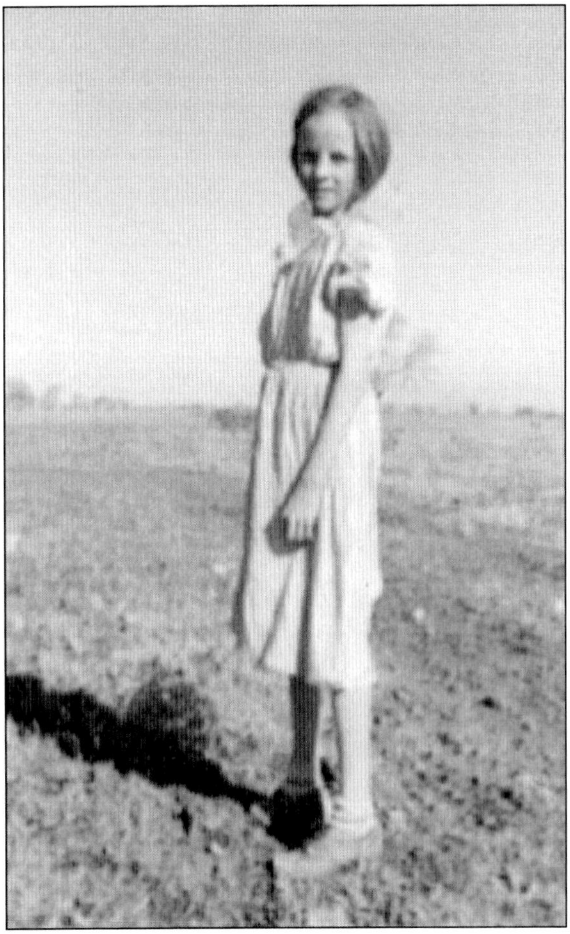

In this photograph, workers dig the main ditch that fed irrigation water to the smaller acequias to irrigate fields in Bosque Farms. In the late 1920s, the Middle Rio Grande Conservancy District was created to establish a series of dams and canals to provide water for crop irrigation in the central Rio Grande Valley between Albuquerque and Socorro. (Photograph by Arnold Rothstein, courtesy of the US Department of Agriculture, Farm Security Administration.)

This girl, pictured in 1935 in Bosque Farms, New Mexico, resettled with her family from Mills County, Oklahoma, to Taos Junction, New Mexico, and from there to Bosque Farms. She took care of a neighbor's cattle for 5¢ a day. (Photograph by Dorothea Lange, courtesy of the US Department of Agriculture, Farm Security Administration, Negative No. 34.)

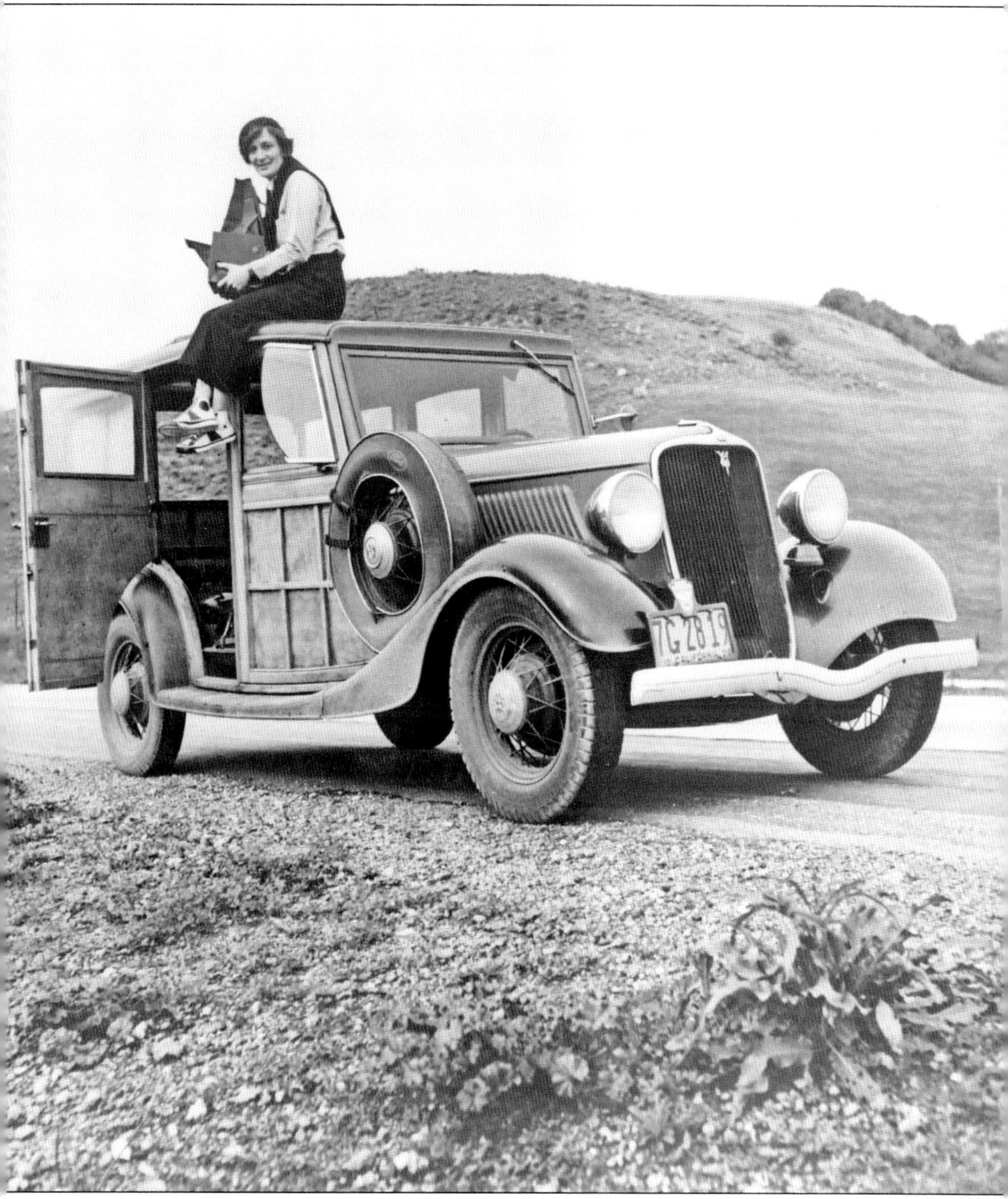

Roy Stryker sent photographers working for the Historical Section of the Farm Security Administration into rural areas of the country in the 1930s and 1940s to document the impact of the Depression on rural America. FSA photographers Arthur Rothstein and Dorothea Lange made many photographs in Los Lunas. Dorothea Lange is shown in this photograph. (Courtesy of the Library of Congress, Negative No. 128944.)

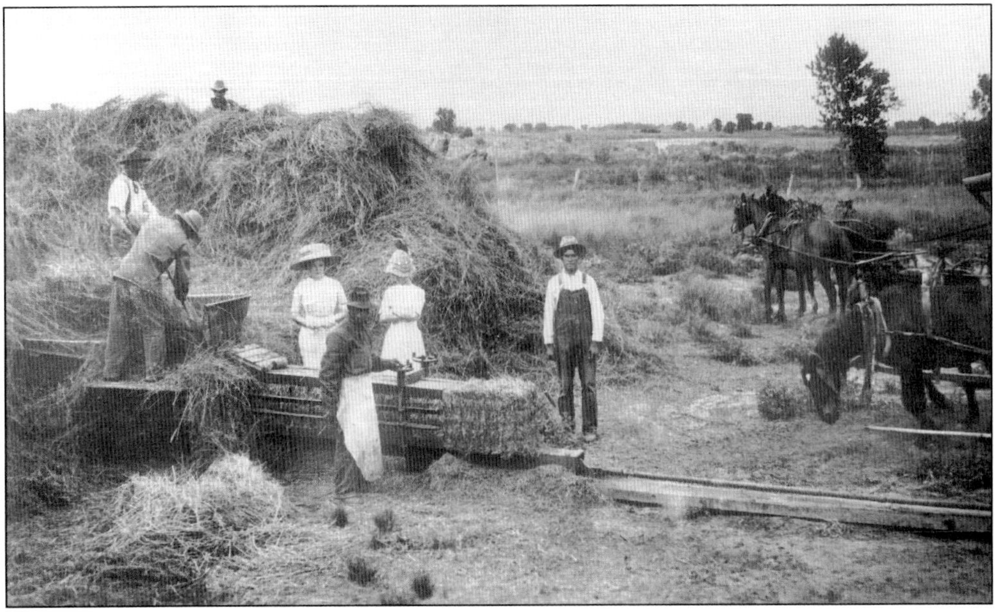

Workers are baling hay at the José Pasqual Sais farm in Los Lentes in this c. 1915 photograph. The hay was cut in the field using horse-drawn mowers and then transported by wagons to the baling site, where it was stacked. The hay was then fed into the baling machine to be compressed and tied with baling twine. (Courtesy of the Valencia County Historical Society)

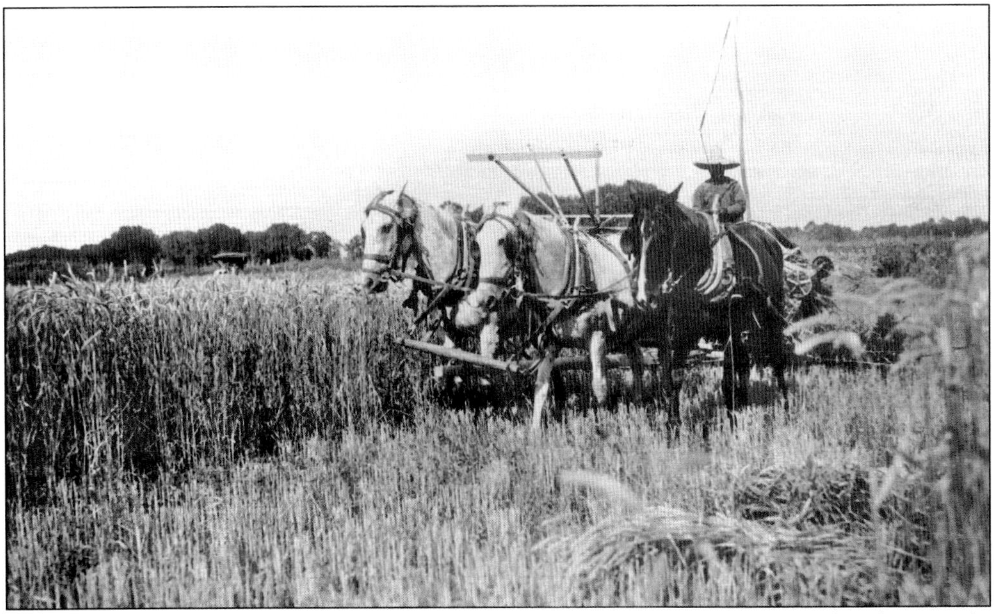

Horse-drawn mowers were used to cut wheat as well as hay. Wheat is being cut in this photograph. The cut wheat was loaded onto a wagon using pitchforks and transported to a central location where it was threshed, a process that removed the grain from the stalk. The grain was then gathered in bags and transported to a mill where it was ground into flour. The wheat stalks were baled for feeding livestock. (Courtesy of the Valencia County Historical Society.)

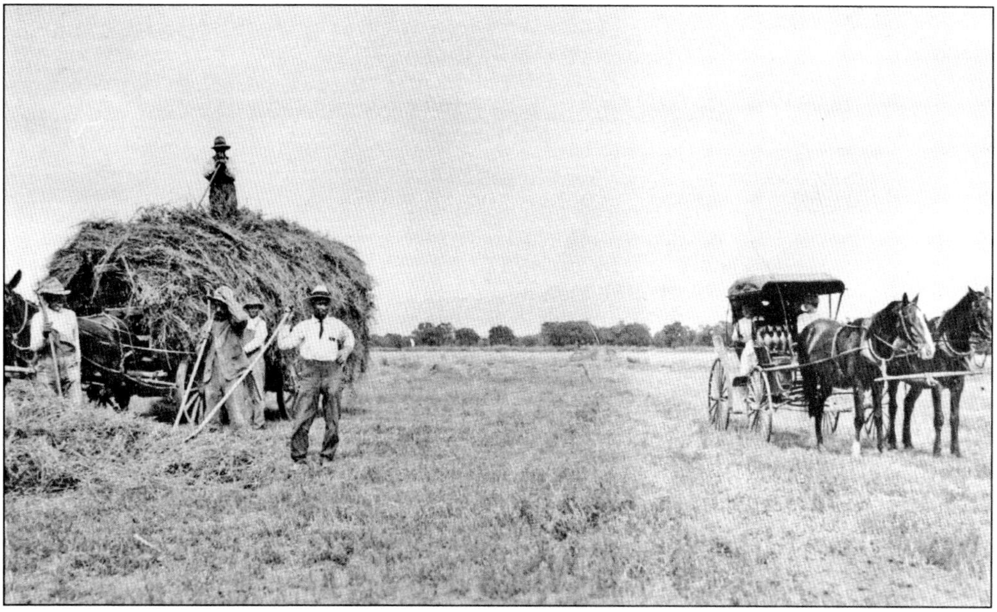

Mowed hay was left in the field to dry after cutting. The cured hay was raked into piles, placed on a wagon, and transported to the baling machine. This photograph was taken around 1910. (Courtesy of the Valencia County Historical Society.)

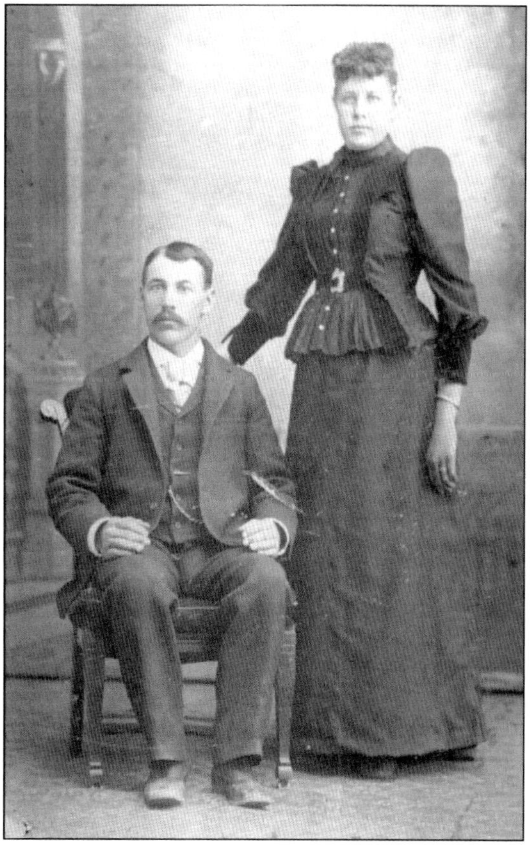

George Andrew and John Adam Sichler came to the Los Lentes area from Tuttlingen, Germany, in the mid-1800s. Pictured here are George Andrew Sichler and his wife, Mary. Their son Ernest F. Sichler was born on July 20, 1899. Ernest served on the Los Lunas School Board and as a member of the Valencia County Commission. Ernest's sister Ernestine married Silverio Sais, the grandson of José Pasqual Sais, thus joining two prominent Los Lentes farming families. (Courtesy of the Valencia County Historical Society.)

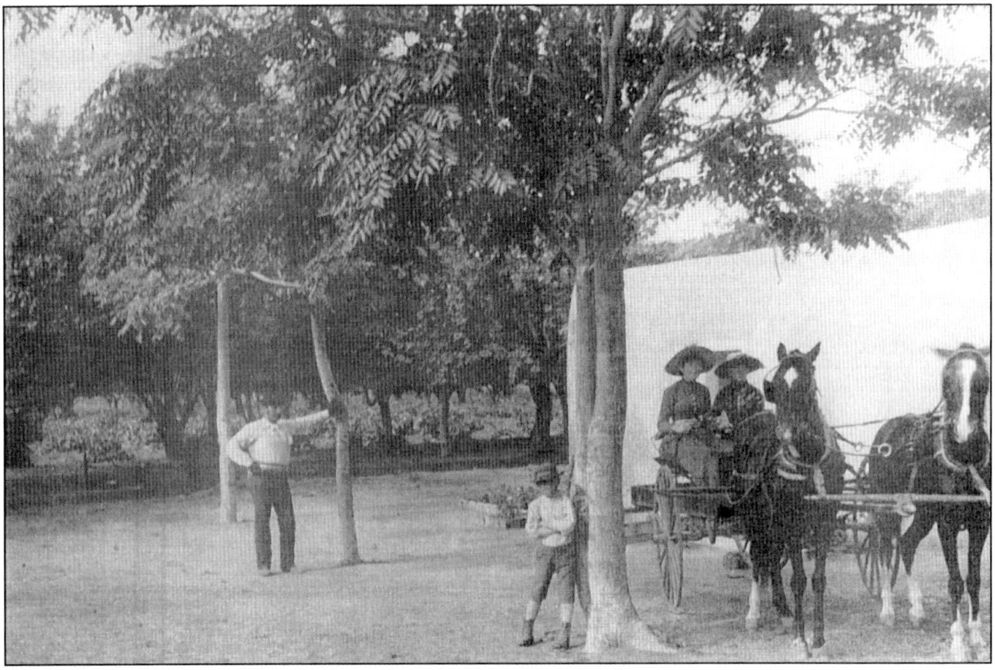

The ranch of Joseph Frank and Josephine Tondre was also located in Los Lentes. In addition to growing alfalfa, wheat, and corn, the Tondre ranch was well known for its fine wines. (Courtesy of Los Lunas Museum of Heritage and Arts.)

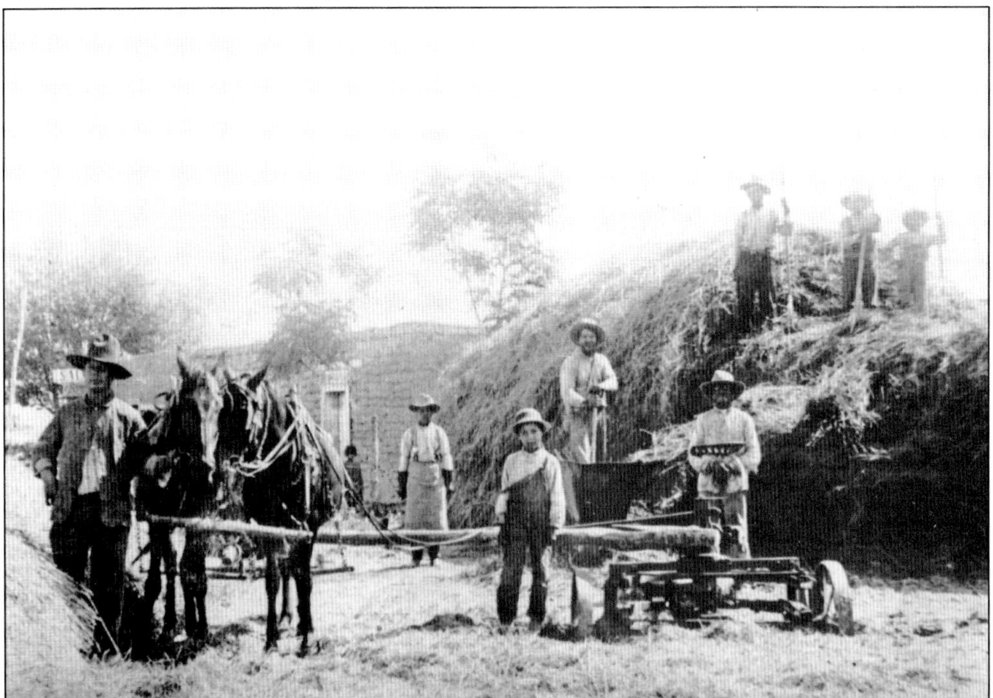

A team of horses turned the driveshaft that powered the baling machine located next to the stack of hay waiting to be baled. (Courtesy of the Valencia County Historical Society.)

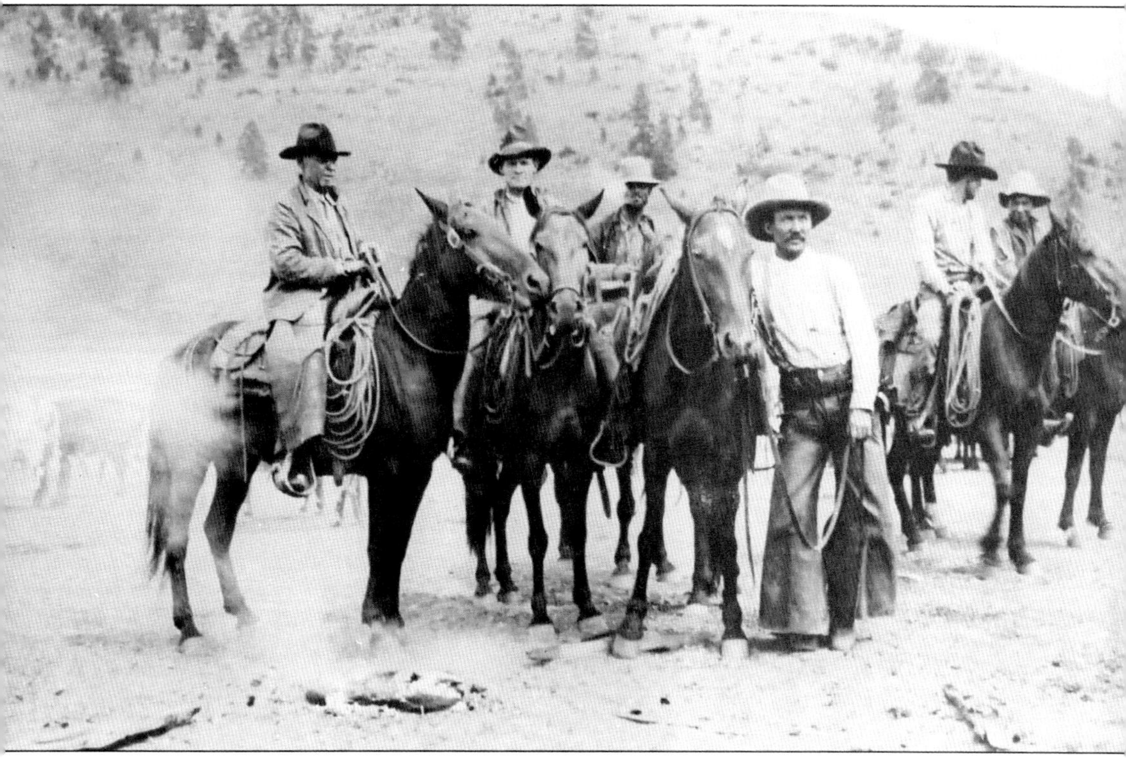

Although sheep were the major focus of the Otero ranching operations, the family also maintained extensive cattle herds. Shown here are several of the cowboys employed by the Otero family. They spent their time moving the herds between pastures as the season and grazing conditions dictated. (Courtesy of Barbara Bergère Nau.)

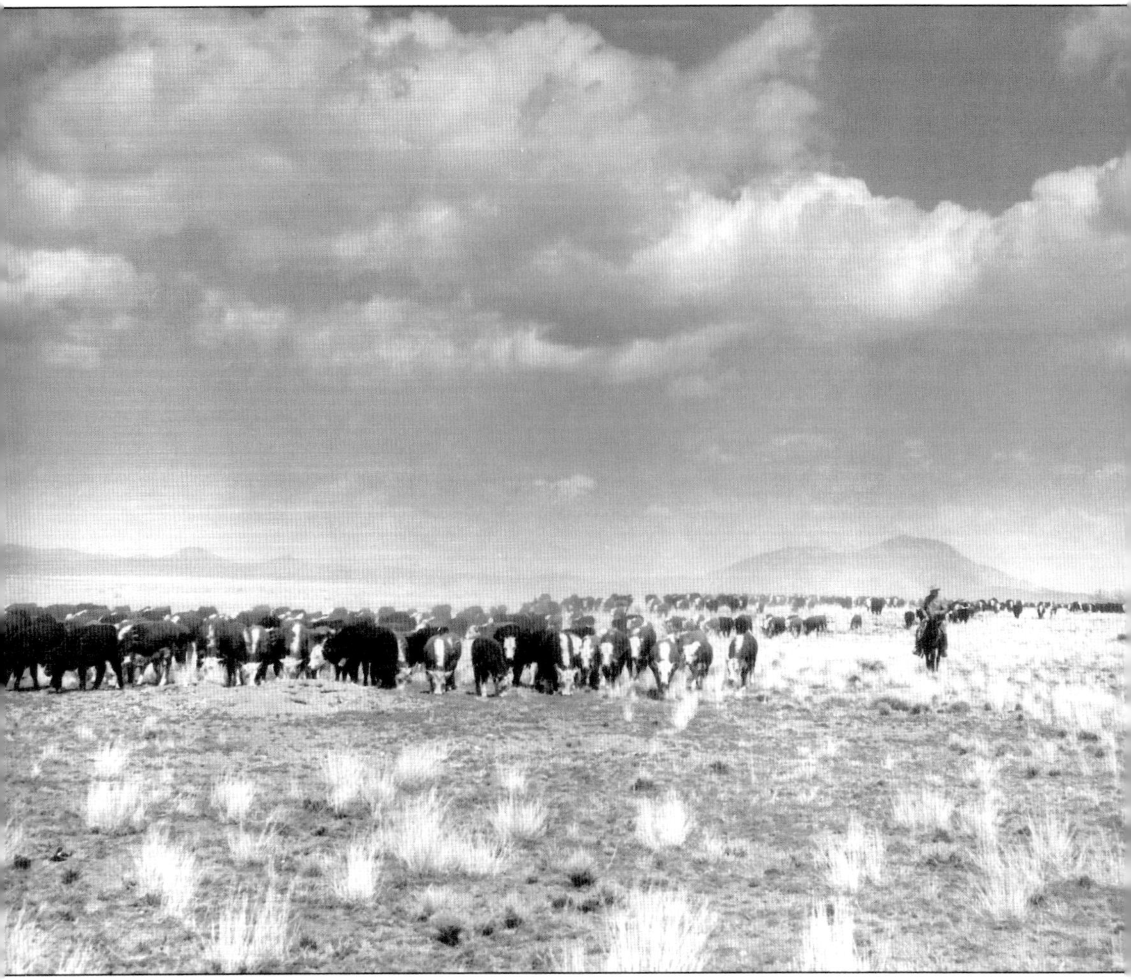

The Major family was one of the most prominent cattle ranching families in the Los Lunas area. This photograph shows one of the cattle drives organized by the Major ranch. More than 2,000 head of cattle were driven east from near the Arizona border to the railhead at Magdalena, New Mexico. The Major cattle drive was documented in a special presentation by CBS News' 60 *Minutes*. (Courtesy of Buddy Major.)

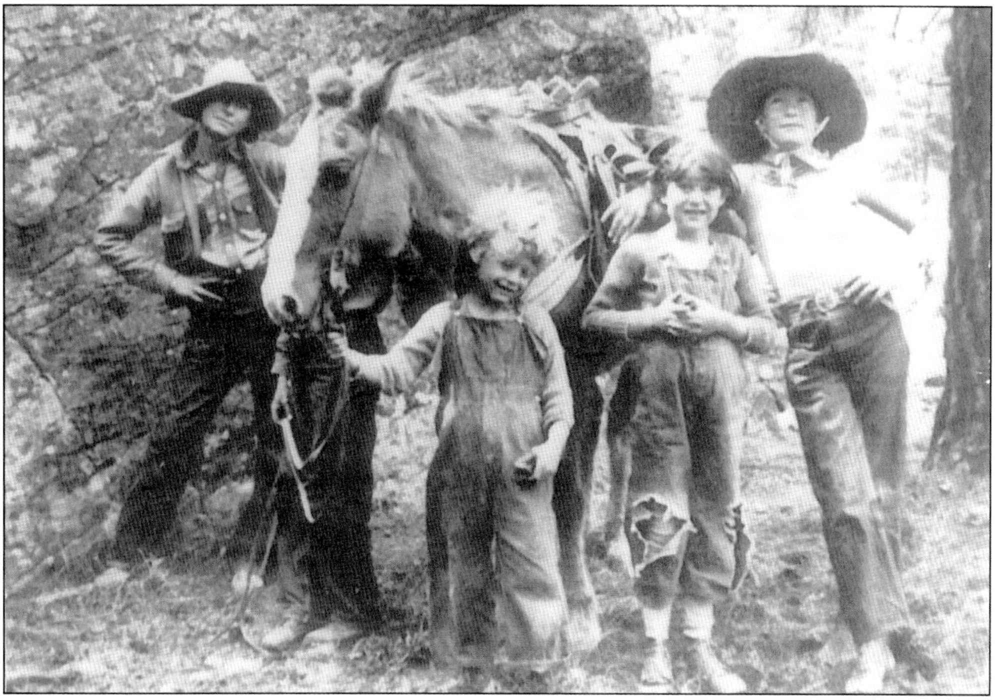

Buddy Major grew up in a ranching family and has worked around cattle his whole life. This photograph shows Major and his four sisters around 1926. Buddy is mostly hidden by the horse's head. A quick count, however, reveals 10 feet on the ground. (Courtesy of Buddy Major.)

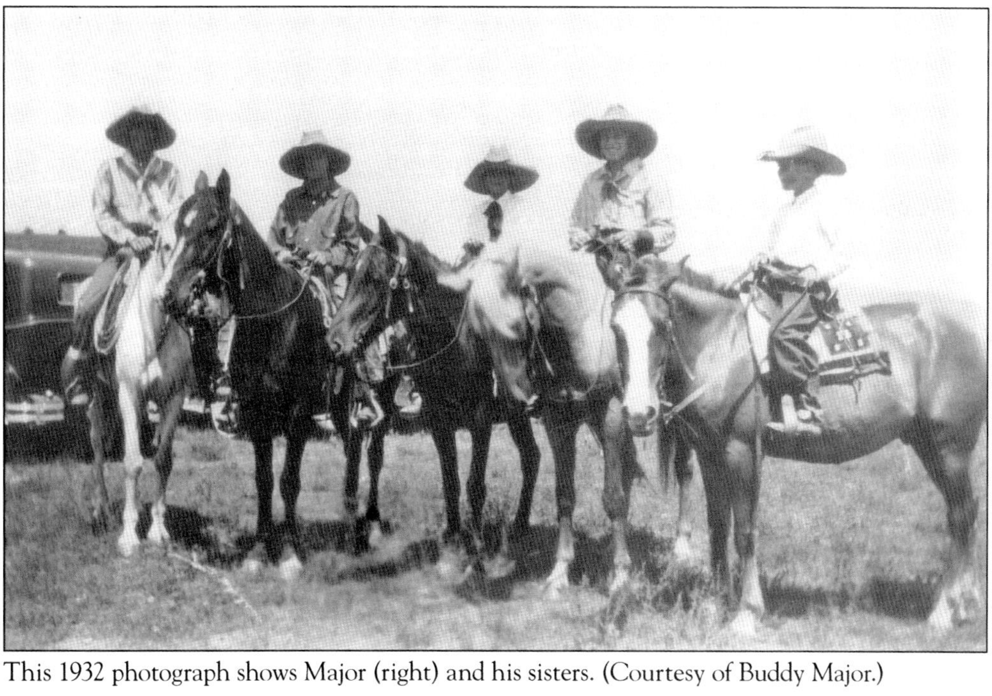

This 1932 photograph shows Major (right) and his sisters. (Courtesy of Buddy Major.)

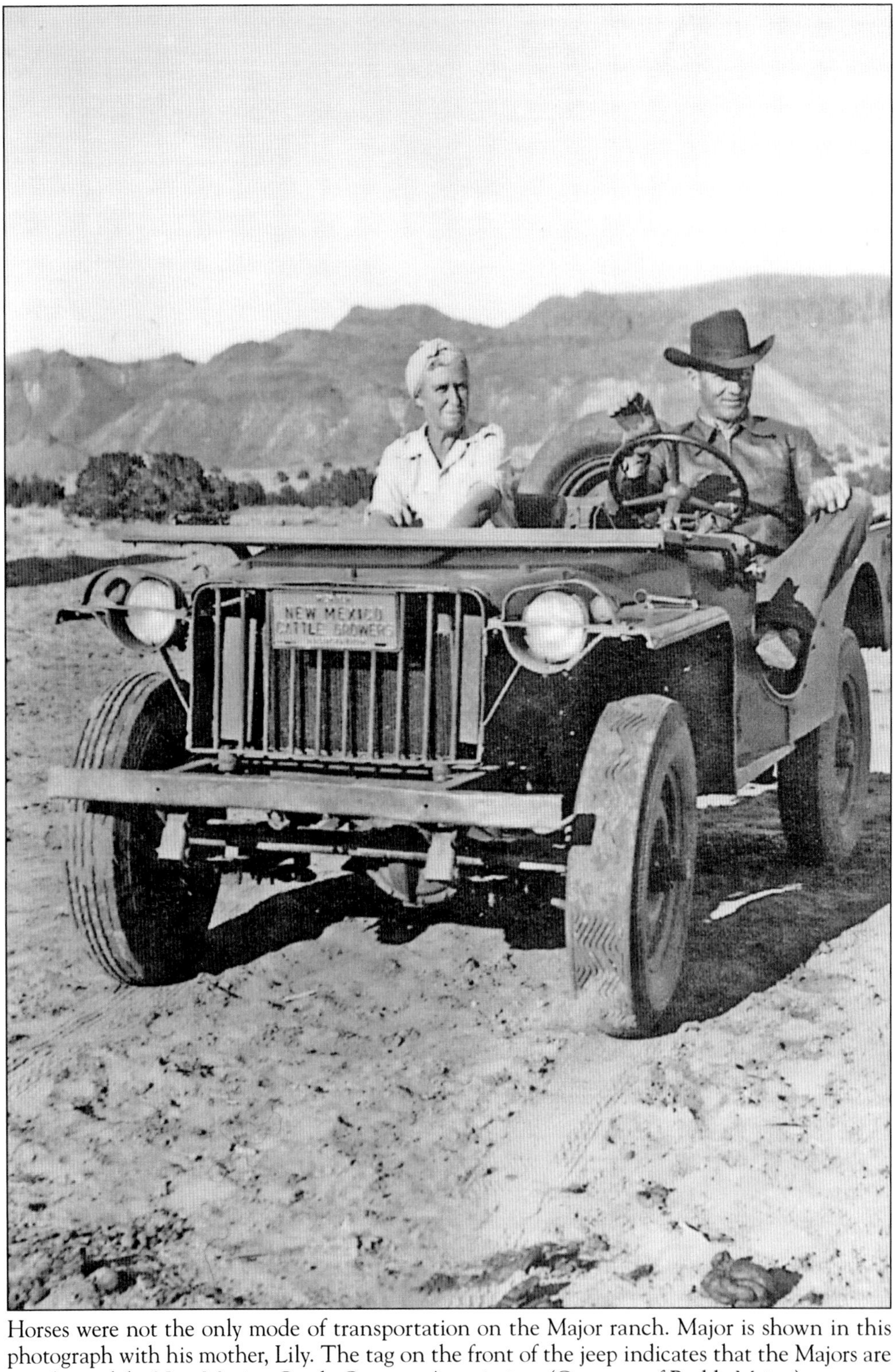

Horses were not the only mode of transportation on the Major ranch. Major is shown in this photograph with his mother, Lily. The tag on the front of the jeep indicates that the Majors are members of the New Mexico Cattle Growers Association. (Courtesy of Buddy Major.)

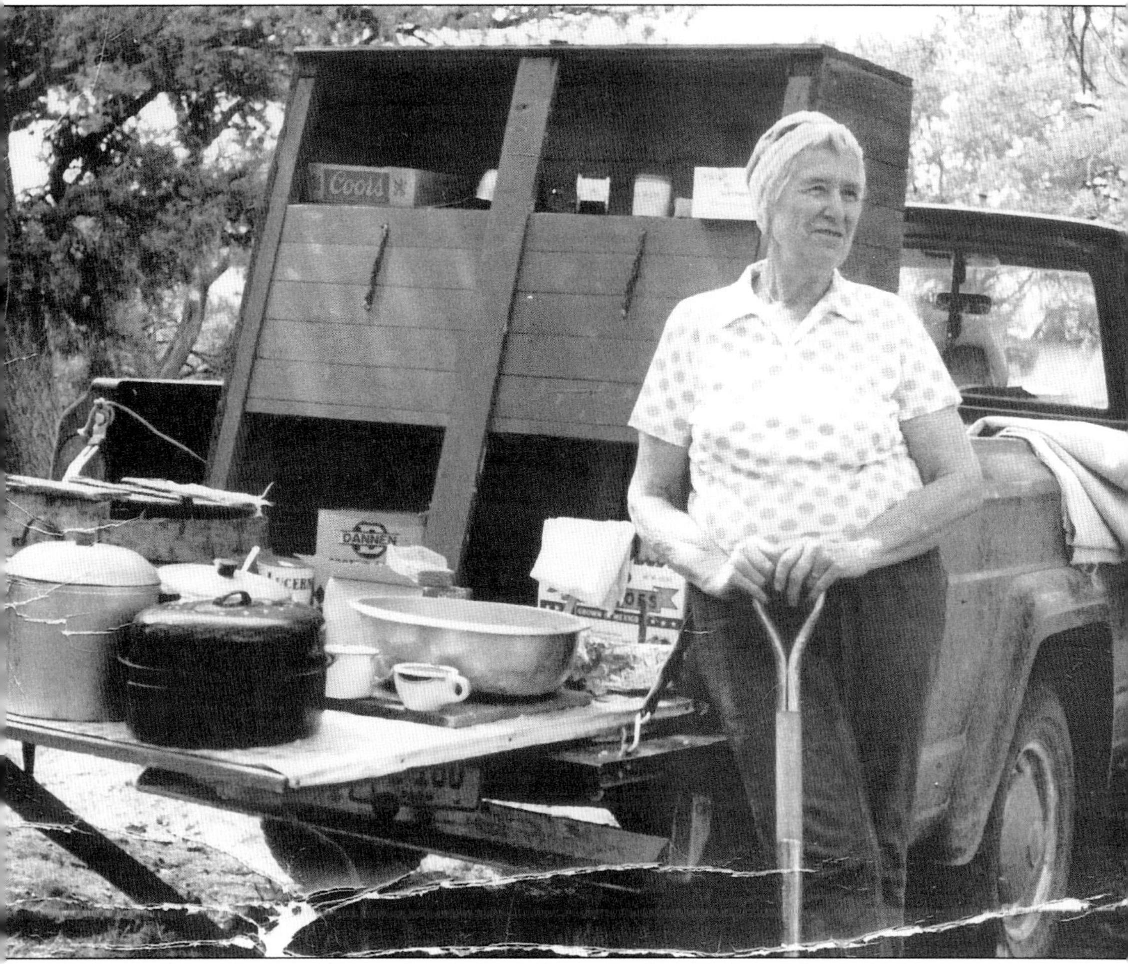

Major's mother, Lily, served as camp cook on the cattle drives. She is shown here setting up the modern version of the chuck wagon—a chuck box mounted to the back of a pickup truck. (Courtesy of Buddy Major.)

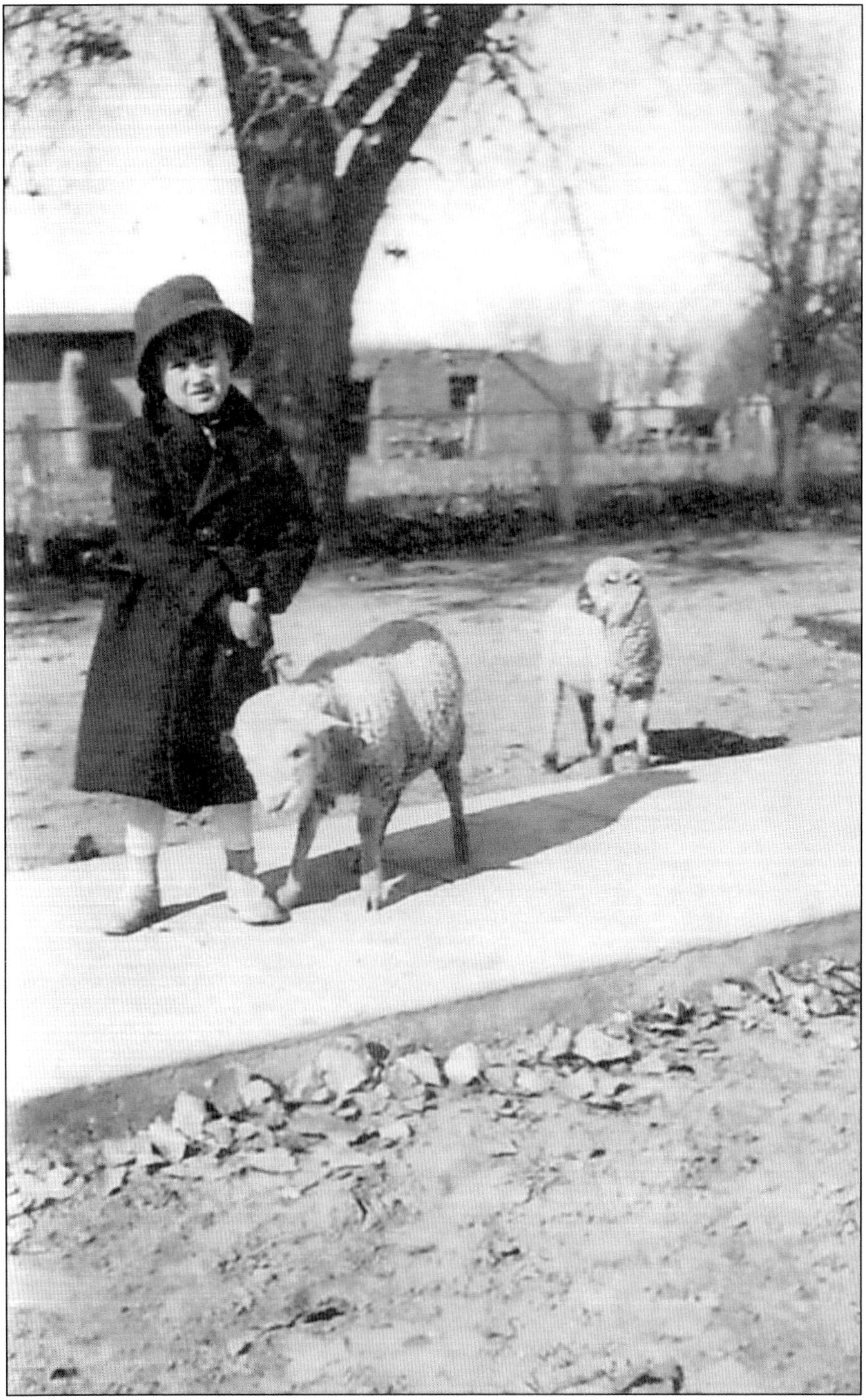

Fred Huning is shown here with his pet sheep. He grew up to manage the Huning Mercantile Company and to serve as mayor of Los Lunas. In a rural community like Los Lunas, it was not unusual for young children to be responsible for the care of farm animals. (Courtesy of the Huning family.)

Three

Merchants

During the 1860s, members of the Huning family immigrated to New Mexico from their native Germany. Franz Huning came first, settling in Albuquerque. He was soon followed by his brothers Louis, Henry, and Carl. Louis Bismark Huning established a mercantile store in Los Lunas that was operated his descendants until the 1990s. The Huning Mercantile sold groceries, household goods, farm implements, grain, and hardware to residents throughout Valencia County.

In addition to their own children, Louis and Henrika Huning also raised Emiliano Castillo Sr. from the time he was 11 years old. The Hunings taught young Emiliano the mercantile business, and he eventually opened his own meat market, which grew into a general merchandise business. Emiliano Castillo's son, Emiliano Castillo Jr., carried on the business and established the first public transportation company in the area with a route that went from Belen to Albuquerque.

Simon Neustadt was another successful German immigrant who established a mercantile business in Los Lunas. Along with his wife, Leah, and his partner, Joseph Tondre, Simon Neustadt built the Simon Neustadt Company into a very successful establishment.

Merchants in the village of Los Lunas provided access to Anglo goods and culture from the eastern United States. This availability reinforced the residents' desire for statehood.

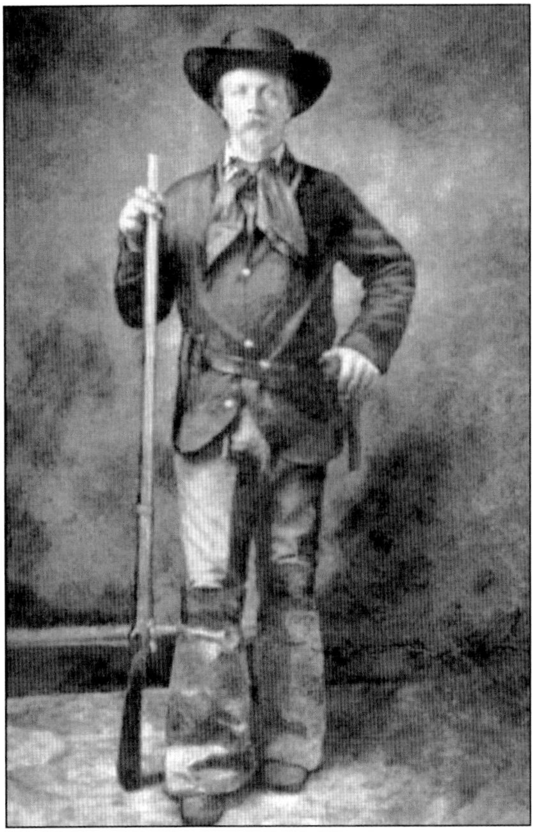

Born in Germany in 1827, Franz Huning came to New Mexico Territory with his brothers around 1860. While the Huning family established a mercantile store in Los Lunas, he settled in Albuquerque and opened his store at the location of the present Basket Shop in Old Town. Franz Huning died on November 6, 1905, in Albuquerque. (Courtesy of the Center for Southwest Research.)

In Albuquerque in 1881, Franz Huning built a luxurious home at the corner of Central Avenue (then called Railroad Avenue) and Fourteenth Street. This house came to be called Huning Castle. It was converted to a private school in the 1930s and served that purpose until 1954, when it was condemned. Huning is pictured here in front of Huning Castle around 1890. (Courtesy of the Center for Southwest Research.)

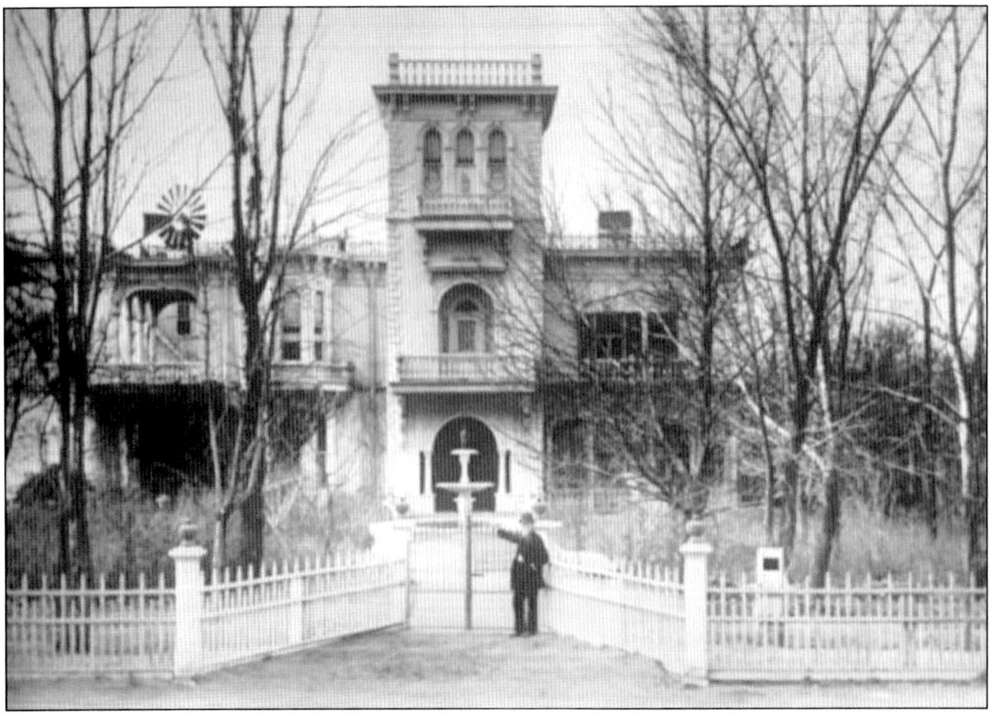

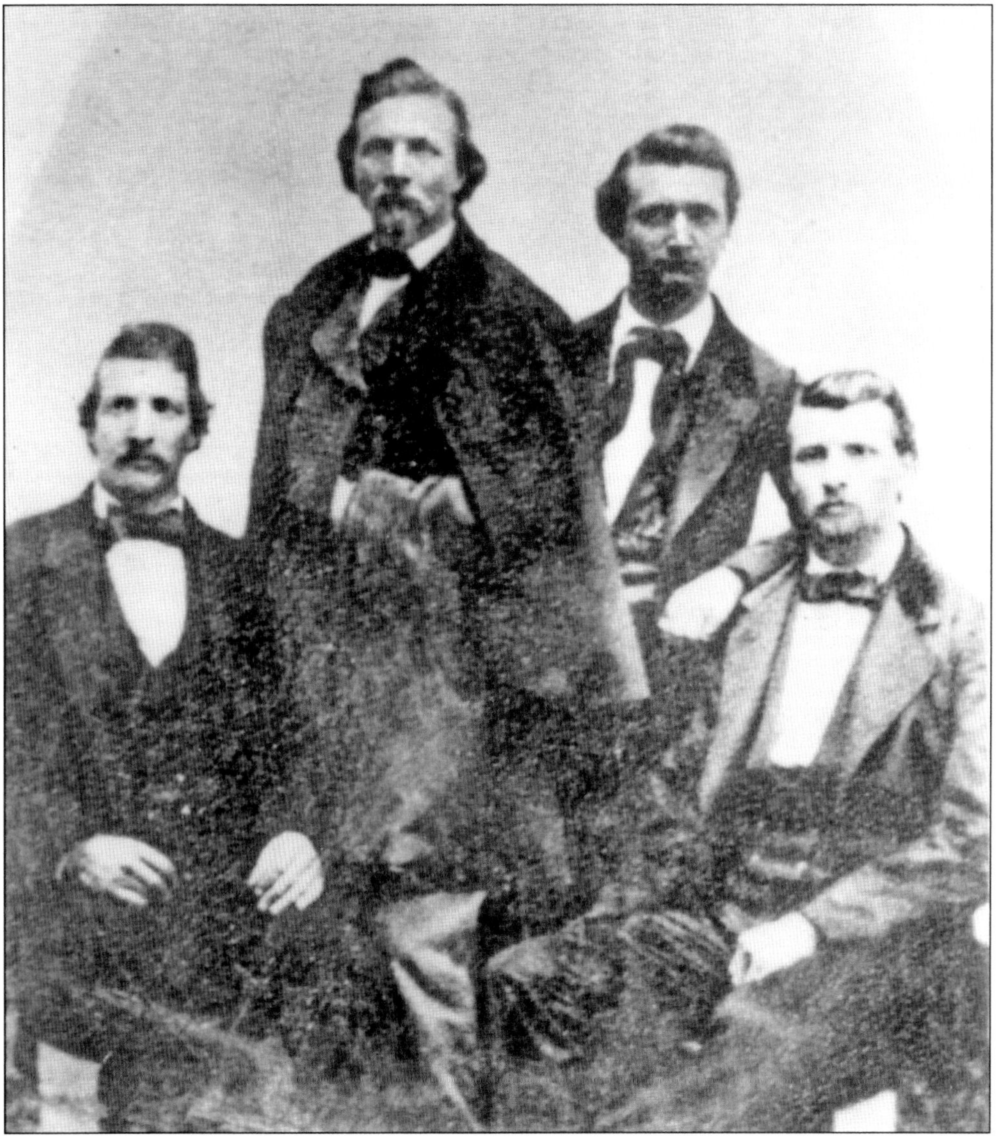

Shown here, from left to right, are Huning brothers Louis, Franz, Karl "Charles," and Henry. The brothers first came to New Mexico Territory from their native Germany around 1860. By 1871, the Huning brothers had established six branch stores in various communities in New Mexico and Arizona. Their government contracts alone amounted to more than $150,000 annually. They also had extensive livestock holdings, including 60,000 head of sheep and 8,000 head of cattle. Their yearly wool production amounted to 200,000 pounds. The Huning Mercantile store in Los Lunas was operated continuously by the Huning family from 1860 until 1994. (Courtesy of the Huning family.)

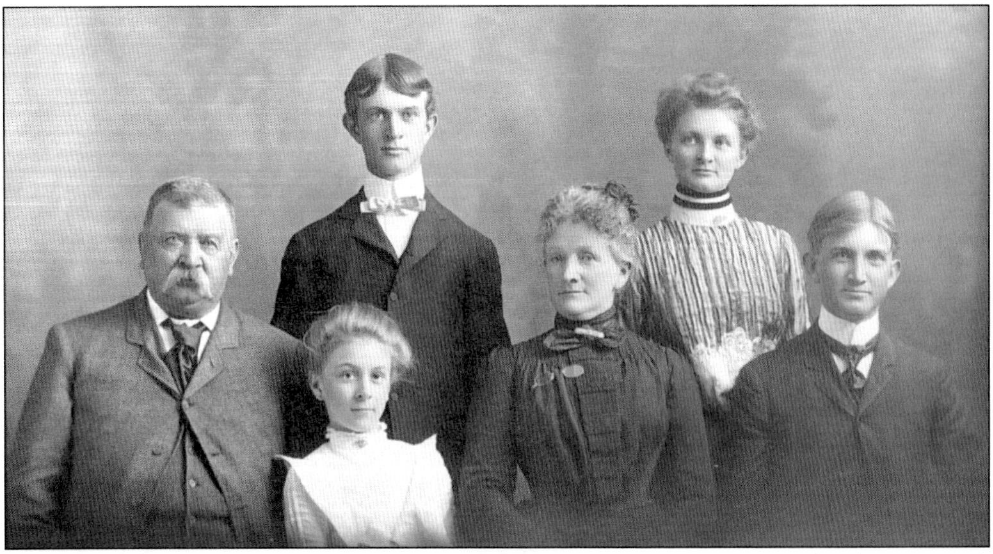

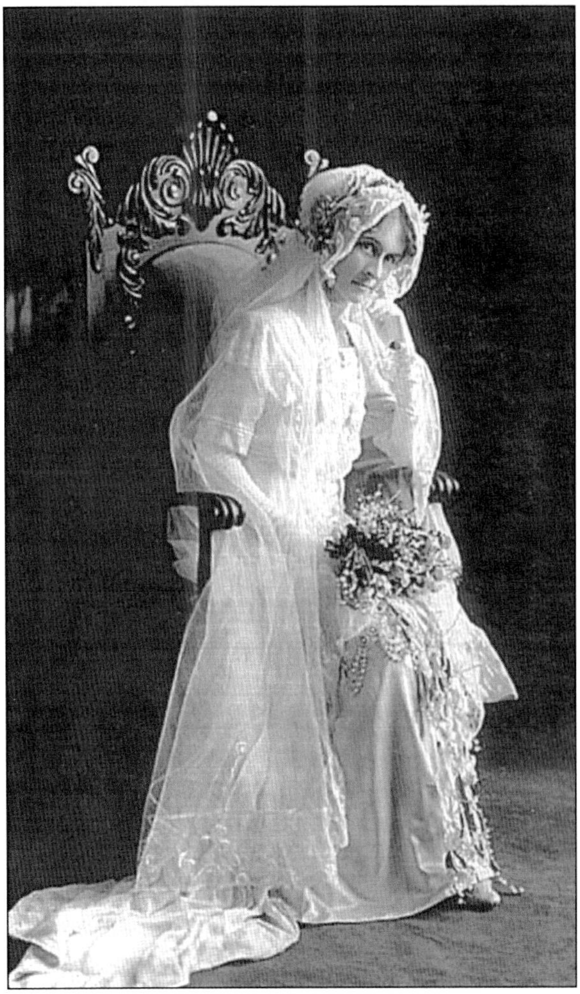

The Louis Huning family is pictured here around 1890. The family members are, from left to right, Louis B. Huning, daughter Lolita Huning, son Louis D. Huning Jr., wife Henrika "Henny" Busch Huning, daughter Emma Huning, and son Frederick Huning. Henny, from the prominent Busch brewing family of St. Louis, Missouri, was Louis's second wife. Louis came to New Mexico following his brother Franz around 1860. (Courtesy of the Huning family.)

Lolita Huning was born on October 21, 1889, in Los Lunas. She married Frank C.W. Pooler, a regional forester with the US Forest Service, and they had two children, Clay and Louise. She was a graduate of the University of New Mexico with a master's degree in foreign language. She taught Spanish and German at the University of New Mexico. She also taught at the Sandia Girls School and Manzano Day School in Albuquerque. (Courtesy of the Huning family.)

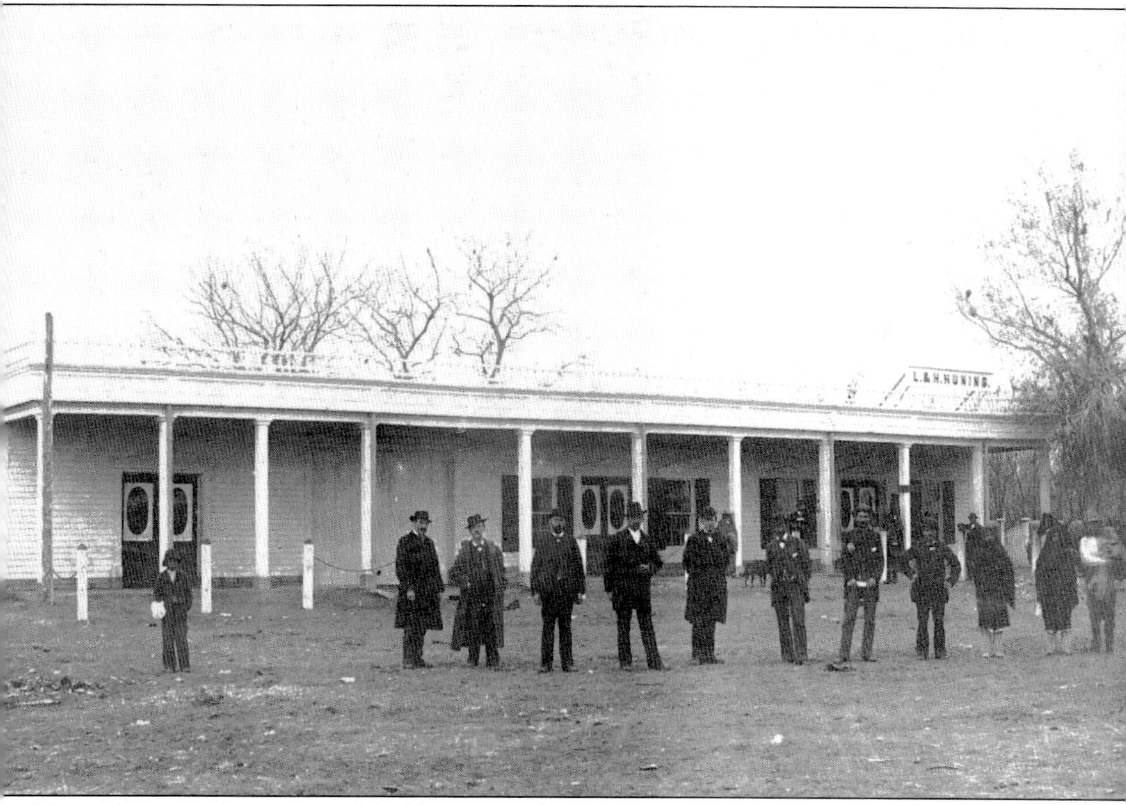

From 1860 to 1994, members of the Huning family operated the Huning Mercantile store in Los Lunas. The store was (and still is) located on the northwest corner of Main Street and Los Lentes Road. The main building is shown here shortly after it was opened by Louis and Henry Huning. (Courtesy of the Center for Southwest Research.)

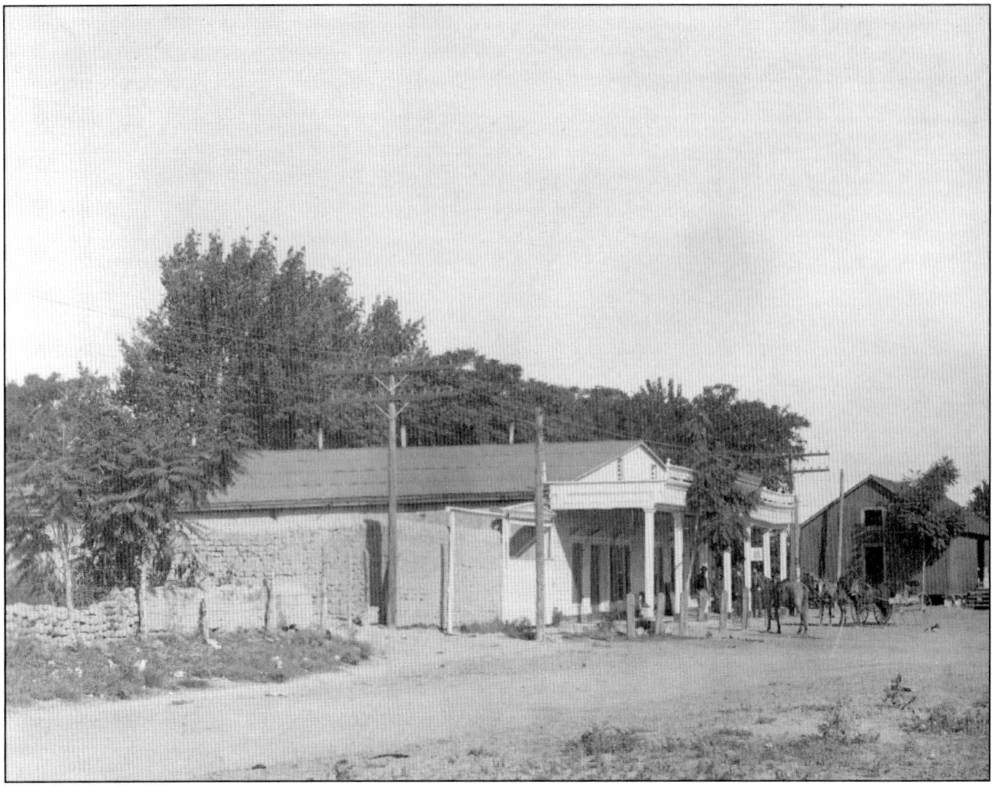

This photograph shows the Huning Mercantile store around 1880. Some of the utility outbuildings can be seen to the right of the main store. The main building is little changed from the original, with the exception of the addition of a pitched roof. (Courtesy of the Huning family.)

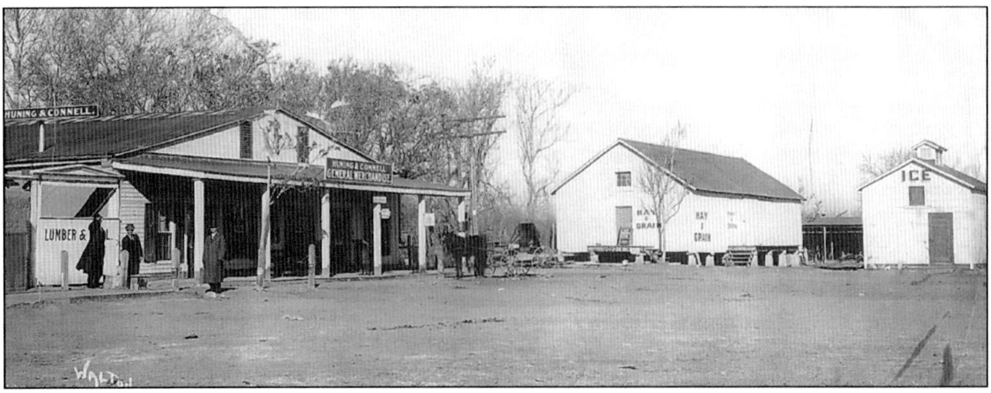

Later, Fred Huning joined in a partnership with Walter Connell, who had married Fred's sister Emma Huning. A grain and hay building and an icehouse were added to the complex of buildings. This photograph was taken around 1900. (Courtesy of the Huning family.)

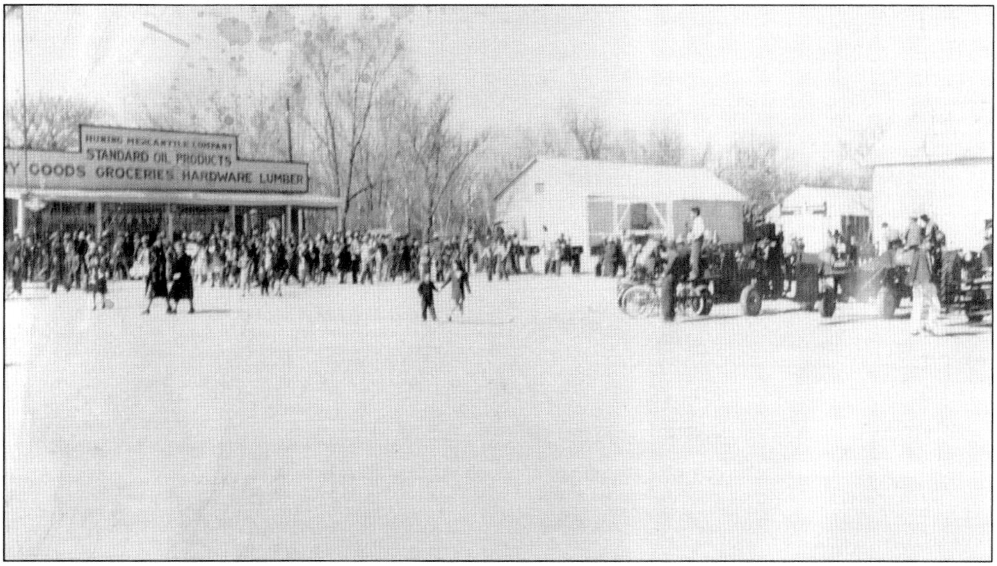

For many years, the Huning family held a customer appreciation day celebration. The event, pictured here in 1925, became an unofficial town fair, with food, prizes, contests, and product demonstrations. In 1928, a cross-country foot race called the "Bunion Derby" was staged, and the race route ran through Los Lunas. Bunion Derby racers slept in tents on the grounds of Huning Mercantile. (Courtesy of the Huning family.)

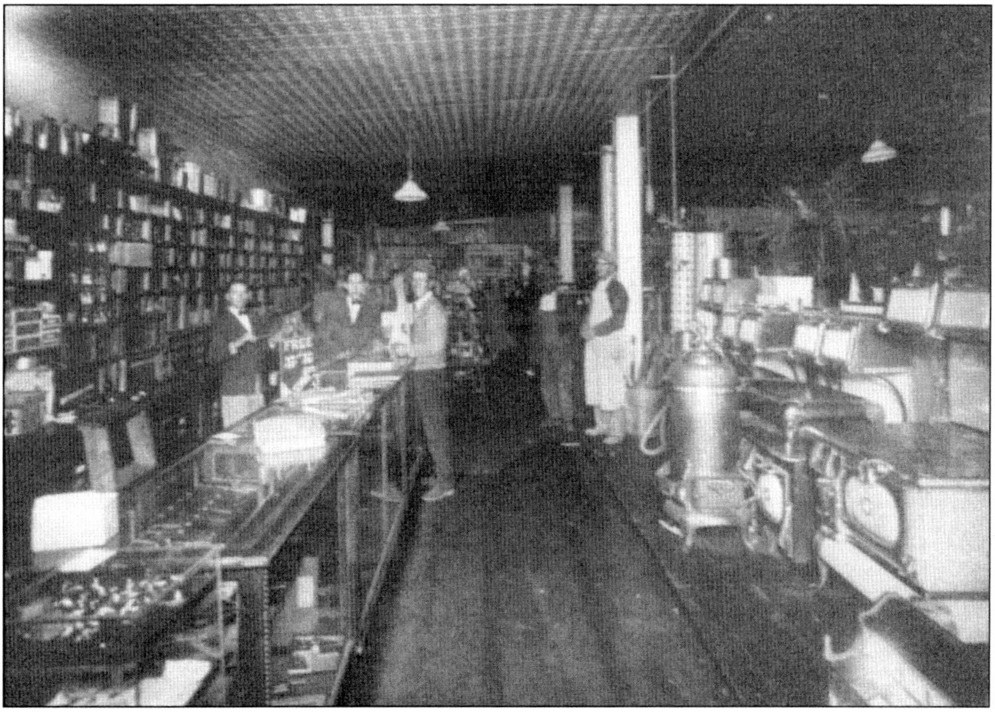

This c. 1910 photograph shows the interior of the Huning Mercantile store. Huning's was truly a general store, selling canned goods, hand tools, cooking stoves, linoleum, and just about anything else a family might need. Local farmers would exchange their crops for credit at the store. (Courtesy of the Huning family.)

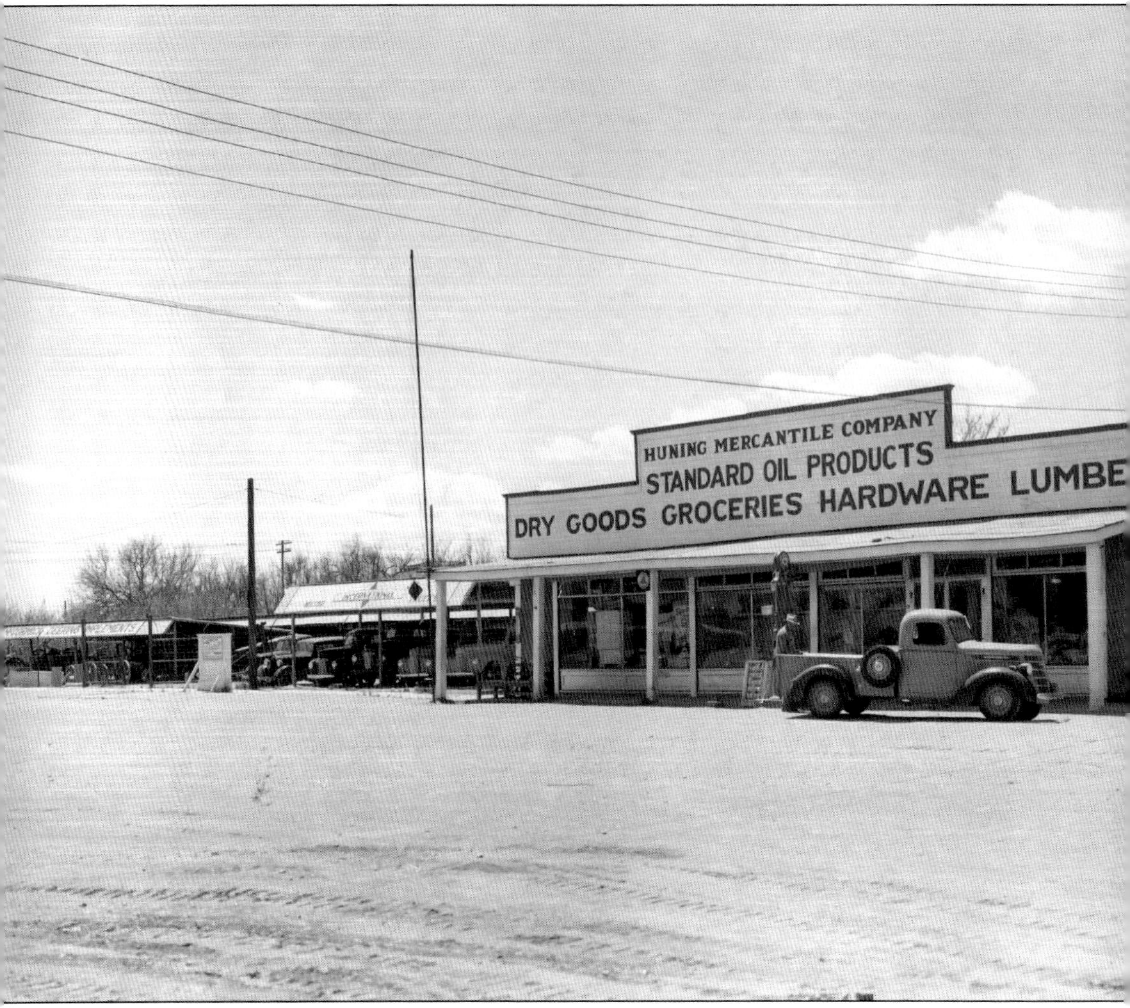

By the late 1930s, Huning Mercantile was also selling tractors, pickup trucks, and automobiles. The pitched roof has been removed and replaced with the original flat roof. Otherwise, the main building is little changed. (Courtesy of the Huning family.)

John Becker came from Germany and worked for the Huning brothers in their Los Lunas store. The Hunings sent him to Belen, New Mexico, to manage their store. Prominent Belen citizen Felipe Chaves, called "El Millionario" because of his vast business and ranching holdings, offered to support Becker in opening a general store of his own. (Courtesy of the Valencia County Historical Society.)

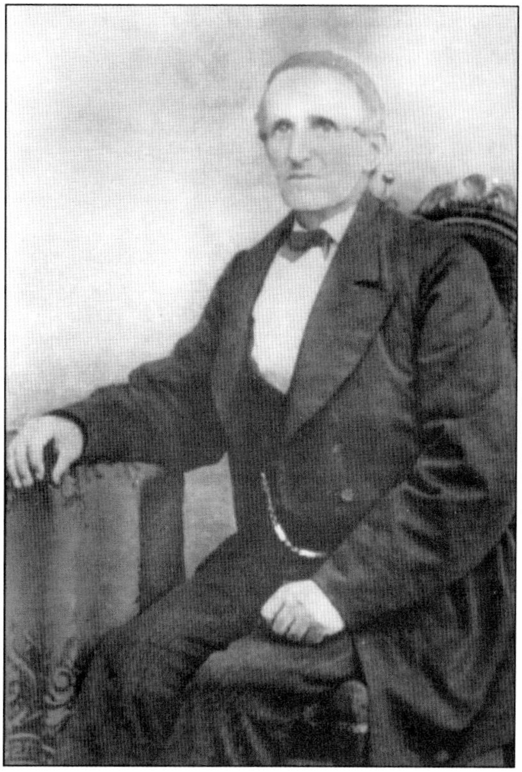

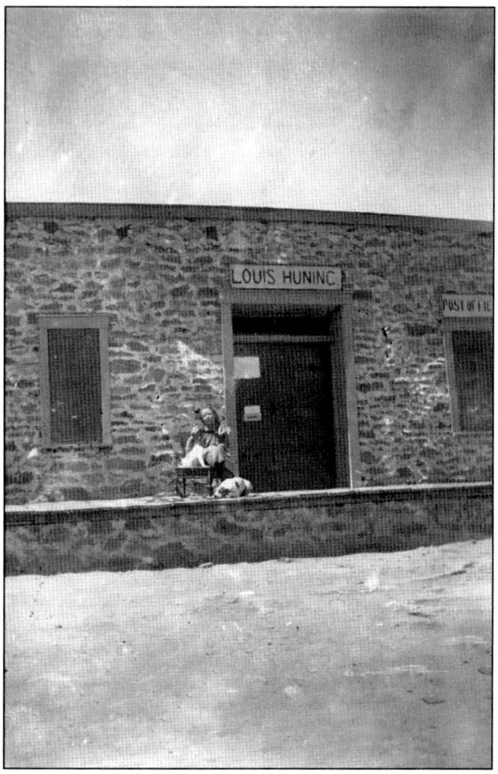

In addition to its mercantile operations, the Belen Huning store also served as the post office for the town of Belen. The building was constructed of stone and mortar, an unusual arrangement for the area, since most buildings were made of either terrone or traditional fired clay bricks. When John Becker built his own mercantile store, it was constructed of clay brick. (Courtesy of H.O. Becker.)

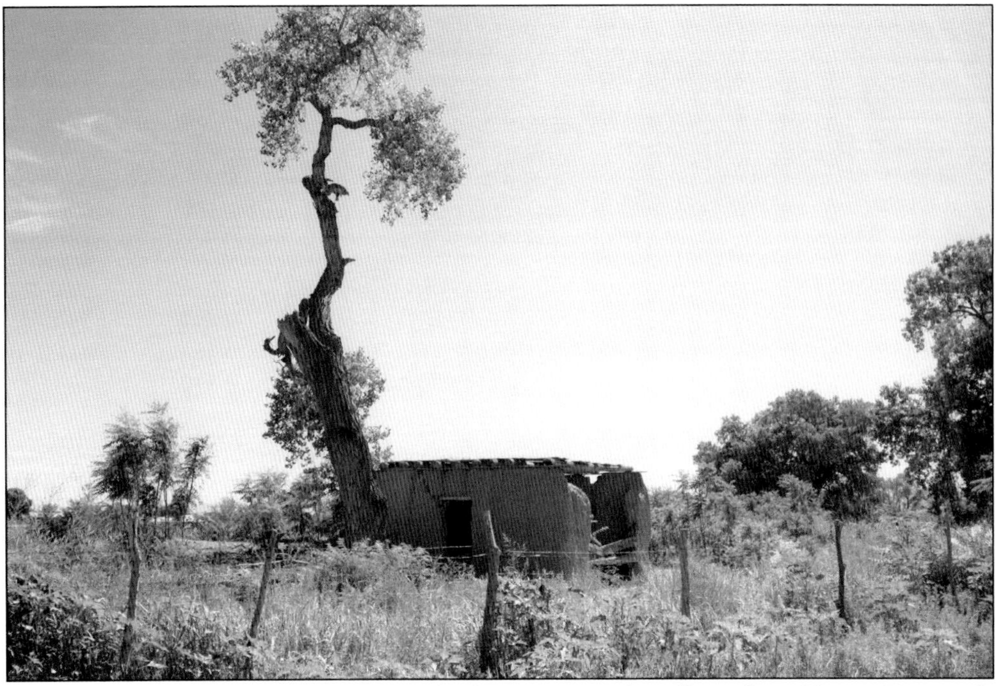

Louis Huning constructed a flour mill south of Los Lunas in the village of Los Chávez. To provide power for the mill wheel, Huning dug a seven-mile-long ditch from the Rio Grande to the mill to build up a proper head of water pressure. This water source ensured inexpensive power to the mill and made it highly competitive with the roller mill owned by John Becker in Belen. Competition between flour mills all along the Rio Grande between Albuquerque and Belen became intense around 1890. In early 1892, the Huning Mill was burned to the ground. Pictured here, the ruins are all that remains. Pictured below is another flourmill, owned by Andres A. Romero Sr. The mill was built in Los Lunas in 1915. (Above, courtesy of the author; below, courtesy of Los Lunas Museum of Heritage and Arts.)

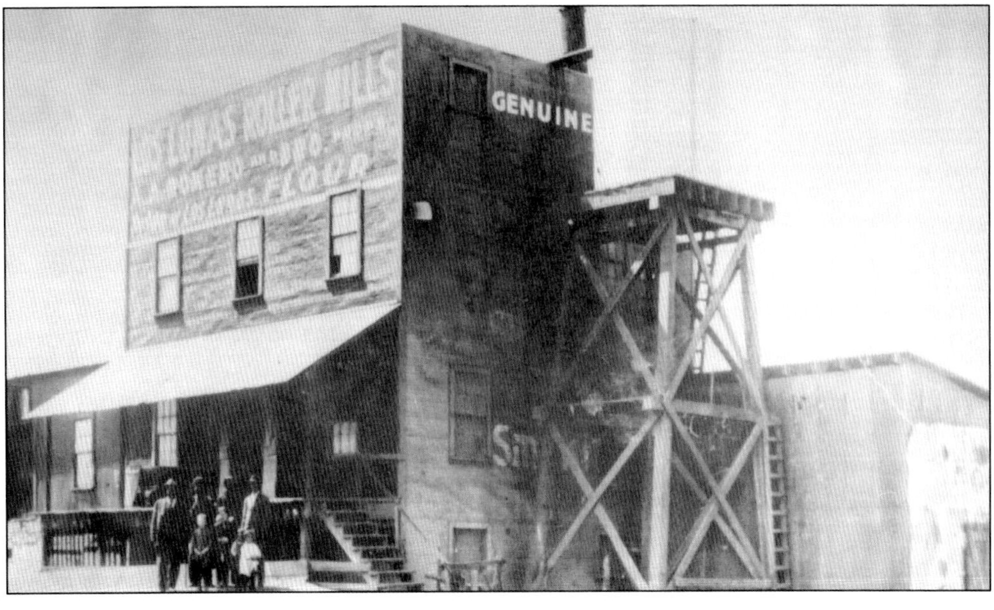

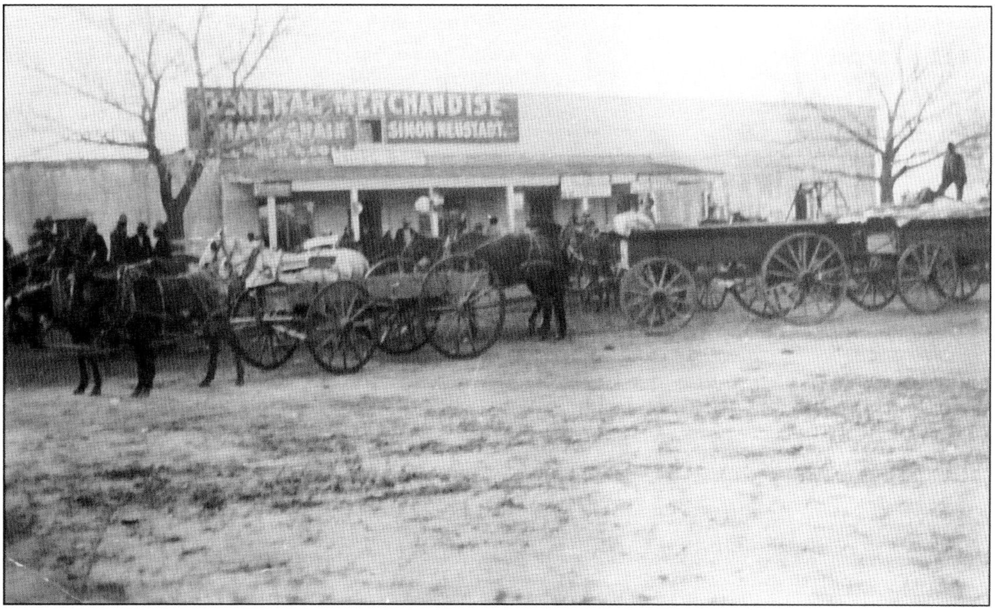

Along with the Hunings, Simon Neustadt and Emiliano Castillo Sr. were successful merchants in Los Lunas. Shown here at the corner of Main Street and Los Lentes Road, the original store was established in 1867 in Los Lunas by Simon Neustadt. (Courtesy of the Valencia County Historical Society.)

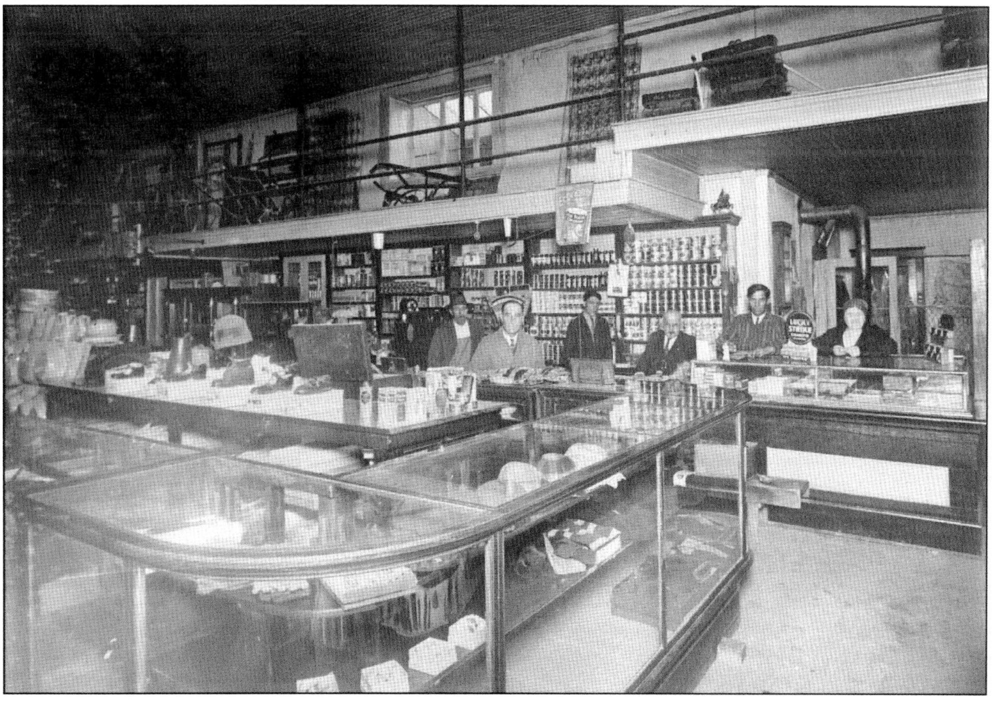

This 1918 photograph shows the interior of the Simon Neustadt mercantile store. Pictured here, from left to right, are two unidentified men, Tomas Sena, Simon Neustadt, Robert Sanchez, and Leah Neustadt. (Courtesy of the Valencia County Historical Society.)

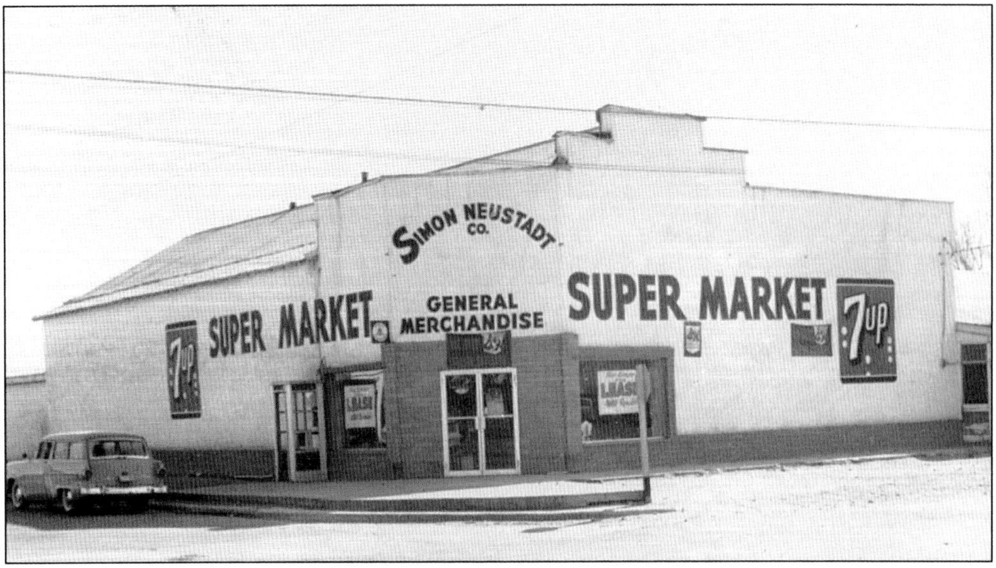

At the same Main Street and Los Lentes Road location (where the Village Inn Pancake House is now), the Simon Neustadt Company had transformed into a supermarket in the 1950s. (Courtesy of the Valencia County Historical Society.)

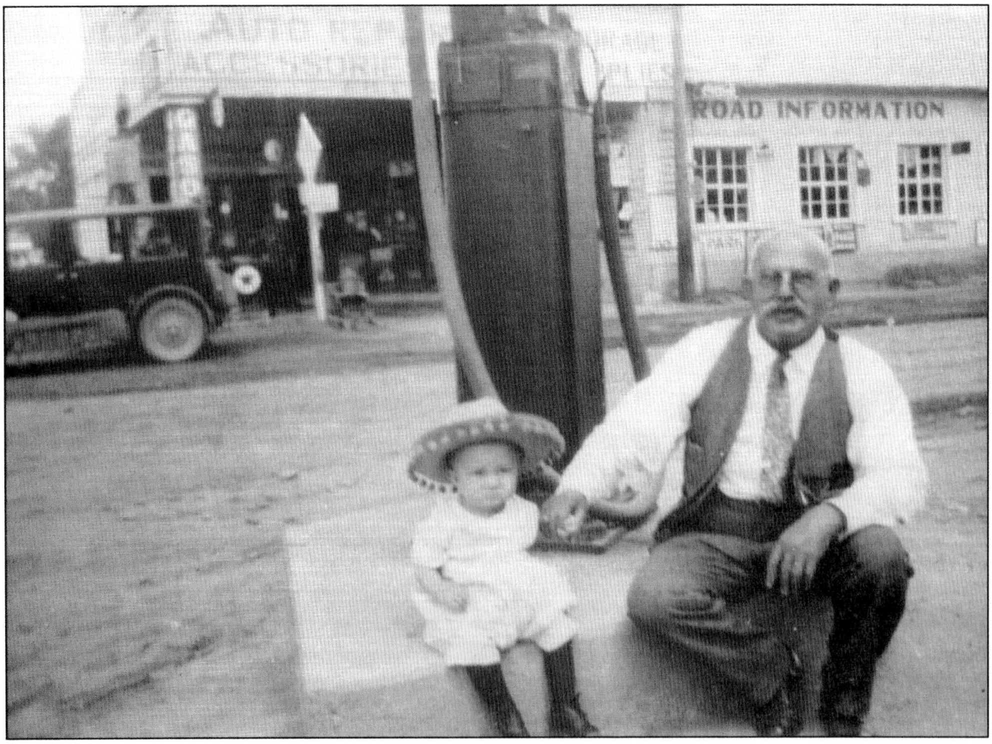

By 1925, Simon Neustadt and Joseph Tondre Sr. had joined in partnership. Tondre, who was raised at Isleta Pueblo and whose mother, Josephine Tondre, was the business manager and banker for the pueblo, was himself a prominent Valencia County political figure and also served as county sheriff. In this photograph, Simon Neustadt is sitting on the curb with Tondre's son Joe Jr. in front of the store. (Courtesy of Los Lunas Museum of Heritage and Arts, Historic Route 66 Project.)

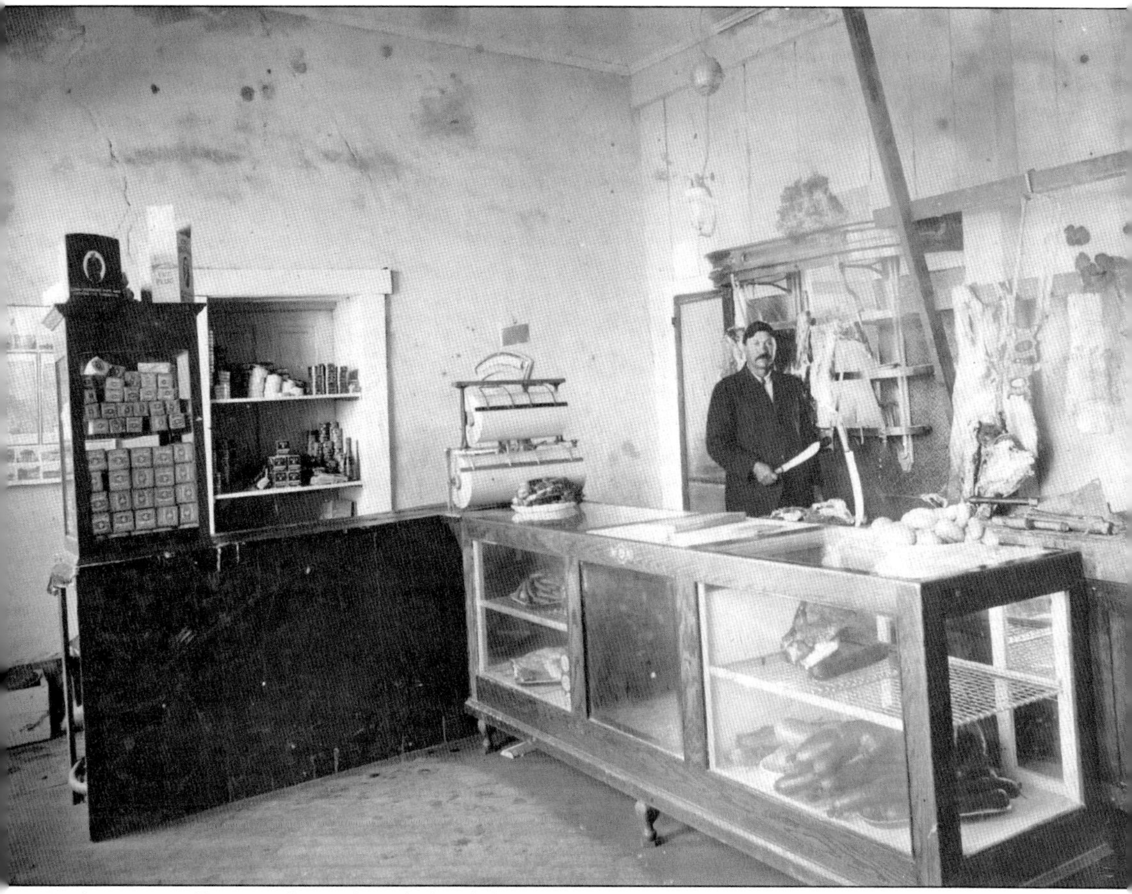

Emiliano Castillo Sr. is shown here behind the counter of the Castillo Meat Market in 1915. The meat market was located in an outbuilding on the Huning Mercantile property. Emiliano Castillo Sr. was born on May 28, 1871, and was raised by the Hunings from age 11. When he grew up, he helped with the Huning businesses. He spoke fluent German, English, and Spanish. Emiliano Castillo Sr. was the first of four members of the Castillo family to be elected mayor of Los Lunas. He served from 1930 to 1932. He was also superintendent of county roads and chairman of the Valencia County Commission for two years. (Courtesy of Barbara Arnold.)

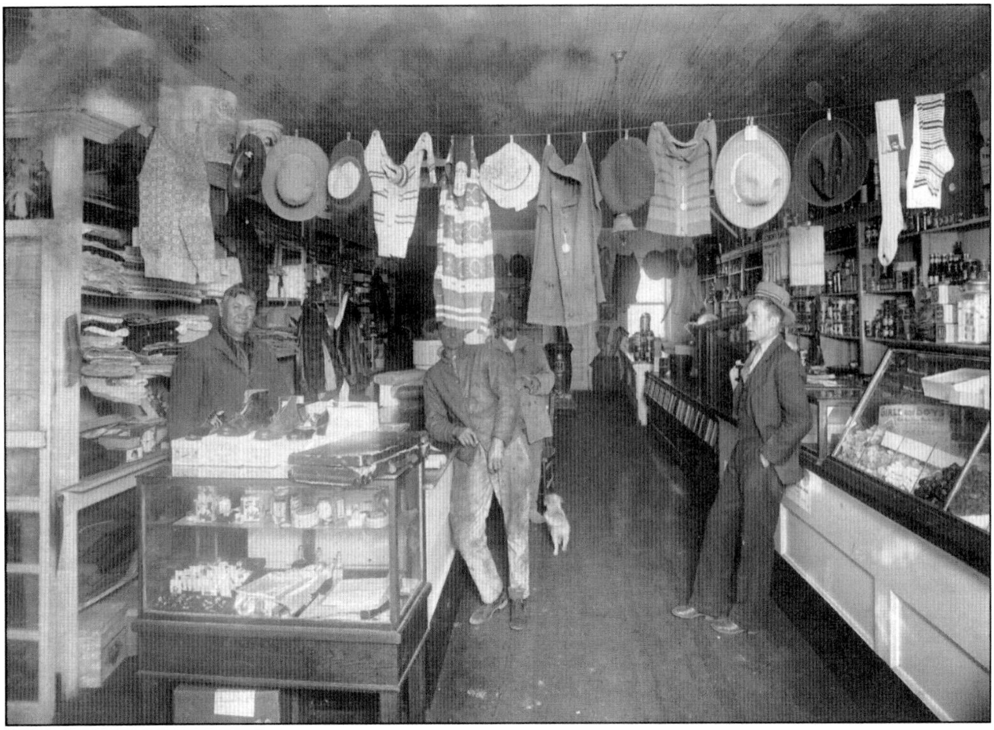

This 1925 photograph shows the interior of the Castillo General Merchandise Company, located on South Los Lentes Road. The range of merchandise sold at the Castillo General Merchandise Company is evident in this photograph. (Courtesy of Barbara Arnold.)

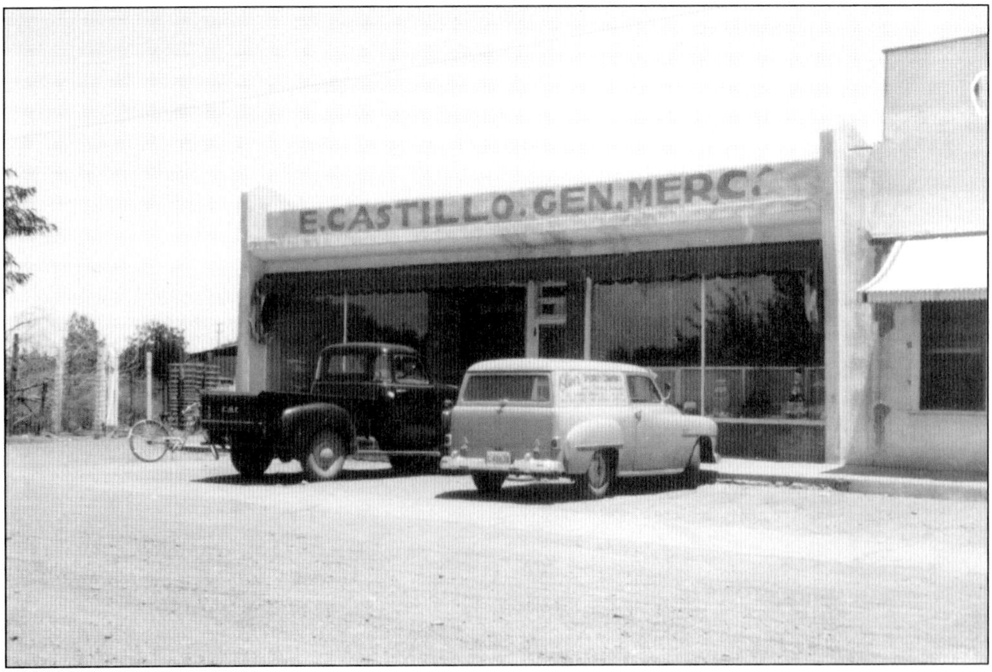

By the 1950s, the Castillo store had become a modern general merchandise establishment. It was still located at the corner of Main Street and Los Lentes Road. (Courtesy of Barbara Arnold.)

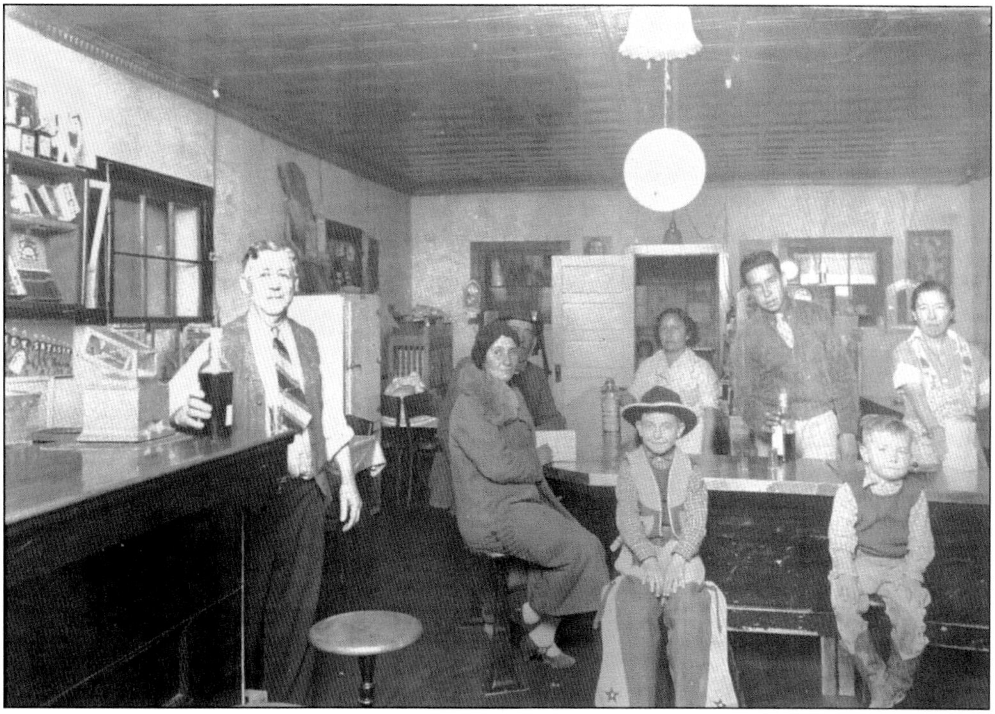

The U and I Diner, owned and operated by Antonio Archuleta, provided food and drinks for local patrons. It also featured billiard tables. The diner was a rest stop for the 1928 transcontinental "Bunion Derby" foot racers. Antonio Archuleta served as the first mayor of Los Lunas from 1928 to 1930. The diner was located at the corner of Main Street and Don Diego Avenue, the present location of an extensive rose garden. (Courtesy of Los Lunas Museum of Heritage and Arts, Historic Route 66 Project.)

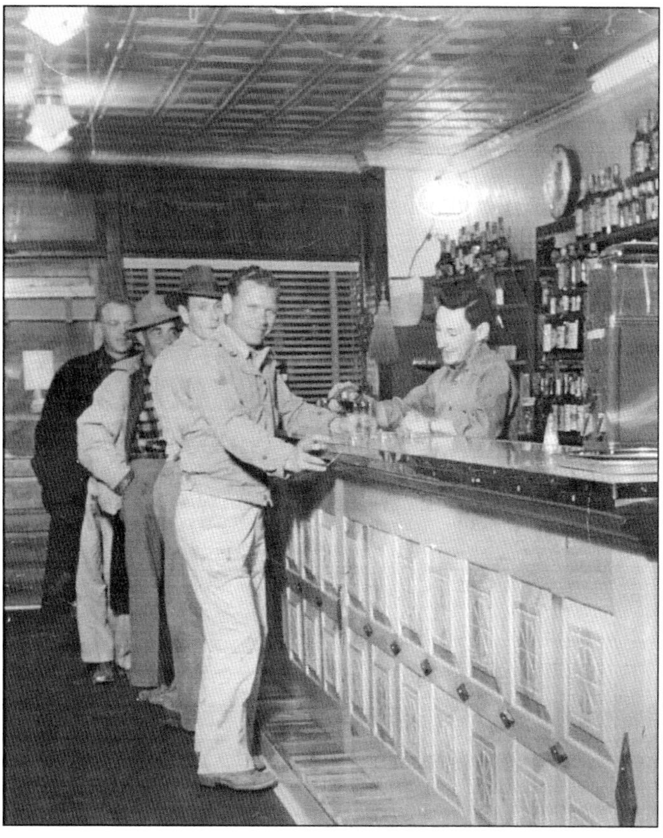

The Archuleta family also operated a bar, located just west of the Luna Mansion on Main Street. (Courtesy of Los Lunas Museum of Heritage and Arts, Historic Route 66 Project.)

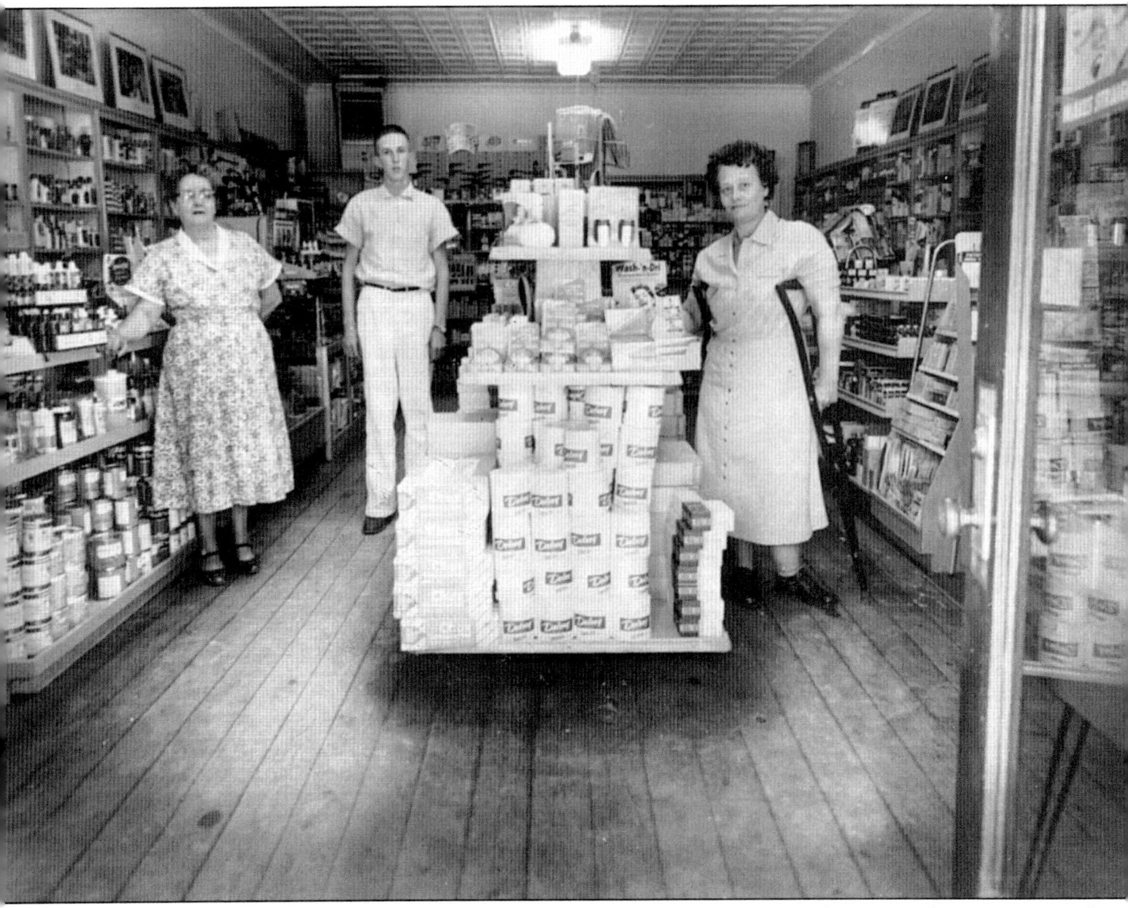

Employees of the Los Lunas Pharmacy, owned by Helen Lucas, are shown in the store around 1940. (Courtesy of the Valencia County Historical Society.)

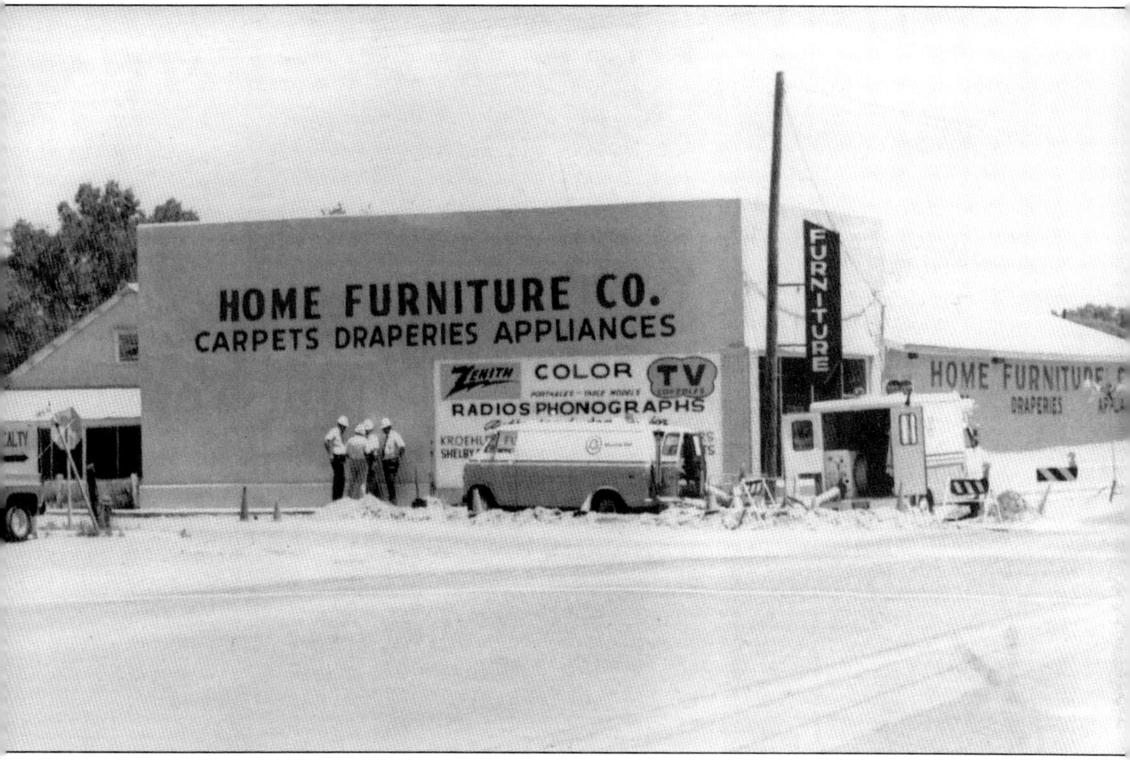

The Home Furniture Company, which has been owned and operated by the Sanchez family for many years, is another long-standing business in Los Lunas. Although this building has been replaced with a newer one, the business is still in the same location at the northeast intersection of Main Street and Los Lentes Road. (Courtesy of Los Lunas Museum of Heritage and Arts.)

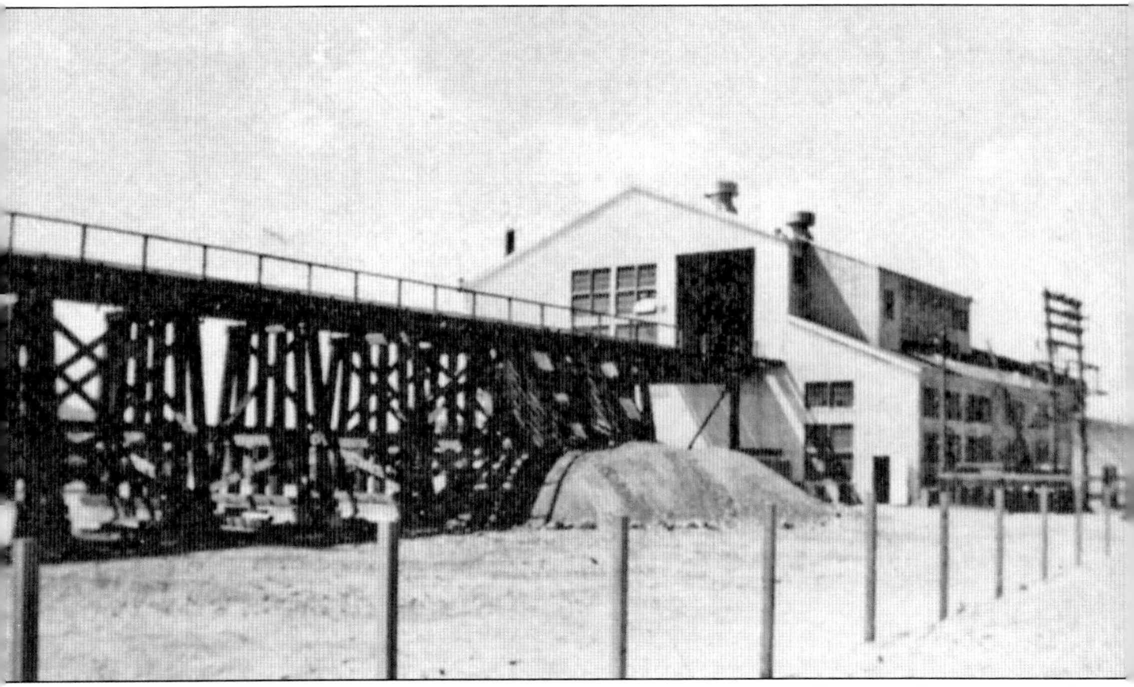

The World War II Defense Plant Corporation constructed the Zuni Fluorspar Plant in 1942. The plant was located in Los Lunas on the east side of Highway 314, south of the present Transportation Center. The mine that provided the fluorspar for the plant was located south of Grants, New Mexico, in the Zuni Mountains. By 1945, the plant was the most efficient and up-to-date fluorspar mill in the western United States. Fluorspar (or fluorite) is used as a flux in smelting operations and in the production of certain glasses and enamels. It is also used in making fluorescent light fixtures. (Courtesy of Los Lunas Museum of Heritage and Arts.)

Four

Getting Around

Because of the rural aspect of life in and around the village of Los Lunas, getting from one place to another efficiently has always been an important consideration. Within the village, people would usually walk to their destination. Travel to nearby communities such as Los Lentes, Los Chávez, Peralta, Valencia, and Tomé would be accomplished on horseback or in a horse-drawn wagon or buggy.

In 1881, the railroad came to Los Lunas using land purchased from Don Antonio Luna as a right-of-way. The railroad provided two major benefits to the residents of Los Lunas and nearby Valencia County communities. First, it provided a means of delivering locally produced agricultural products to more distant (and profitable) markets. Second, the railroad allowed people to travel more easily to places like St. Louis, Chicago, New York, and the West Coast.

The first automobile arrived in Los Lunas around 1910, but poorly maintained dirt roads made travel more difficult than it would have been in a more urban location. In 1925, the Chicago–to–Los Angeles national highway, designated Route 66, passed through Los Lunas. Although this unusual north–south orientation was changed in 1937, for about 10 years the nation's east–west automobile traffic brought hundreds of thousands of travelers to the village of Los Lunas. This traffic, in turn, spurred the creation of many businesses designed to serve the motoring population.

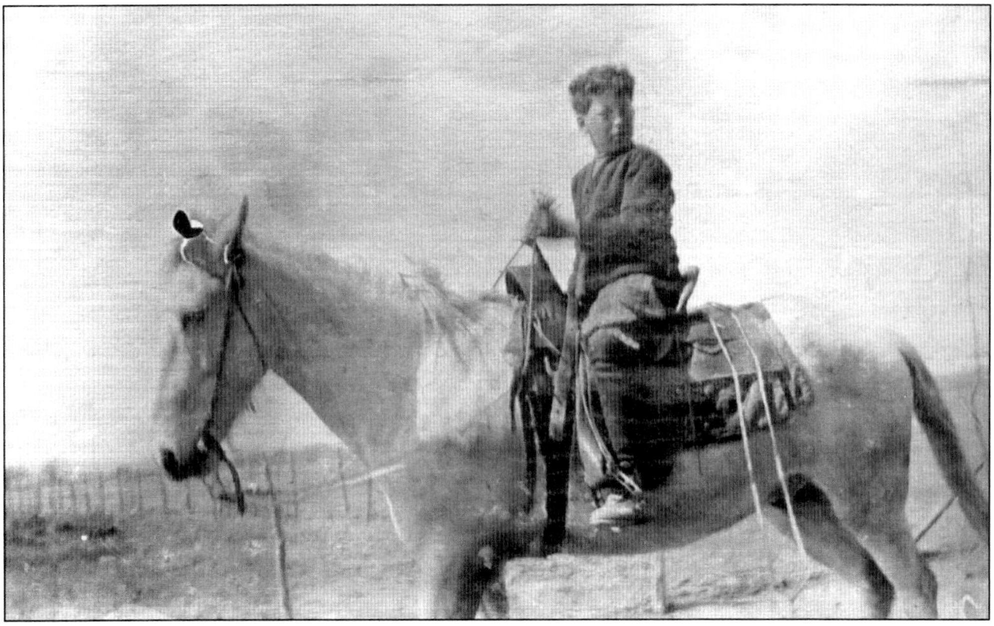

Aside from walking, the most common means of transportation in early Los Lunas was riding a horse or mule. The horse rider in this photograph is Teddy Otero. (Courtesy of Barbara Bergère Nau.)

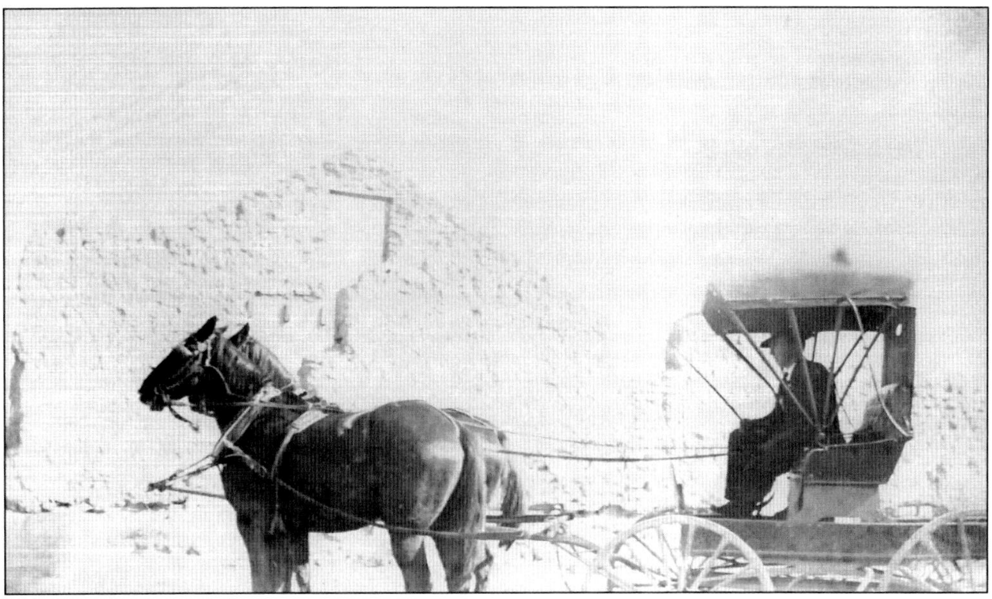

Before motorized transportation, people traveled on horseback or in horse-drawn buggies. Eduardo Otero is shown here driving a team of horses hitched to a Victorian-style buggy. (Courtesy of Barbara Bergère Nau.)

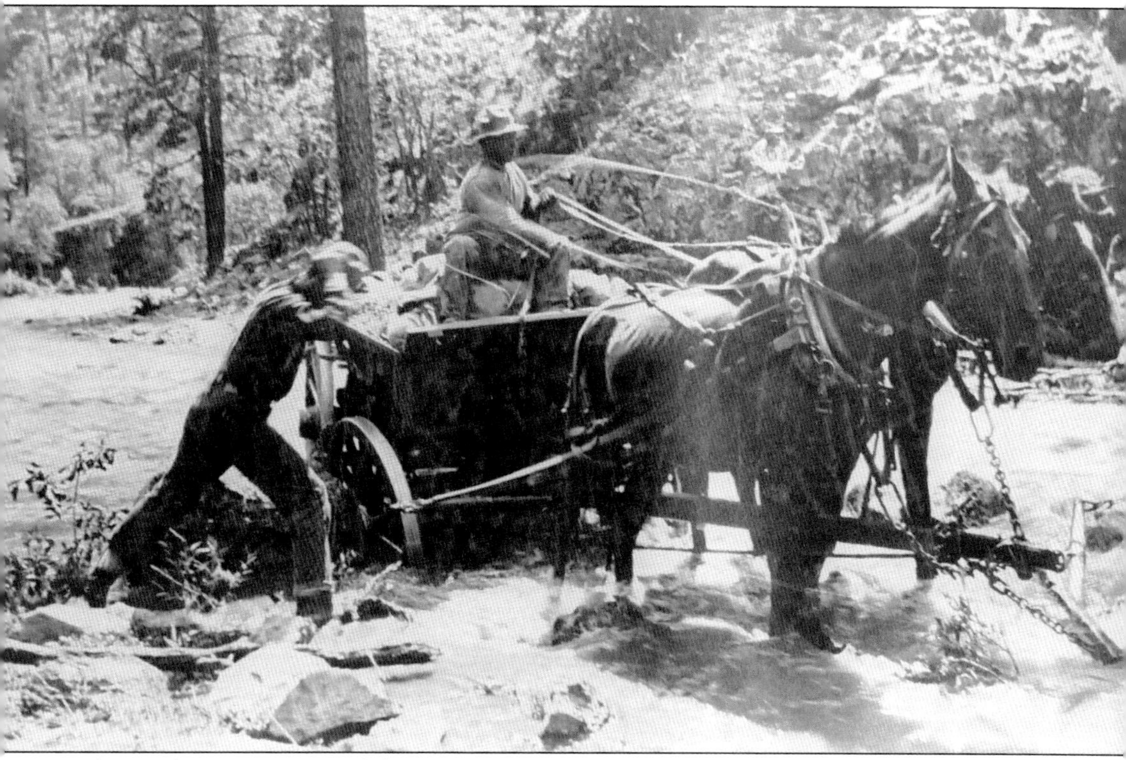

Traveling and transporting goods by wagon was not always a straightforward process. This freight wagon driven by Eduardo Otero is attempting to ford a stream in the Jémez Mountains, north of Los Lunas. A four-horse team pulls the wagon, although only two horses can be seen in the photograph. (Courtesy of Barbara Bergère Nau.)

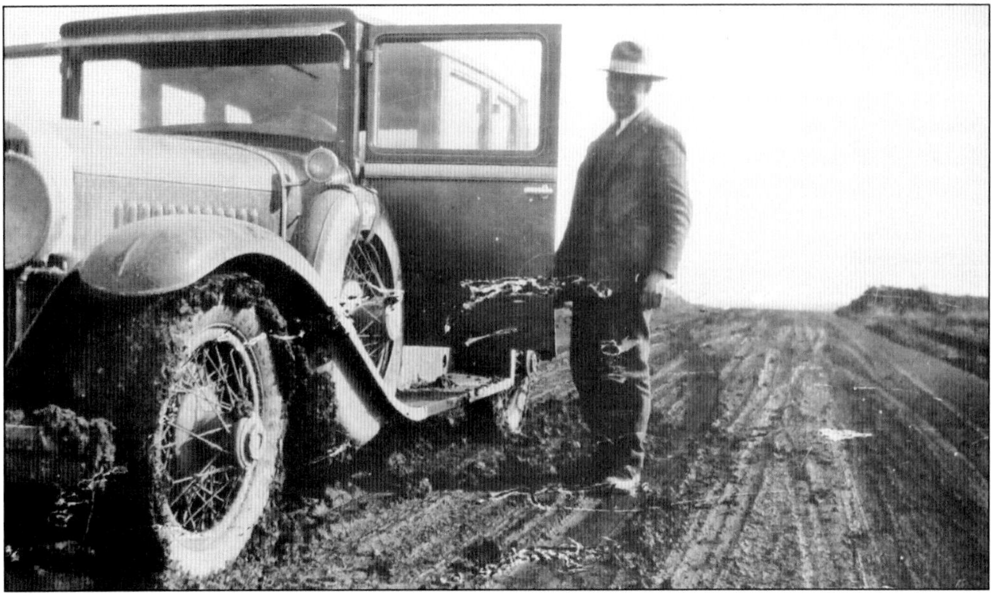

The introduction of the automobile did not necessarily make traveling any easier than it had been in the day of horse-drawn vehicles. Eduardo Otero has mounted chains on the tires of his automobile to provide traction on this muddy road. (Courtesy of Barbara Bergère Nau.)

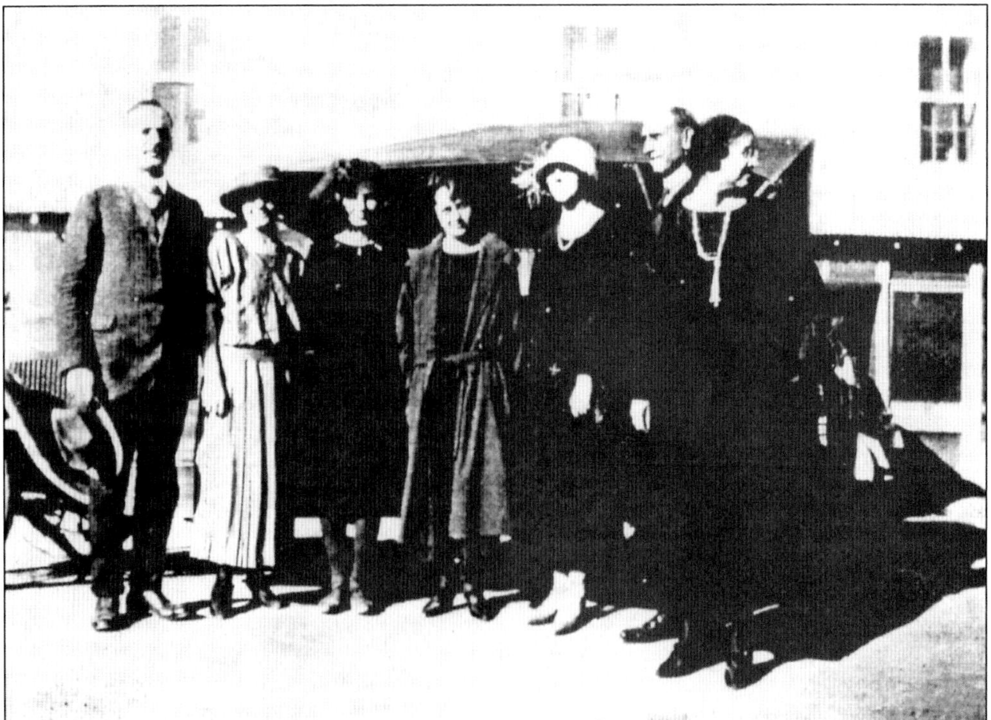

The first automobile in Los Lunas was owned by Dr. William Wittwer, who used his car to make house calls. At first, he could only use the car to serve patients on the west side of the Rio Grande. There was no bridge across the river until 1927. (Courtesy of Los Lunas Museum of Heritage and Arts, Historic Route 66 Project.)

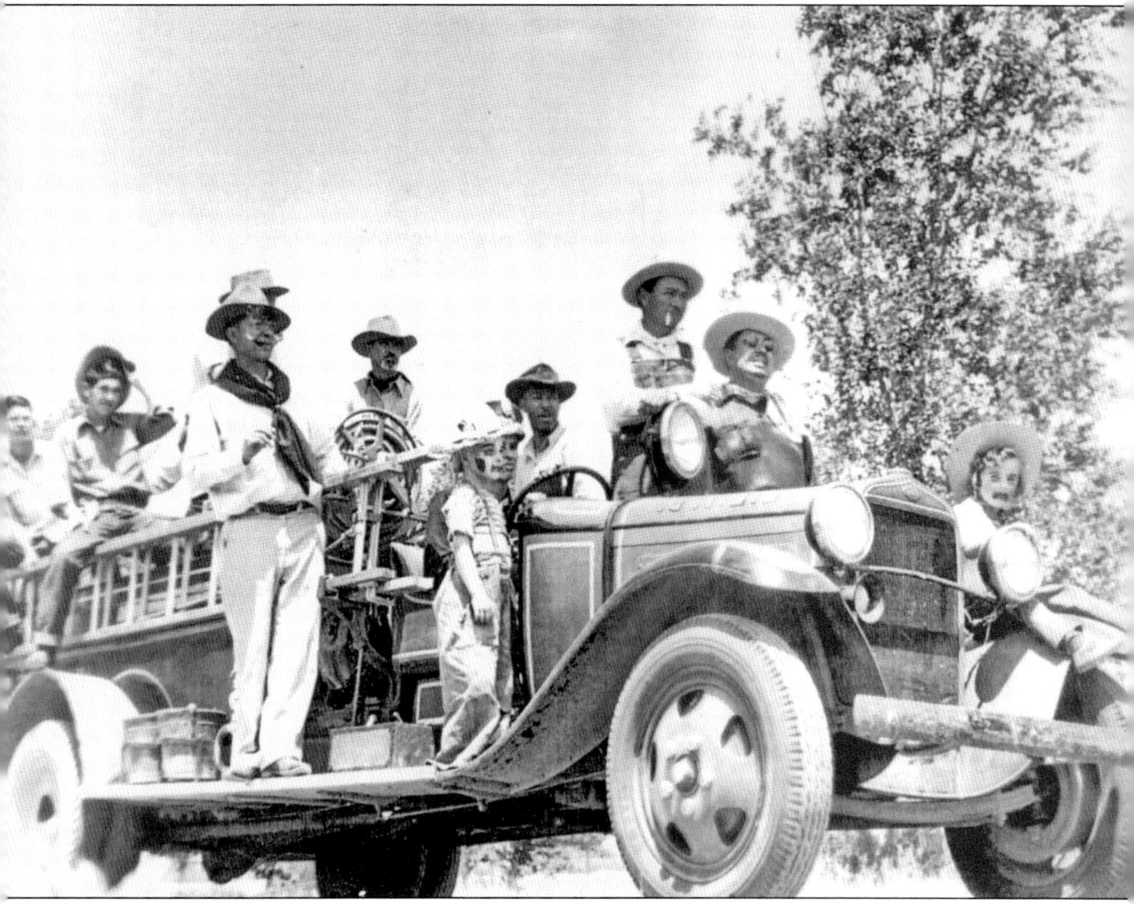

For the 1935 Fourth of July parade in Los Lunas, members of the Los Lunas Fire Department and some friends decided to clown around. (Courtesy of Los Lunas Museum of Heritage and Arts, Route 66 Project.)

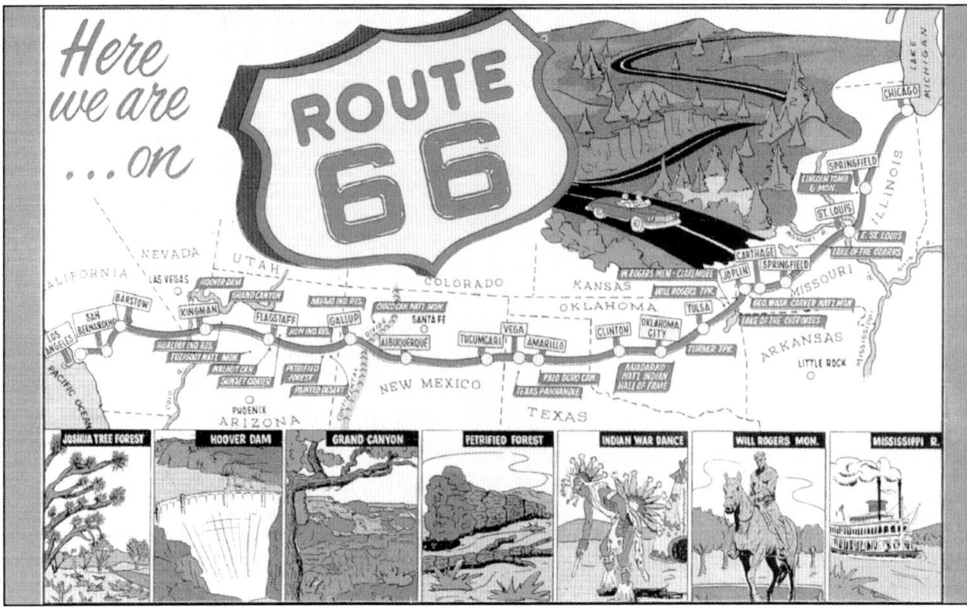

The original US Route 66 in New Mexico went north from Santa Rosa to Las Vegas, then went to Santa Fe, and traveled south through Bernalillo and Albuquerque to Los Lunas. This postcard was produced after 1937, since the map shows the road traveling west from Santa Rosa to Gallup, straight through Albuquerque. (Courtesy Los Lunas Museum of Heritage and Arts.)

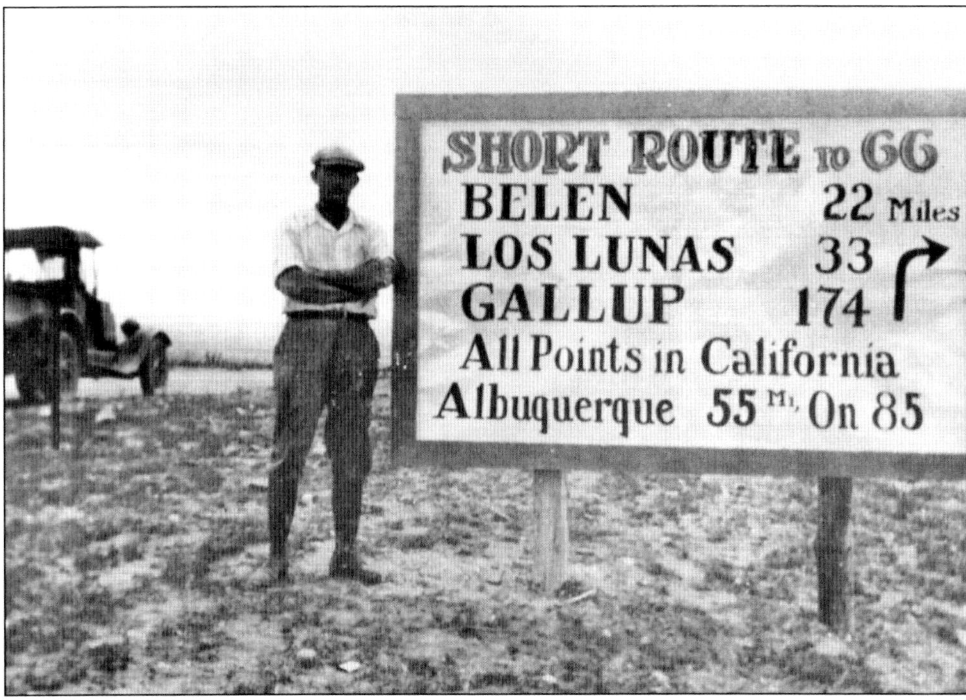

After 1937, as a result of lobbying by the Albuquerque business community, Route 66 was realigned to go from Santa Rosa directly to Albuquerque through Tijeras Canyon. Because of this realignment, Route 66 no longer went through Los Lunas. This rare road sign appeared on US Highway 85 between Socorro and Belen, New Mexico. (Courtesy of Historic Route 66 Project.)

During the Dust Bowl in the 1930s, migrants traveled Route 66 from Oklahoma and Texas through New Mexico on the way to California. Local communities barely had enough resources to take care of their own and did not want travelers lingering too long. (Courtesy of the Library of Congress.)

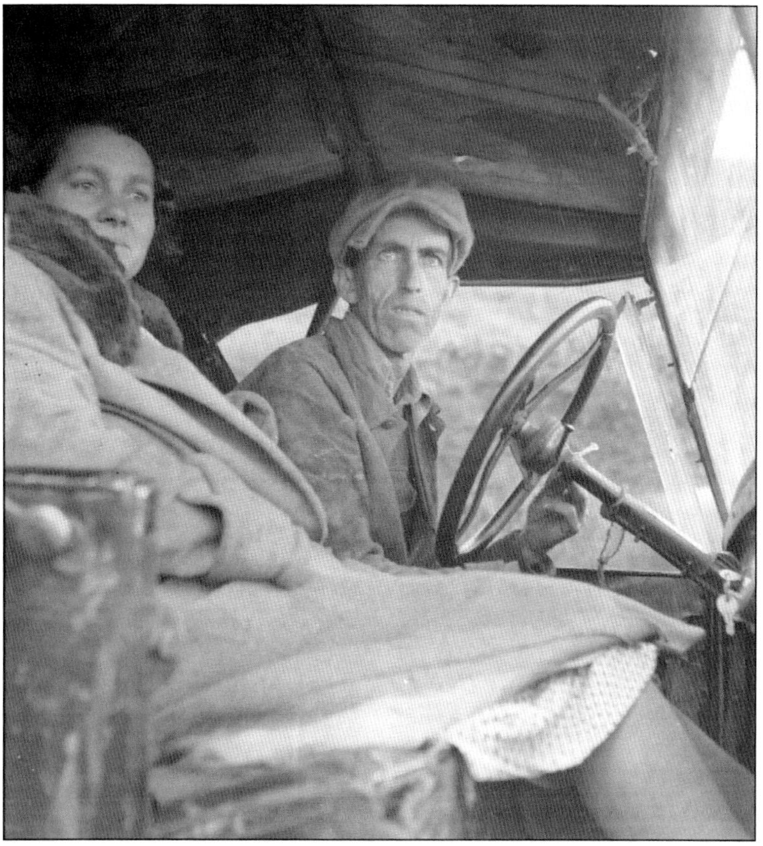

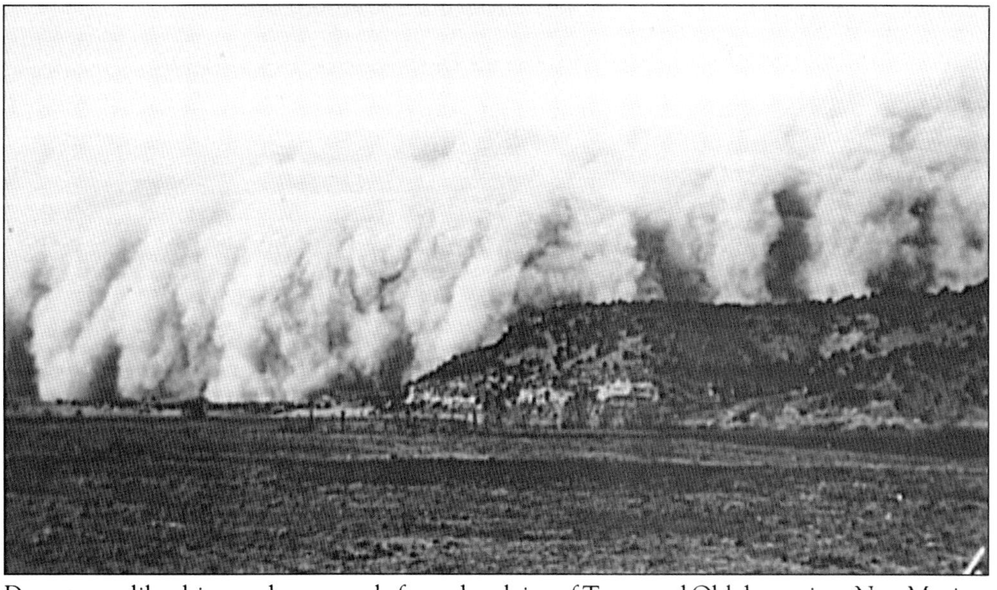

Dust storms like this one drove people from the plains of Texas and Oklahoma into New Mexico, Arizona, and California. In one extended period in 1937 in Oklahoma, the wind blew at 35 miles per hour or more for 100 straight hours. Dust from one of these storms reached as far east as Washington, DC. (Courtesy of the Library of Congress.)

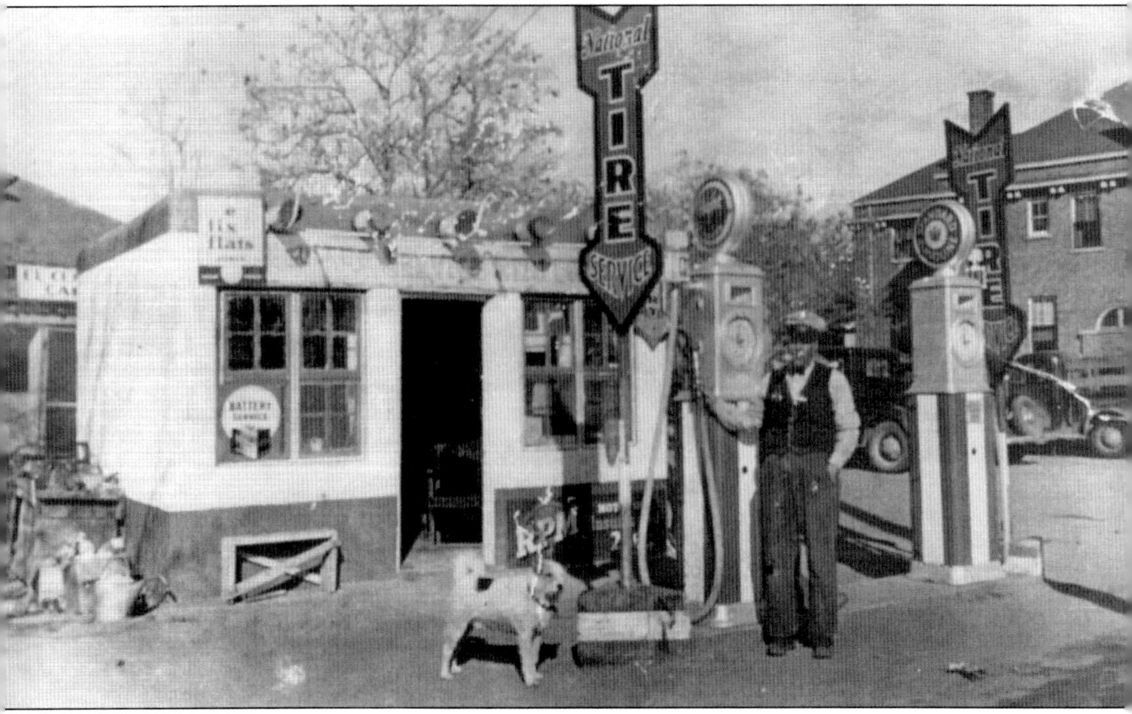

Route 66 brought many travelers through Los Lunas. Climaco Aguirre operated an automobile service station next to the old Valencia County Courthouse. He also served as superintendent of Valencia County Schools and as Los Lunas's village clerk. As village clerk, he issued both automobile licenses and marriage licenses from his service station. His fox terrier, Fifi, followed him everywhere he went. The old courthouse is the two-story brick building to the right in this photograph. (Courtesy of Los Lunas Museum of Heritage and Arts, Historic Route 66 Project.)

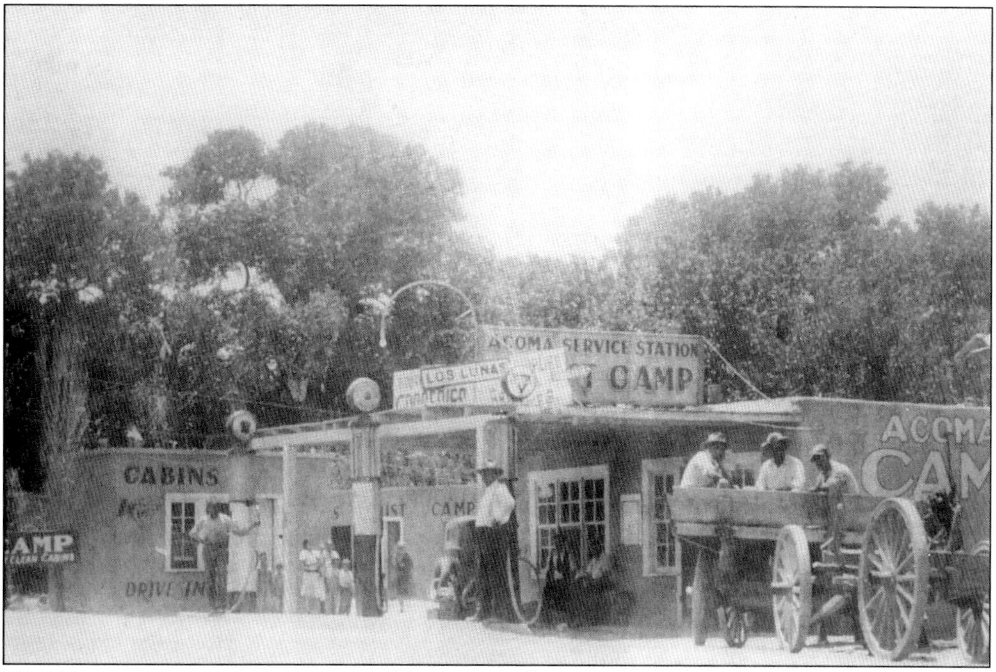

The Acoma service station was owned by Jesús Gallegos. In addition to petroleum products, this business also included a café, grocery store, and tourist cabins. (Courtesy of Charles Griego.)

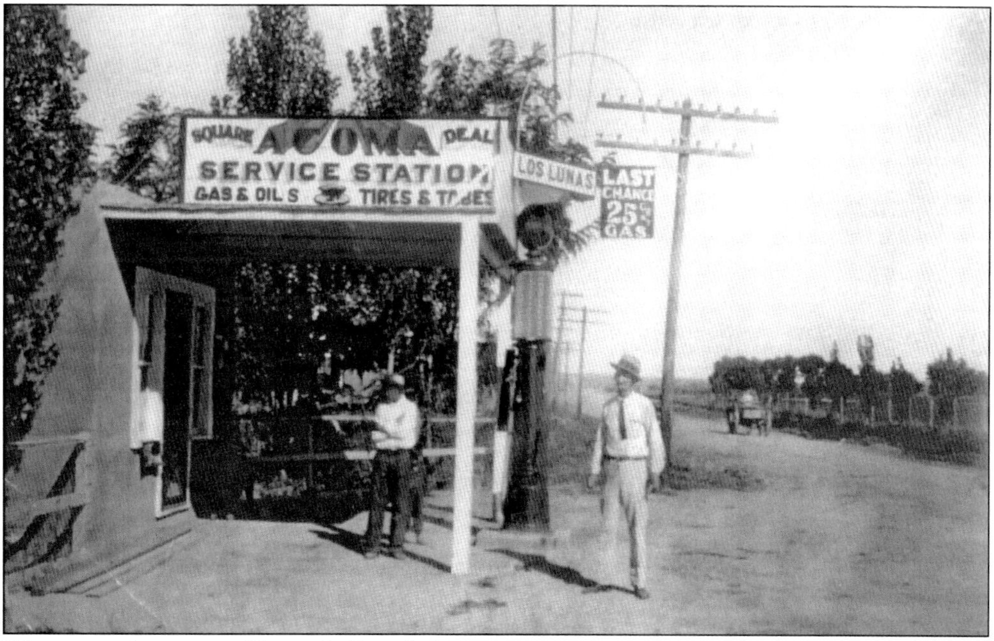

This is another view of Jesús Gallegos's Acoma service station looking north on what is now New Mexico State Highway 314. The sign proclaiming this the "Last Chance" for gas was a bit misleading, since there were other gas stations just west of the Acoma service station location. (Courtesy of Los Lunas Museum of Heritage and Arts, Historic Route 66 Project.)

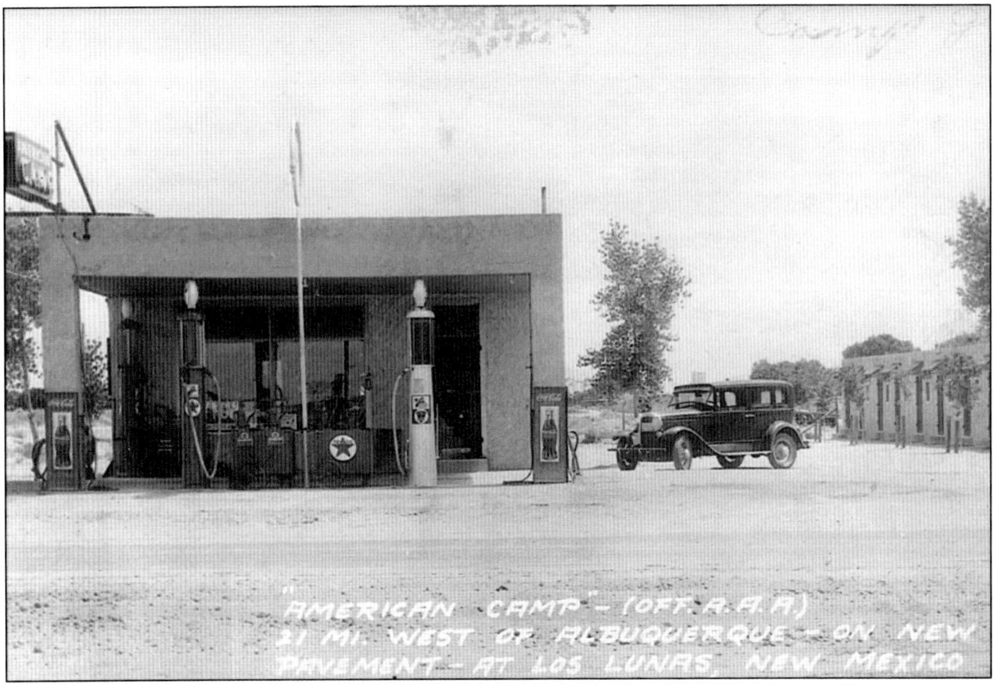

Another typical Route 66 tourist facility in Los Lunas was the American Camp Texaco service station and cabin facility. The hand-lettered caption is technically inaccurate, because Los Lunas is 21 miles south, not west, of Albuquerque. (Courtesy of Los Lunas Museum of Heritage and Arts, Historic Route 66 Project.)

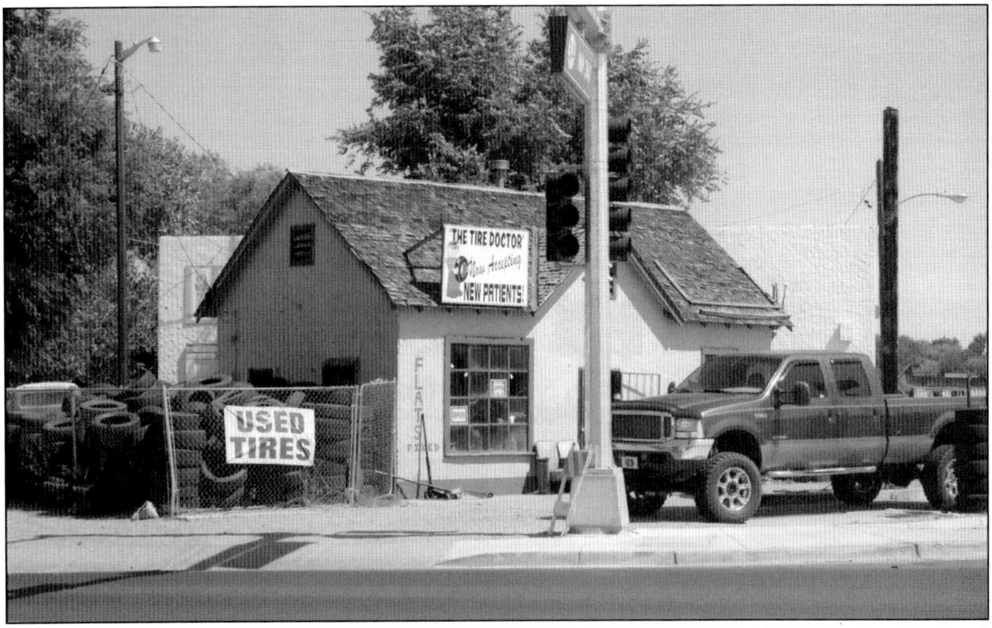

Otero's 66 Service Station (now Sam's Tires) is virtually unchanged from the time it was opened in 1925. This classic Route 66 service station was owned and operated by Frank and Mamie Otero of Peralta for almost 30 years. It has been listed on the National Register of Historic Places since 2003. (Author's collection.)

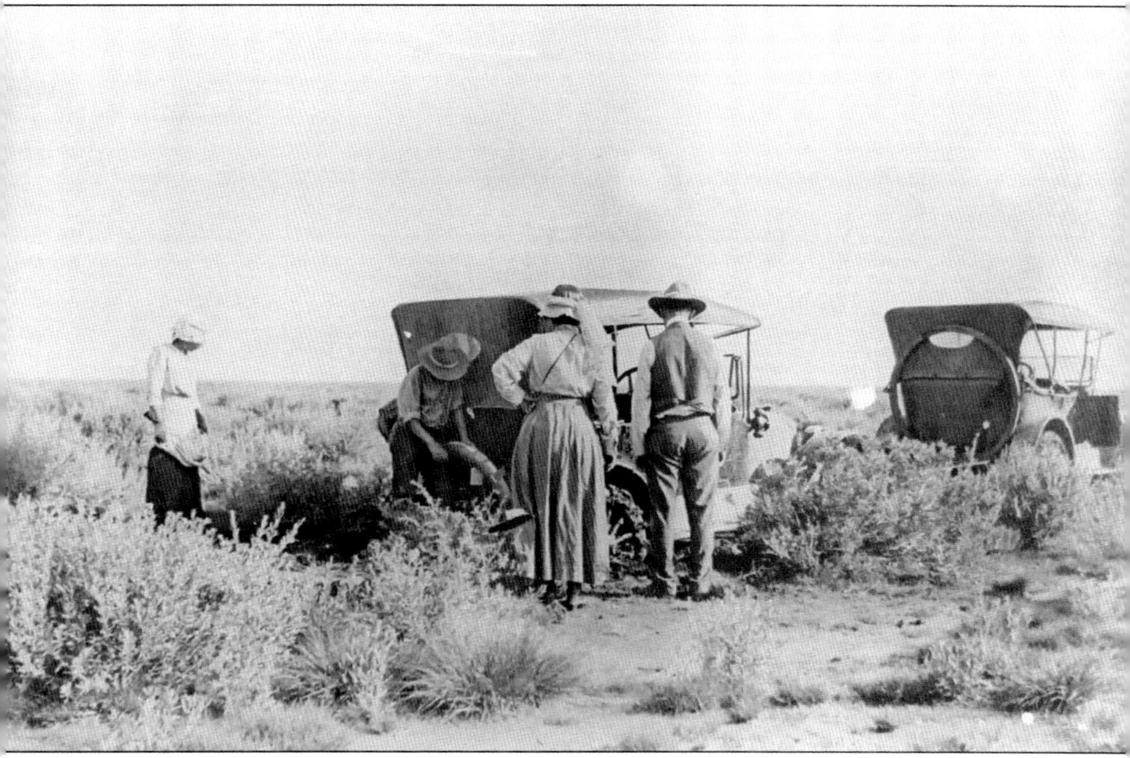

Unpaved roads did not preclude travel by automobile. Here, Eduardo and Josephita Otero watch as attempts are made to free their car from the mud. (Courtesy of Barbara Bergère Nau.)

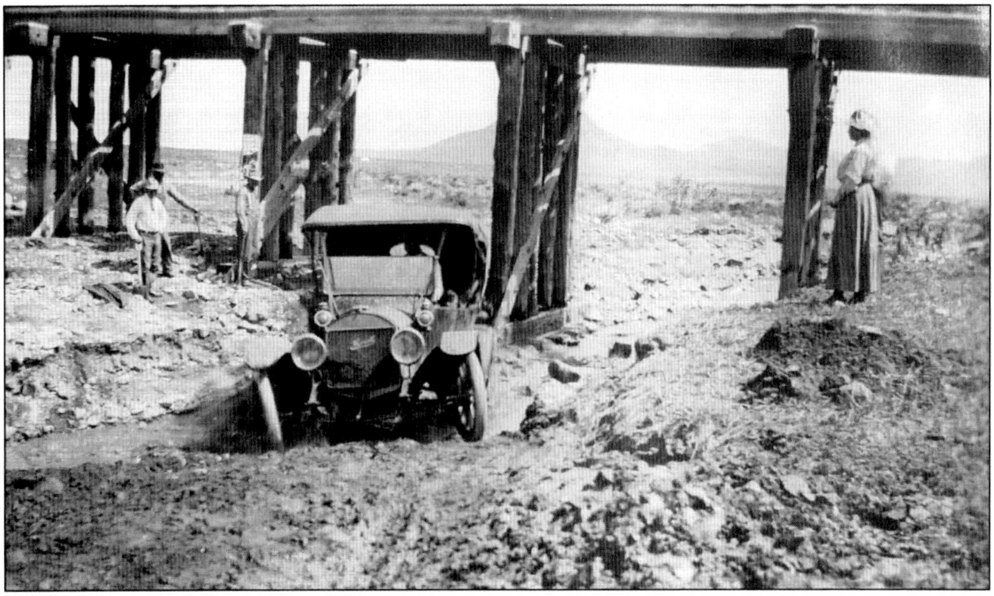

Freight and passenger trains had an easier time traversing this arroyo than Otero's automobile did. Having failed to free the vehicle using shovels and muscle power, the people pictured here are probably waiting for a team of horses to pull the car free of the mud. (Courtesy of Barbara Bergère Nau.)

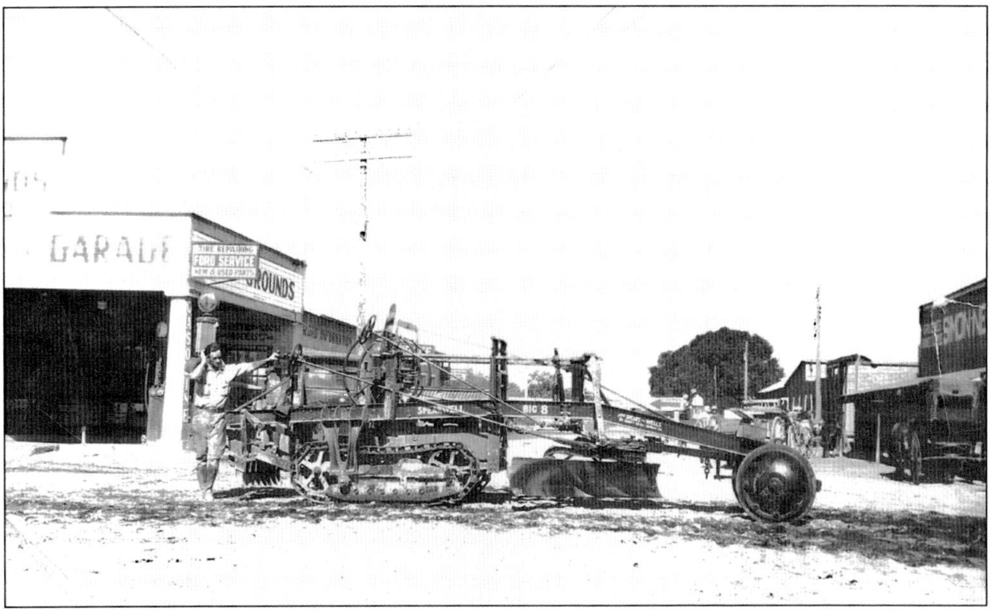

A Spearwell "Big 8" one-man grader is shown here in 1928 grading the intersection of Main Street and Los Lentes Road in Los Lunas. The number of horse-drawn wagons in front of Simon Neustadt Mercantile on the right indicates that wagons were still a popular form of transportation. (Courtesy of Los Lunas Museum of Heritage and Arts, Historic Route 66 Project.)

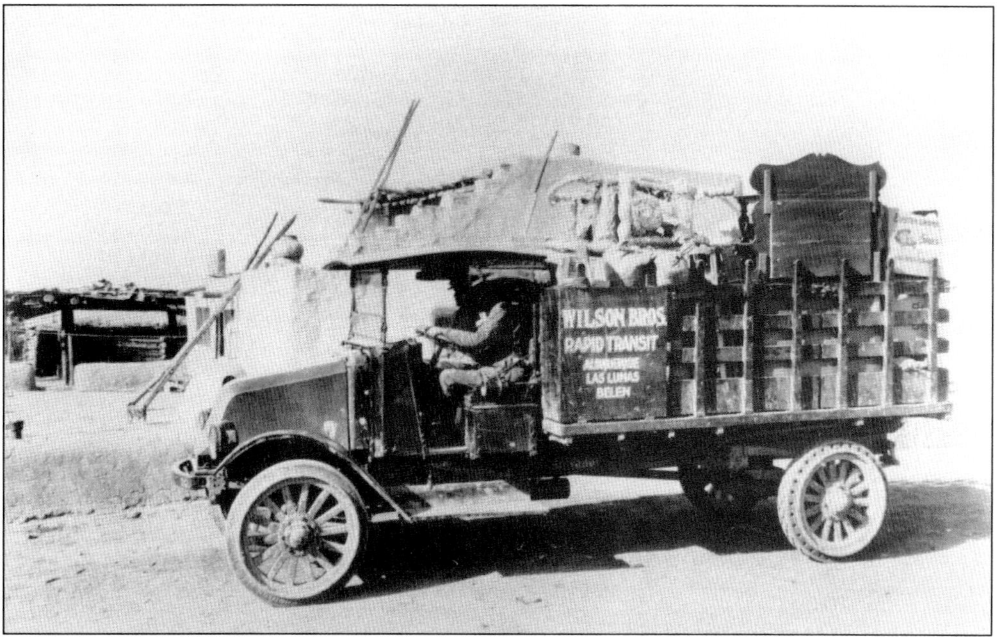

Started in 1917, the Wilson Rapid Transit Company operated out of Frank Wilson's kitchen with three Model A trucks from International and Diamond Rio. The company is still in business today, serving many of its original customers. (Courtesy of the Valencia County Historical Society.)

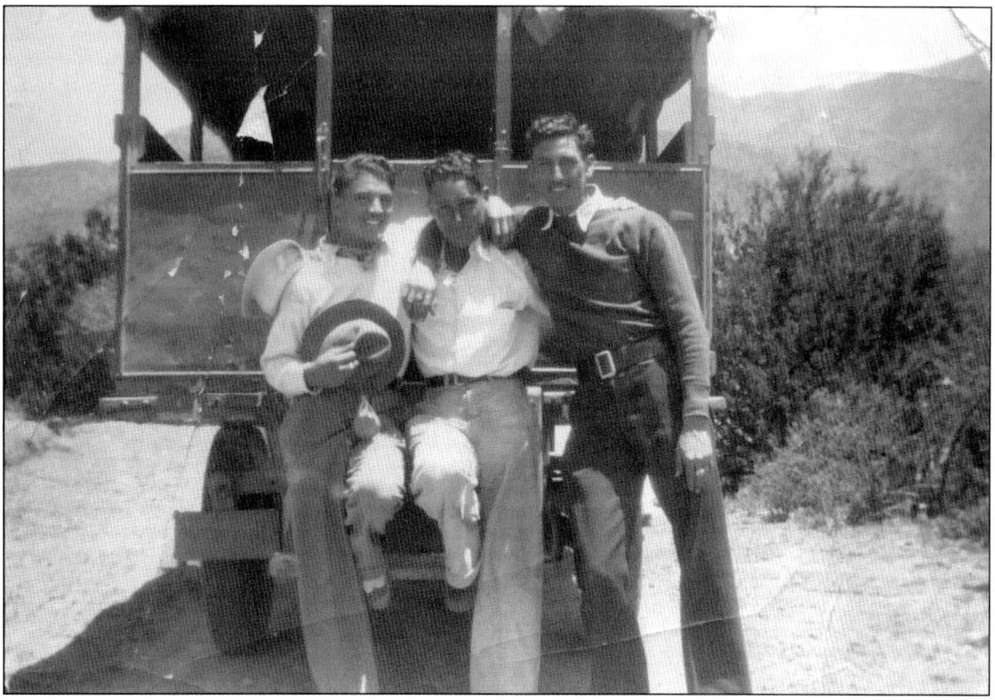

The first regular bus transportation between Los Lunas, Belen, and Albuquerque was provided by the Castillo family. Pictured here from left to right are Alfonso Romero, unidentified, and Emiliano Castillo Jr. Emillano Castillo Jr., his father, and two of his brothers served as mayor of Los Lunas. (Courtesy of Barbara Arnold.)

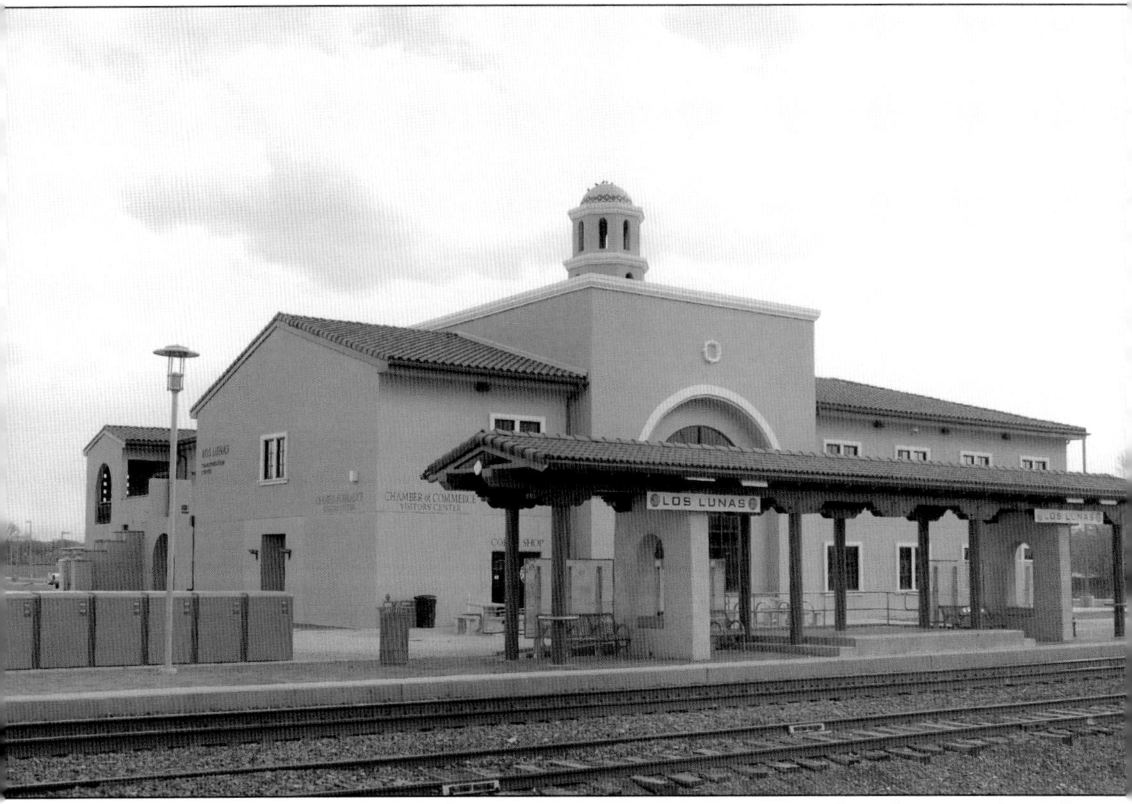

The Village of Los Lunas has built a new Transportation Center to replace the original wooden depot. The New Mexico Railrunner, the commuter train that serves communities from Belen to Santa Fe, stops here. (Author's collection.)

Five

Building Los Lunas

Until quite recently, the most common building material in Los Lunas, for both homes and commercial establishments, was adobe. These earthen blocks were practical because they were structurally sound, could be produced on-site with materials readily at hand, and provided thermal mass that aided in heating and cooling.

Most buildings in the village were (and are) single-story. Notable exceptions are the two remaining courthouses, the Transportation Center, and the signature Luna Mansion. Two-story adobe structures require double-width adobe walls to support the weight of a second story.

The family home that would come to be known as the Luna Mansion was completed in 1881. A typical affluent Victorian home, the mansion was impressive in spite of its adobe construction. A later resident was responsible for the renovation that transformed the house into the mansion that exists today.

Another signature form of adobe architecture was created in Bosque Farms, just north of the village of Los Lunas. Adobe blocks formed on-site were used to construct 42 nearly identical two- and three-bedroom homes for clients of a federal resettlement project during the Great Depression. Adobe blocks were also used to construct the Bosque Farms Elementary School, which is still in operation.

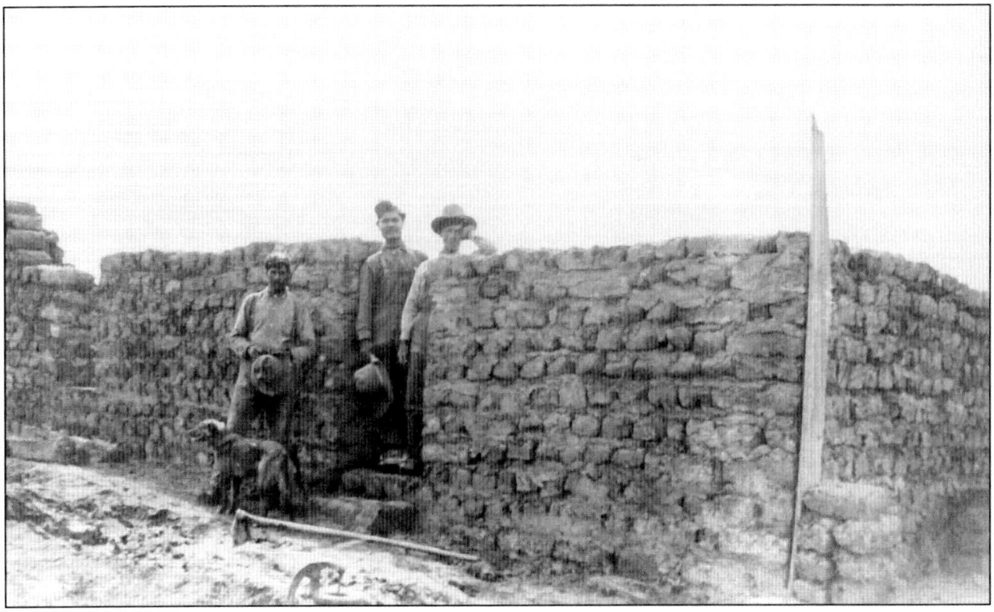

The most common building material in Los Lunas, from the earliest time, was an earthen block. Terrone blocks were cut from the soil, while adobe blocks were formed by pouring mixed water, clay, sand, and straw into a mold. Walls constructed of terrone were unusually strong because the still-growing sod would send roots into the next course, and the whole wall would literally grow together. (Courtesy of Barbara Bergère Nau.)

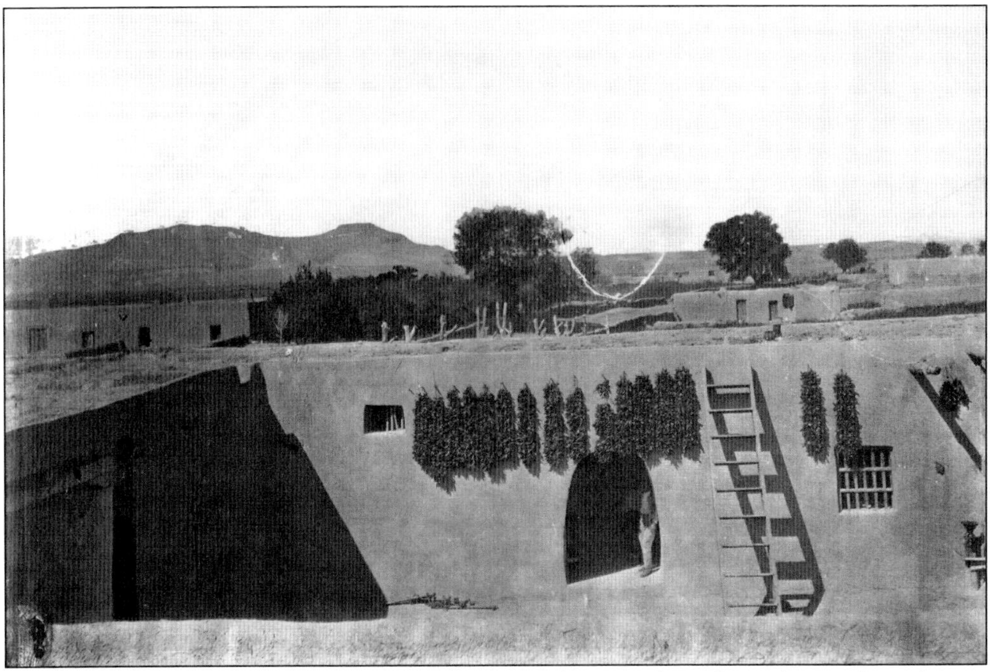

This 1867 photograph, taken by renowned Civil War photographer Alexander Gardner, shows a single-story hacienda built around a *placita*, or central courtyard. The Los Lunas hills can be seen in the background. It is possible that this is the original Luna family compound that was torn down to provide a right-of-way for the Santa Fe Railroad. (Courtesy of the Museum of New Mexico.)

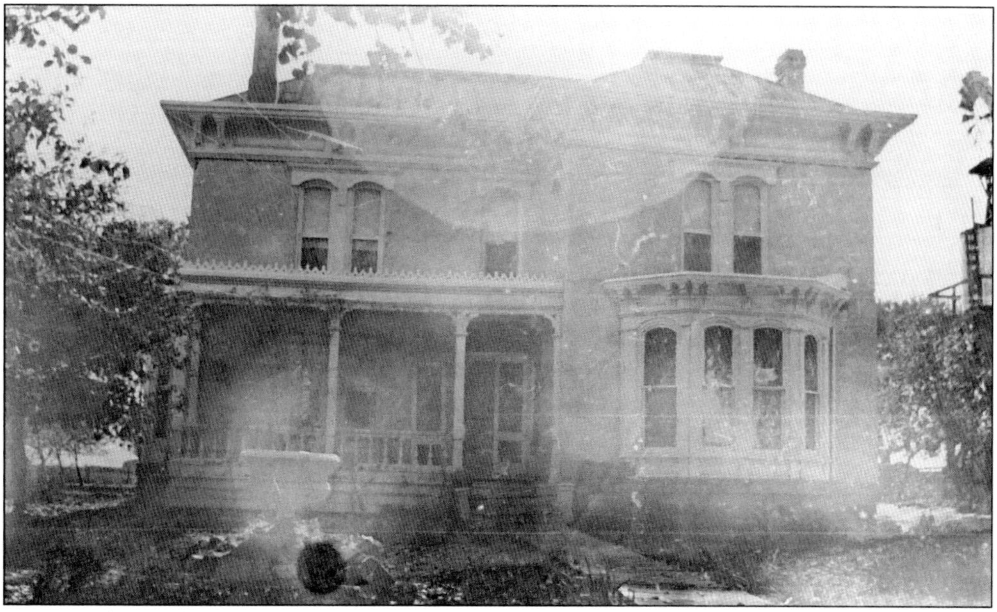

In 1880, the Atcheson, Topeka & Santa Fe Railroad purchased the Luna family hacienda for $13,000 for a right-of-way through Los Lunas. The family used the funds to build a new home on land they owned to the west of the old site. The new house followed the Victorian bonanza style, more popular in the East and Midwest. The house was two stories, with a large bay window and ornate gingerbread accents. The construction material was adobe, however, in keeping with the southwestern locale. By 1920, Eduardo Otero and his wife, Josephita Manderfield, were living in the Luna house. She was a woman of great artistic sensibilities and undertook a major renovation of the house. She replaced the former single-story front porch with soaring two-story columns, reminiscent of a Southern mansion. (Both, courtesy of Barbara Bergère Nau.)

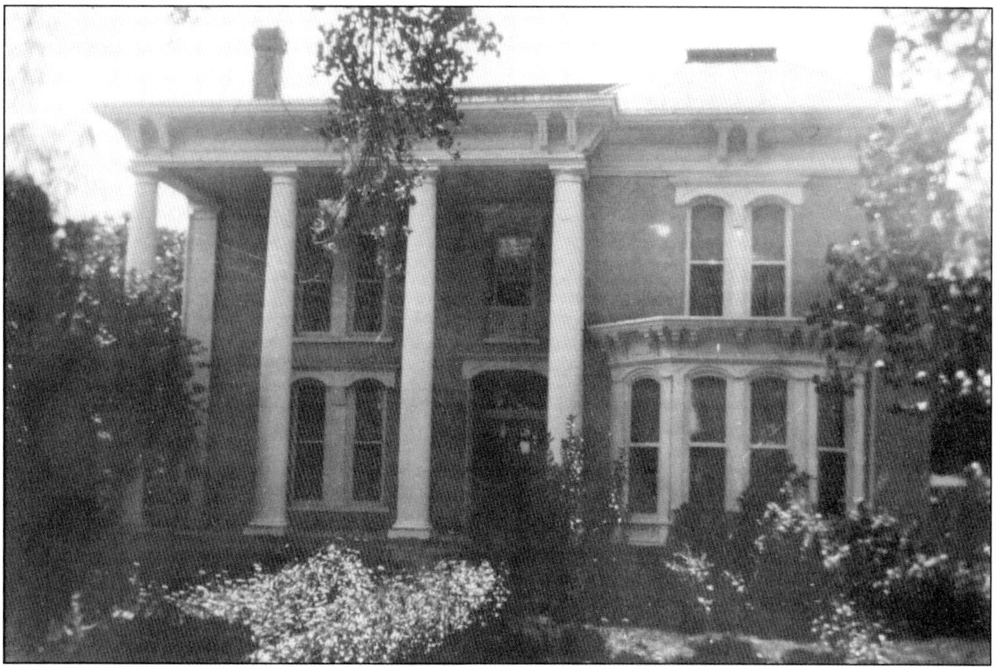

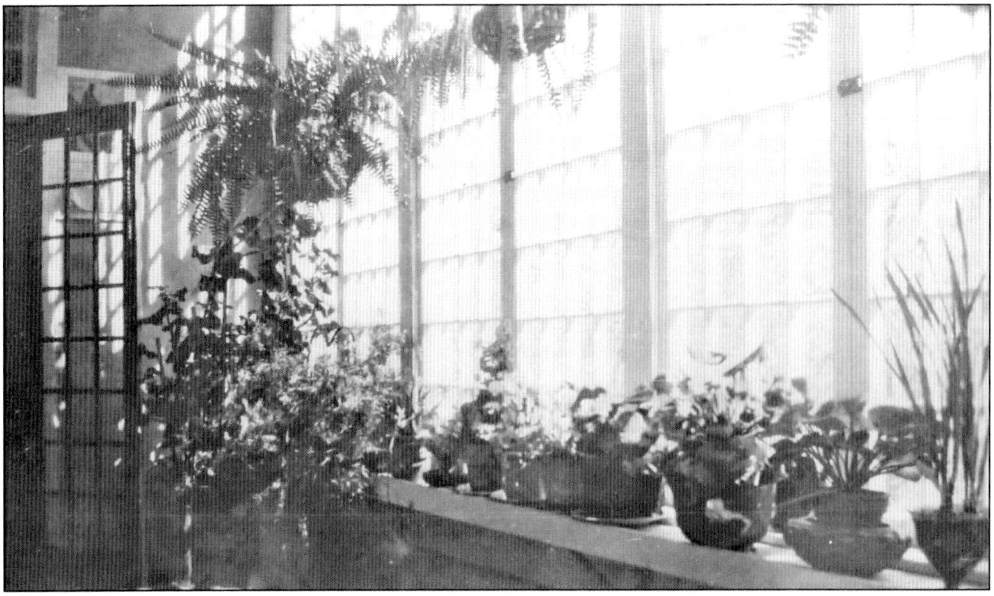

In addition to adding the columns to the front of the home, Josephita also added a glass-walled conservatory on the east side of the house. This photograph shows how this light-filled room looked shortly after it was constructed. (Courtesy of Barbara Bergère Nau.)

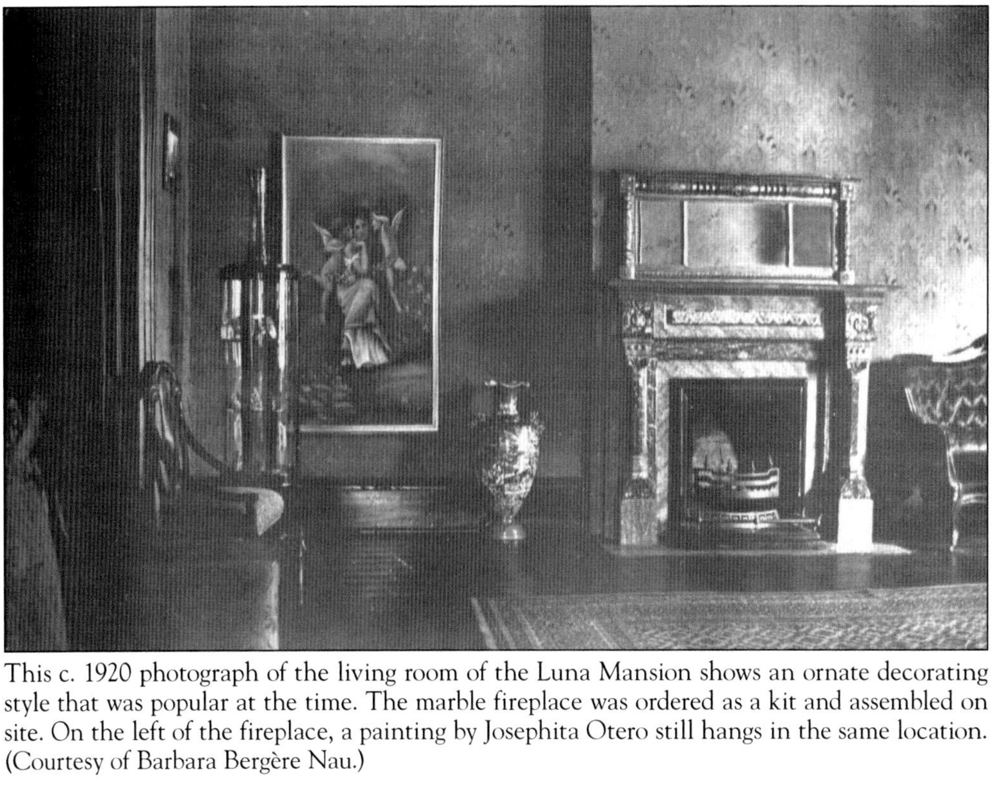

This c. 1920 photograph of the living room of the Luna Mansion shows an ornate decorating style that was popular at the time. The marble fireplace was ordered as a kit and assembled on site. On the left of the fireplace, a painting by Josephita Otero still hangs in the same location. (Courtesy of Barbara Bergère Nau.)

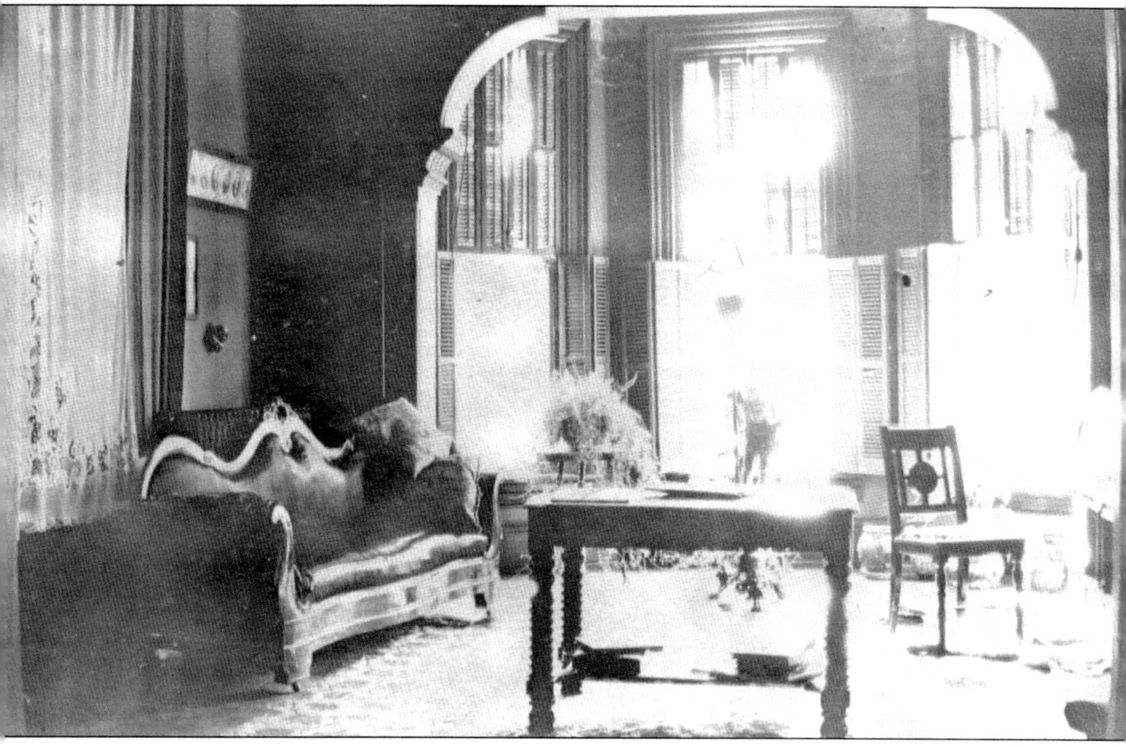

One of the most striking features of the Luna Mansion is the large bay window in the front of the house. The bay window was damaged when a Christmas tree that was lit with candles caught fire. When it was rebuilt, the design details were changed slightly, but the original overall appearance was retained. This photograph shows the bay window from the inside of the parlor. (Courtesy of Barbara Bergère Nau.)

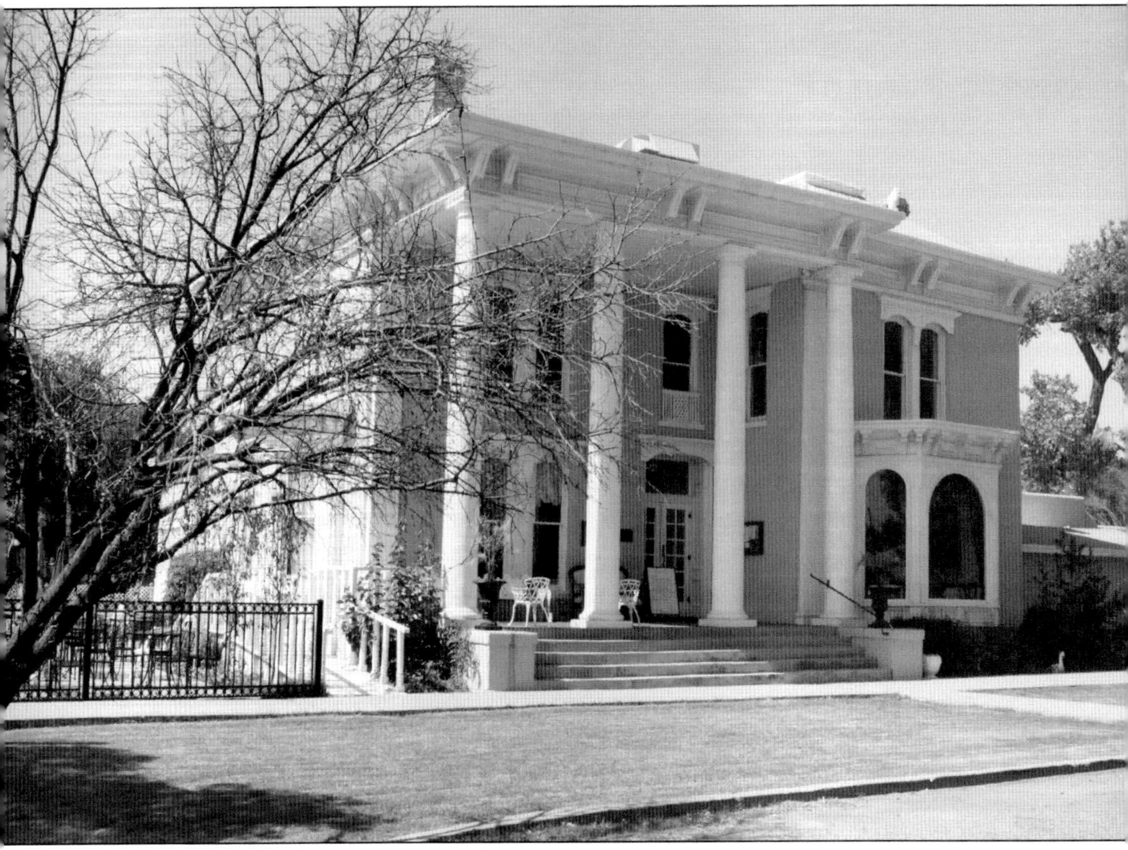

In the mid-1970s, the Luna home underwent an extensive historic renovation and was converted to a fashionable restaurant, appropriately named the Luna Mansion. It is currently owned and operated by the Torres family. (Author's collection.)

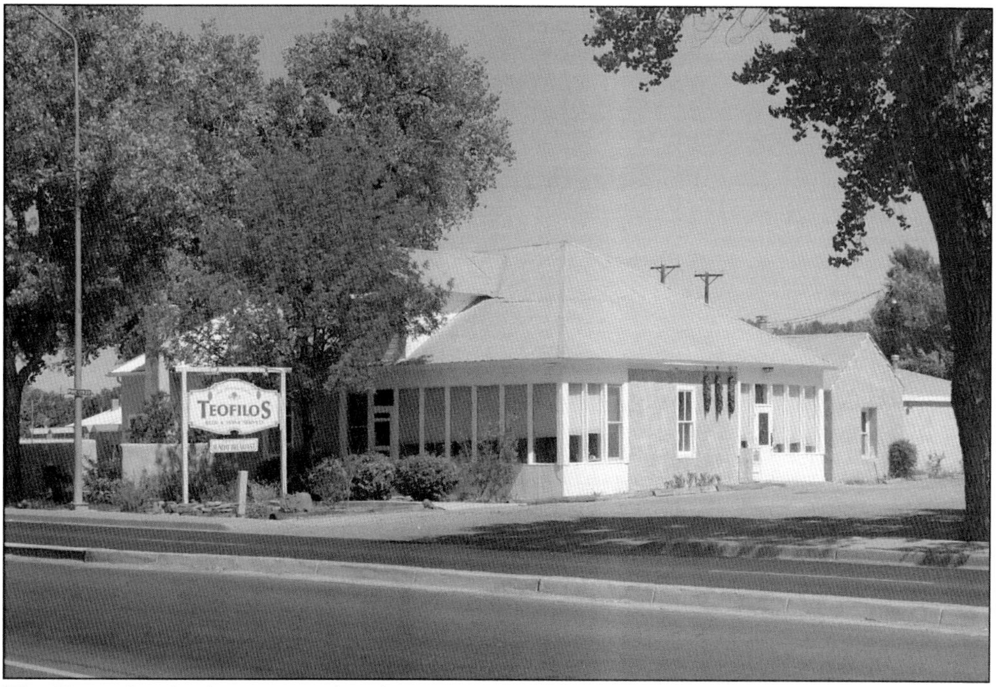

The Torres family also preserved and renovated Dr. William Wittwer's home, converting it to a restaurant named Teofilo's. The Wittwer house is located directly across Main Street from the Luna Mansion. In 1899, Dr. Wittwer came through Los Lunas on his way to El Paso to become a doctor for the railroad. He was persuaded to establish his medical practice in Los Lunas by the Luna family. Dr. Wittwer charged $15 to deliver a baby, and as often as not, was either paid in goods or was not paid at all. Dr. Wittwer is credited with the elimination of smallpox in Valencia County, and he published a scientific paper on the disease pellagra. The house was built on Luna land by Dr. Wittwer in 1913. (Above, courtesy of the author; right, courtesy of the Valencia County Historical Society.)

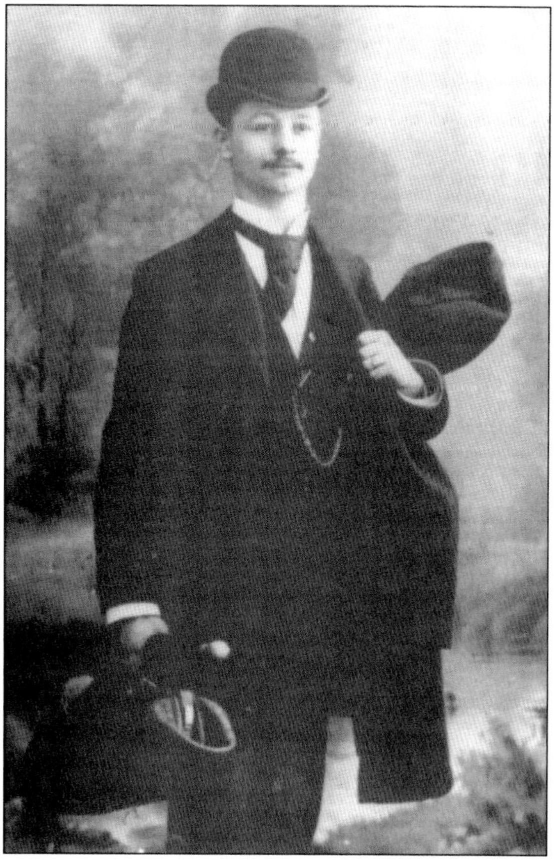

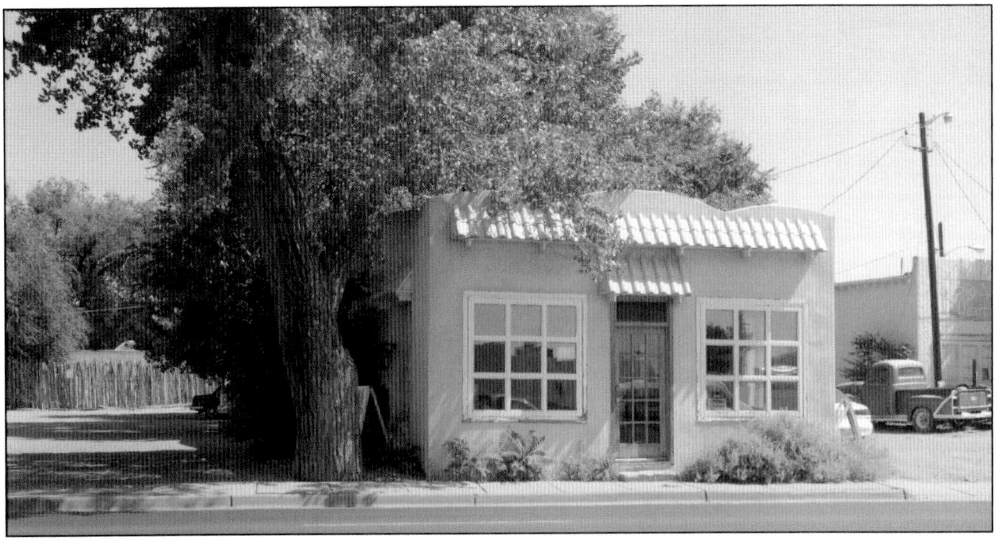

Owned and operated by Paia Romero starting around 1925, the White Café is still located on Main Street, just east of the Wittwer House. The café served travelers following US Route 66, which passed right in front. The building was later renovated by architect John Friedman and became the office of Village Architects. (Author's collection.)

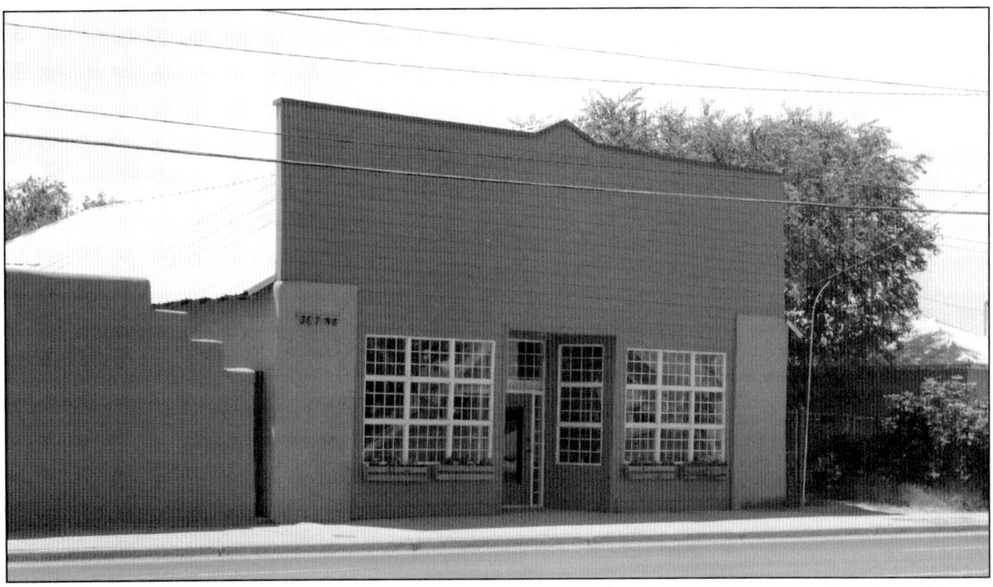

This building, located on the south side of Main Street between Los Lentes Road and Luna Avenue, is another restoration and renovation project carried out by architect John Friedman. It was a popular dance hall in the 1920s and 1930s and later saw use as an electronics manufacturing facility, an exercise studio, and even a residence. (Author's collection.)

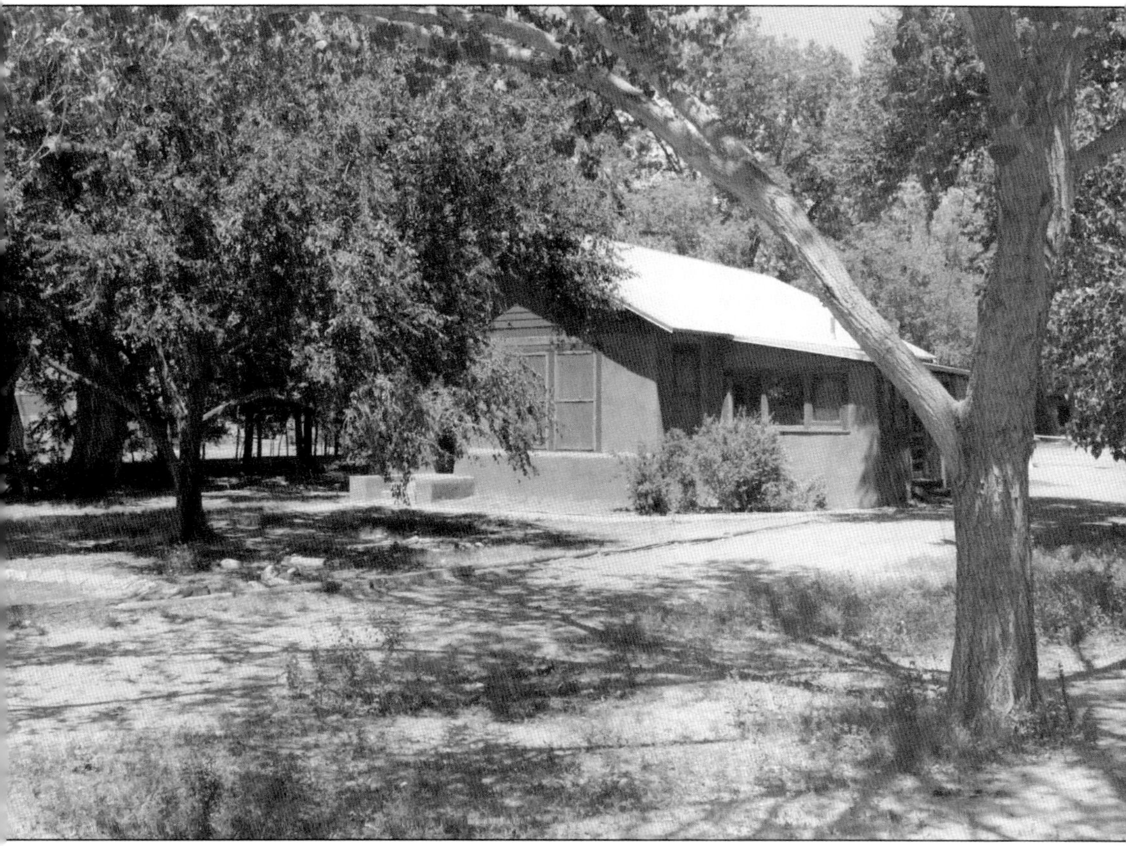

This house, located on Main Street, is typical of the many fine adobe homes throughout the village of Los Lunas. This particular house was built around 1900 by the Hunings as a wedding present for a family member. It is lovingly maintained by the present owners. (Author's collection.)

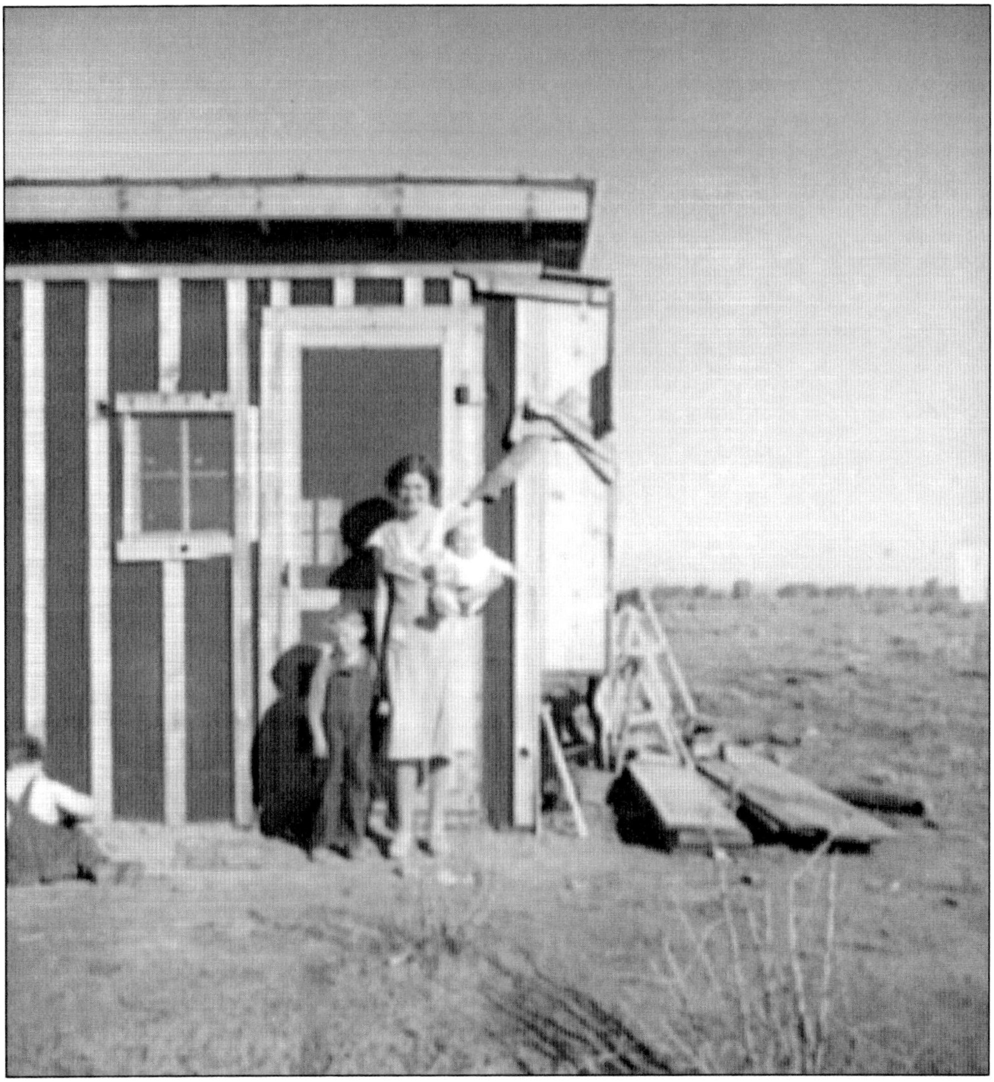

When the original families arrived at Bosque Farms as clients of a federal relocation project, they lived either in tents or in tar paper structures such as this one. This housing was to serve as temporary shelter until more permanent dwellings could be constructed of adobe bricks. (Courtesy of the Library of Congress, Negative No. 8b27353u.)

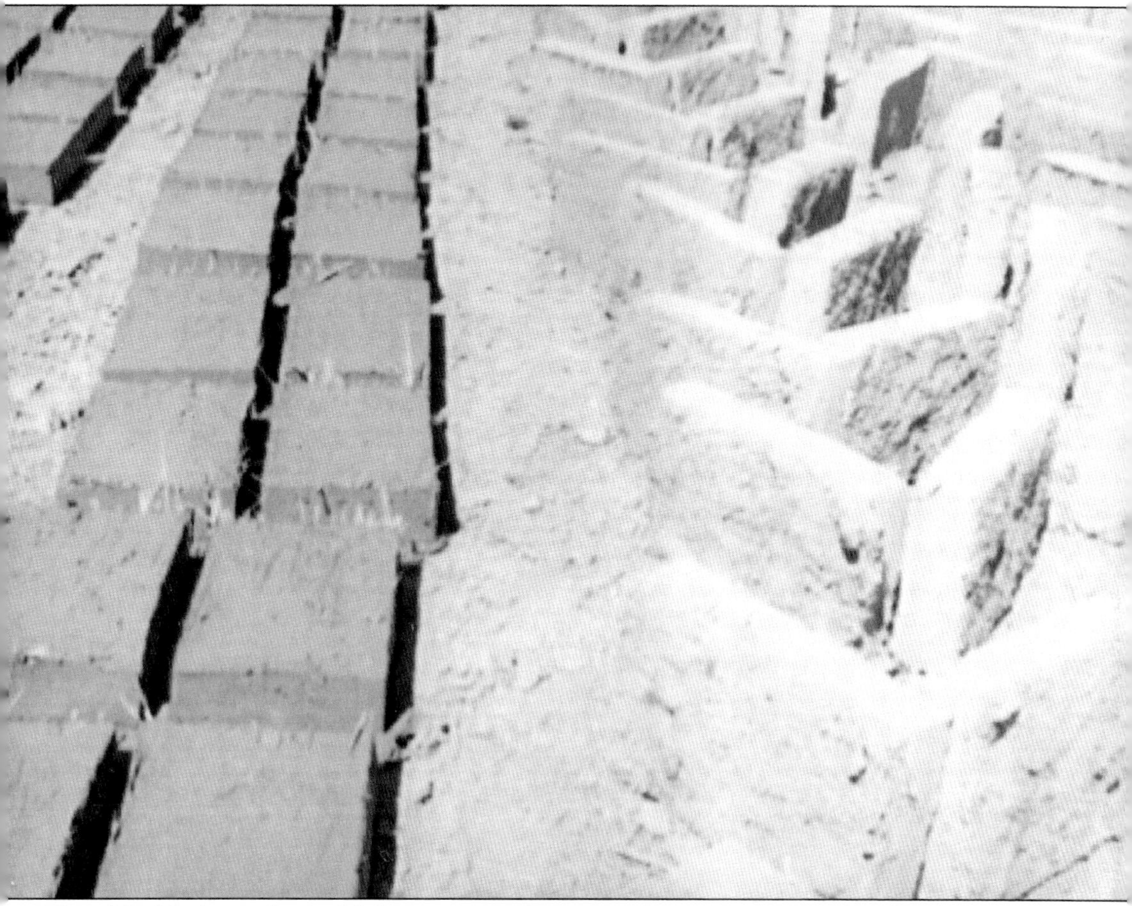

The adobe blocks used to build the permanent housing at Bosque Farms were handmade on the building site. Clay was mixed with water, sand, and straw and then poured into tin-lined wood molds to form the bricks. Once the blocks had set up in the mold, they were removed and placed flat on the ground to dry. Once they were sufficiently dry, they were tipped up and allowed to harden completely. (Courtesy of the Library of Congress, Negative No. 8b38270b.)

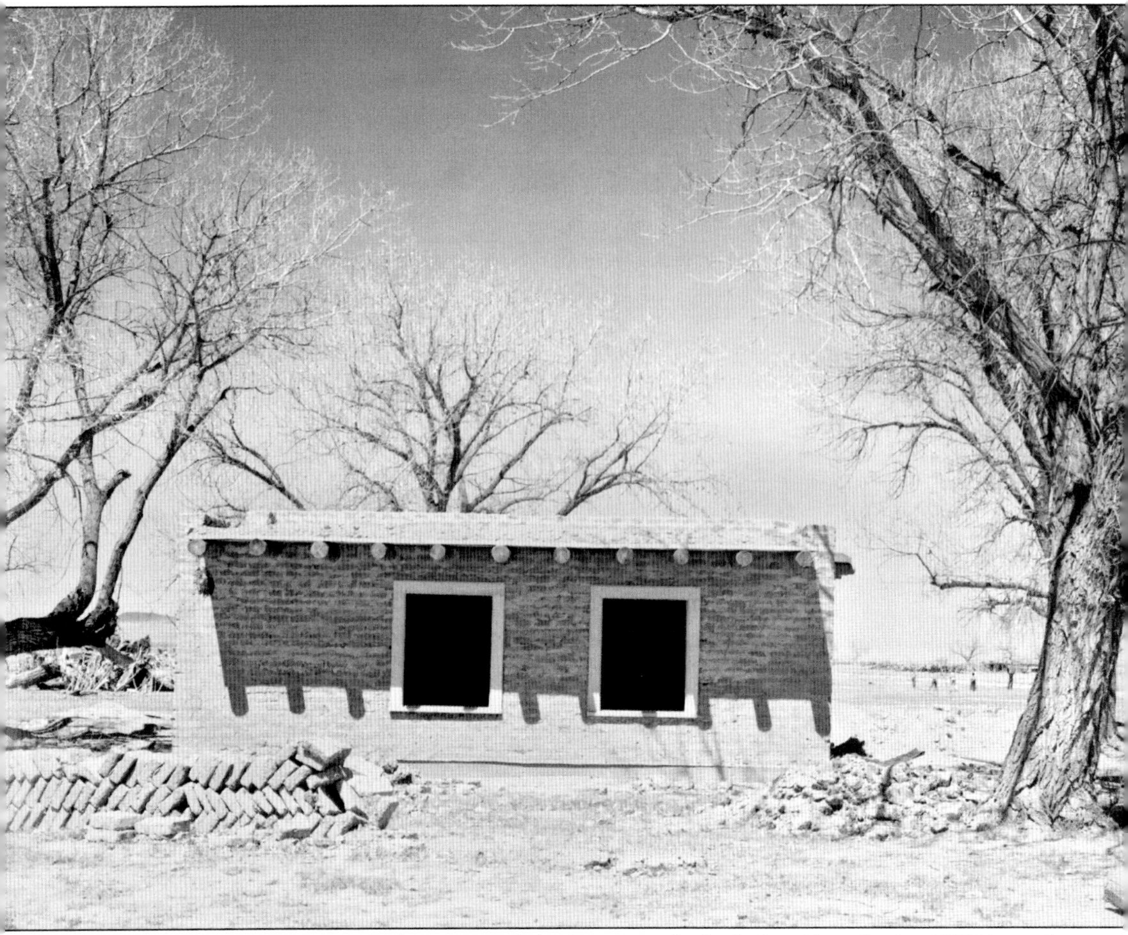

Bosque Farms clients made their own adobe homes with the help of hundreds of WPA workers. There were only two floor plans—a two-bedroom and a three-bedroom configuration. The adobe blocks were laid on a cement foundation and the flat roof was supported by vigas, sturdy pine logs. All 42 of the original Bosque Farms houses are still standing, though many of them have been extensively remodeled. (Courtesy of the Library of Congress, Negative No. 8b38338u.)

Six

Government and Services

Serving from 1928 to 1930, Los Lunas elected Don Antonio Archuleta as its first mayor on August 7, 1928. Archuleta was followed by Emiliano Castillo Sr., who was mayor from 1930 to 1932. Three of Emiliano Castillo Sr.'s sons would also be elected mayor of the village of Los Lunas: Emiliano Jr., José, and Fred. Diego Aragón was mayor of Los Lunas from 1932 to 1934. Fred Huning Sr. served as mayor of Los Lunas for 20 years, a tenure eclipsed by his grandson Louis Huning, who served the village for 27 years.

The village has provided law enforcement and property protection services to residents even before formal incorporation. There was a time when the law was enforced by means of Los Lunas's infamous "Hanging Tree." Prominent residents, from Tranquilino and Solomon Luna to Joseph Tondre and Emiliano Castillo, have served the village of Los Lunas and Valencia County as sheriff.

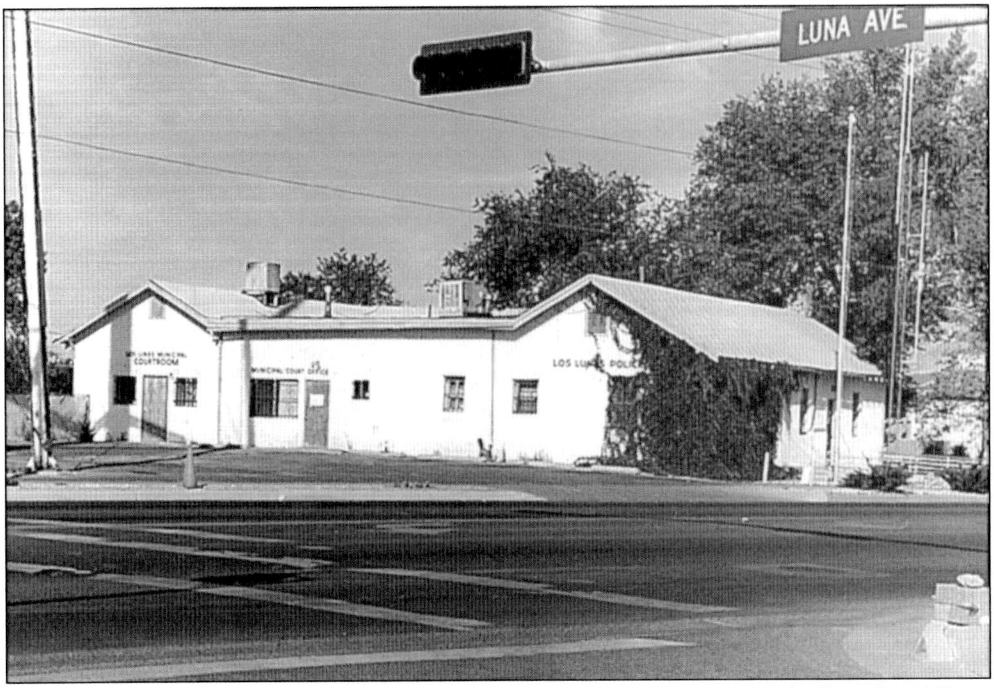

The Archuleta Building, at the corner of Main Street and Luna Avenue, was built in the 1930s as a WPA project. The building served as the village police department and the Los Lunas Municipal Court during the 1950s and 1960s. (Courtesy of Los Lunas Museum of Heritage and Arts.)

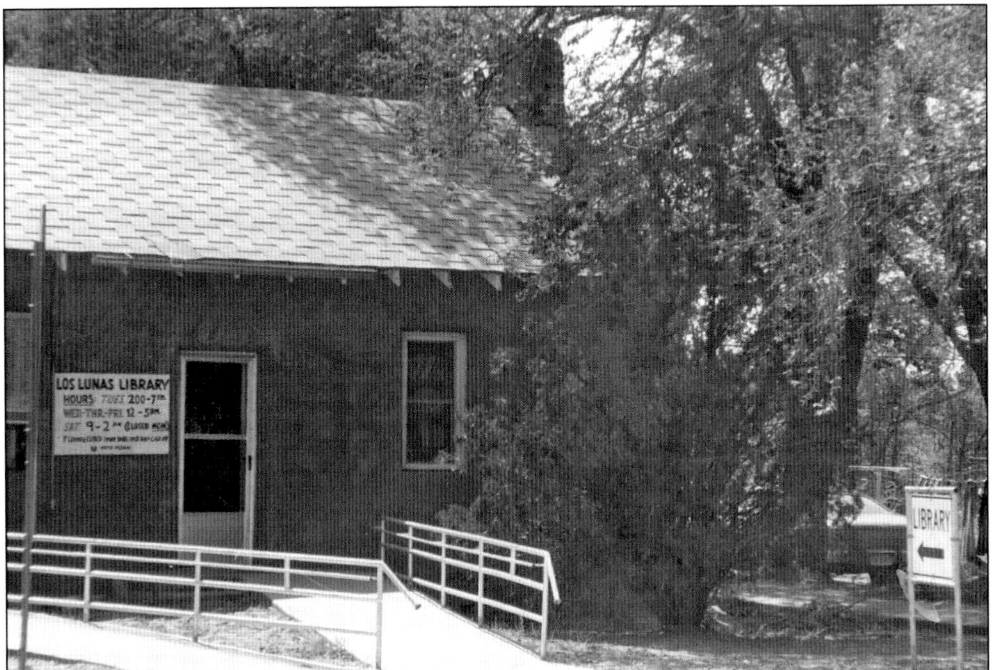

The Archuleta Building housed the village library after the village administrative office and police department. Ramps and railings were added to make the library accessible to those with disabilities. (Courtesy of the Valencia County Historical Society.)

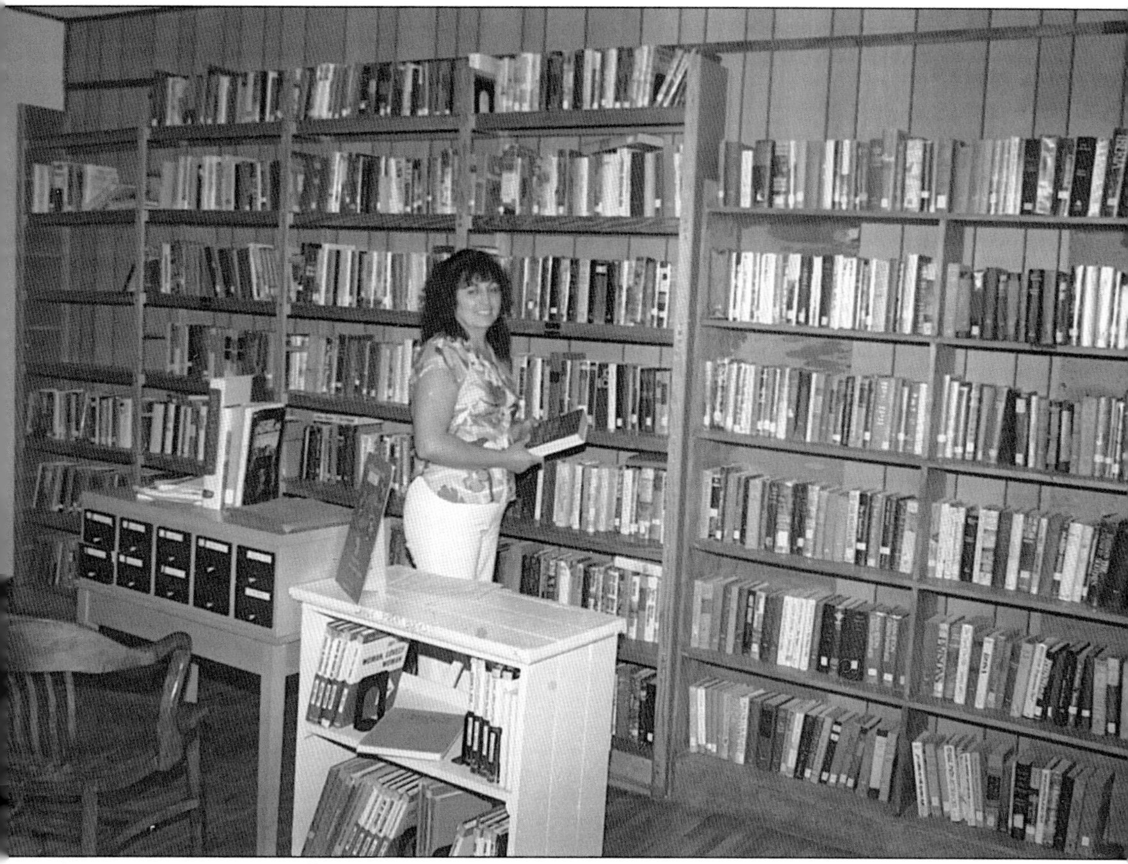

Librarian Carmen Jaramillo-Campos is shown shelving books at the village library, located in the Archuleta Building. The first village library was established by Ruth Tondre in 1959. Also serving as village librarian were Lisa Mitchell, Sylvia Aragón, and Katherine Gallegos (Ruth Tondre's sister). (Courtesy of the Valencia County Historical Society.)

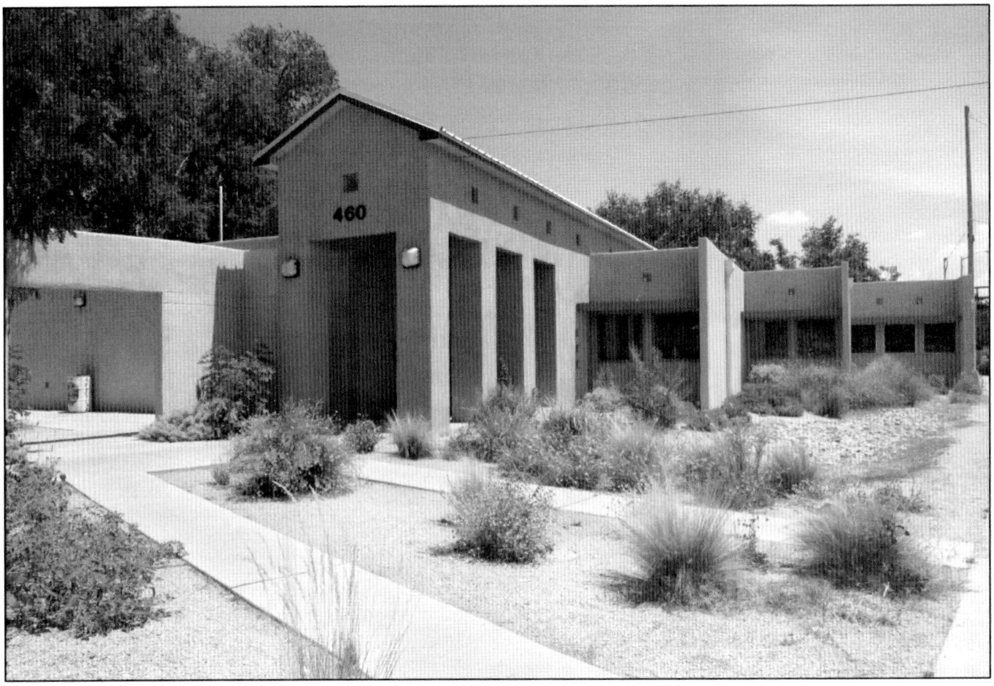

The village of Los Lunas now has a library building designed at the outset to house an extensive collection of books, periodicals, and other media while efficiently serving the library's patrons. The library has a staff of more than 10 employees. (Author's collection.)

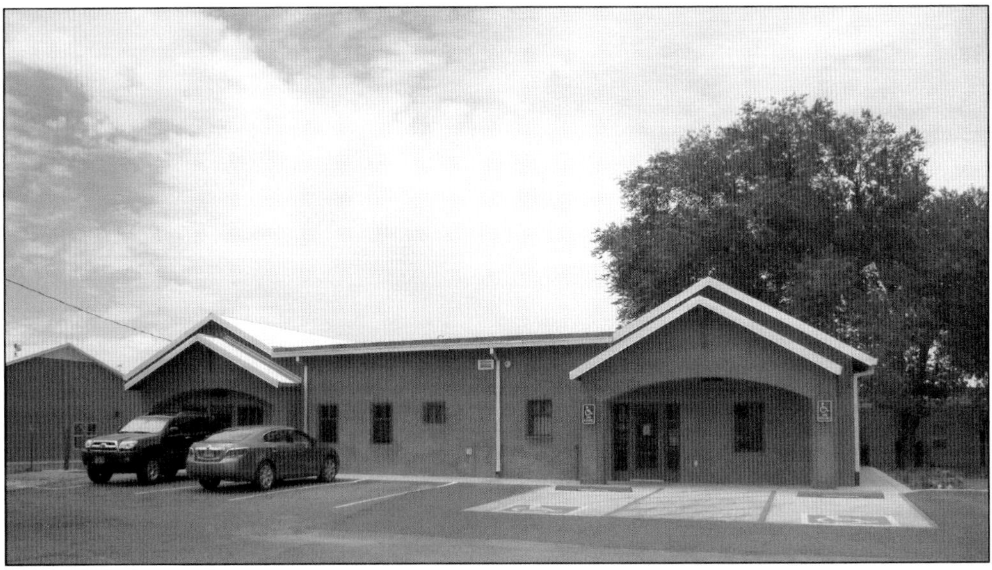

In 2005, Mayor Louis Huning and village councilmembers Charles Griego, Cecilia C.C. Castillo, Bernard Sais, and Richard Lovato supported the establishment of a permanent facility to collect, preserve, and exhibit artifacts relating to the history of the village. The Archuleta Building was completely renovated, inside and out, to serve as the Los Lunas Museum of Heritage and Arts. (Author's collection.)

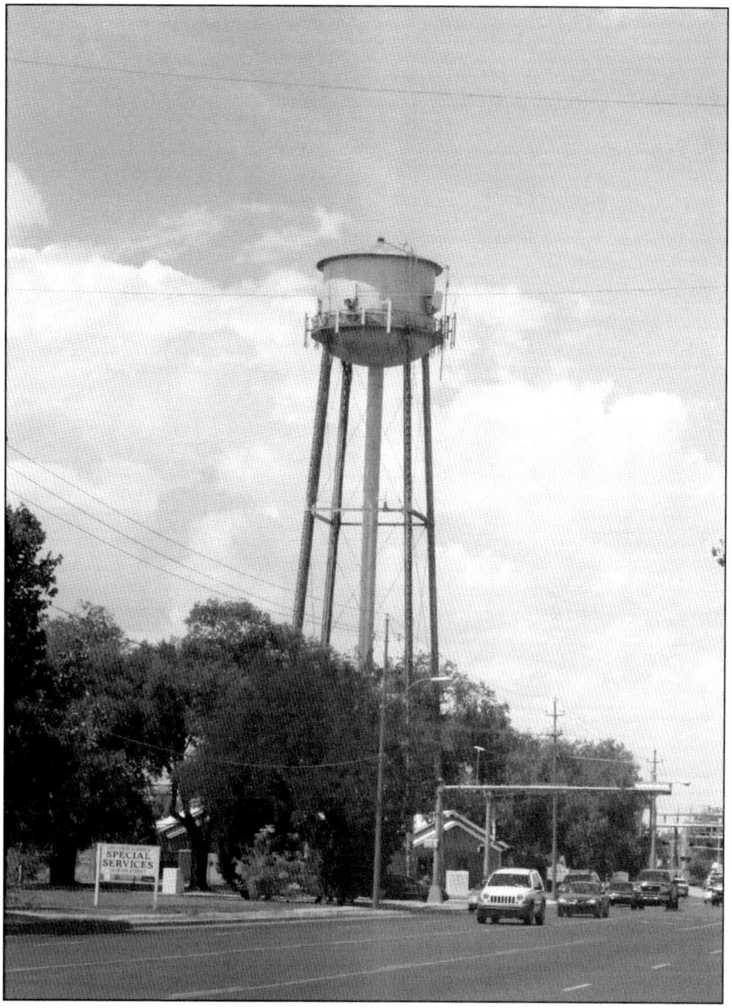

A well and pumping system provided the water that was stored in the Los Lunas water tower. Although it no longer feeds the village water system, the tower is still useful as a telecommunications equipment platform. (Author's collection.)

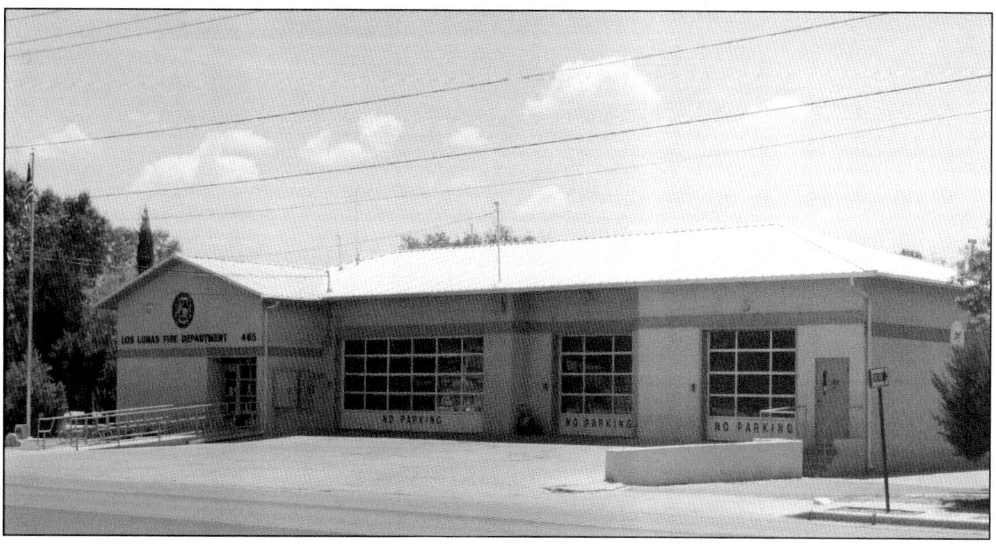

The new fire department facility is located on Main Street between Los Lentes Road and Luna Avenue. The fire department is staffed 24 hours a day and provides emergency medical services as well as firefighting services to village residents. (Author's collection.)

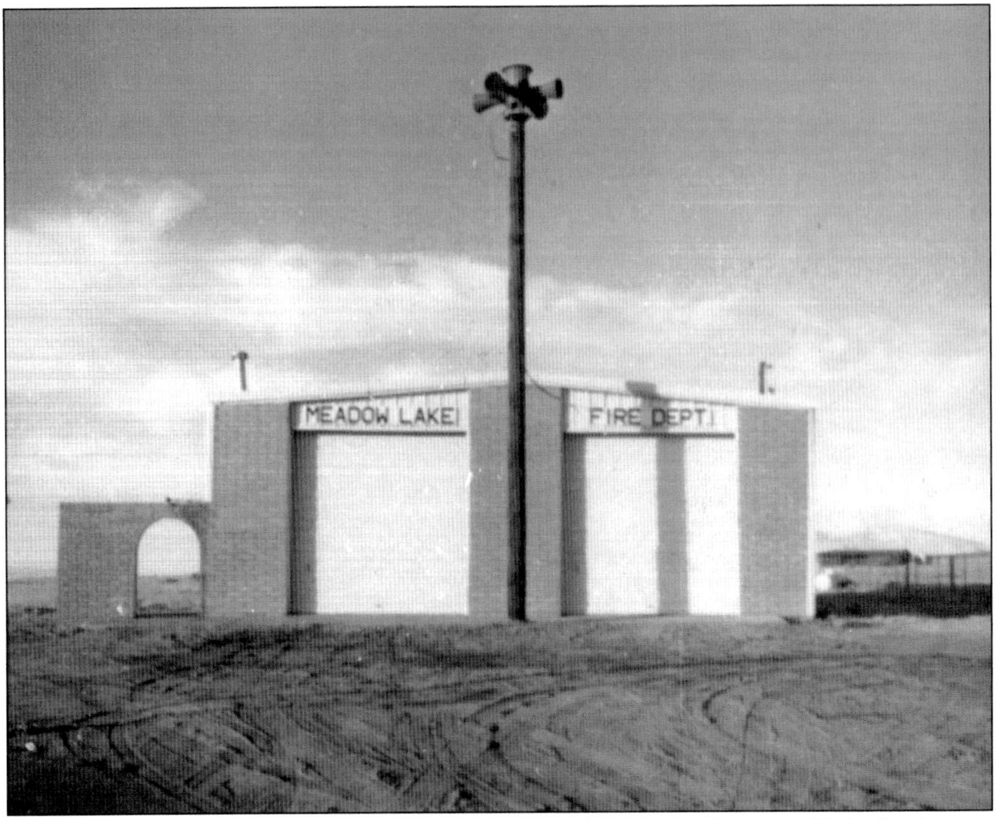

Many of the rural, unincorporated communities around Los Lunas have established volunteer fire departments. This is the Meadow Lake Fire Department building, shown shortly after it was completed in 1972. (Courtesy of the Valencia County Historical Society.)

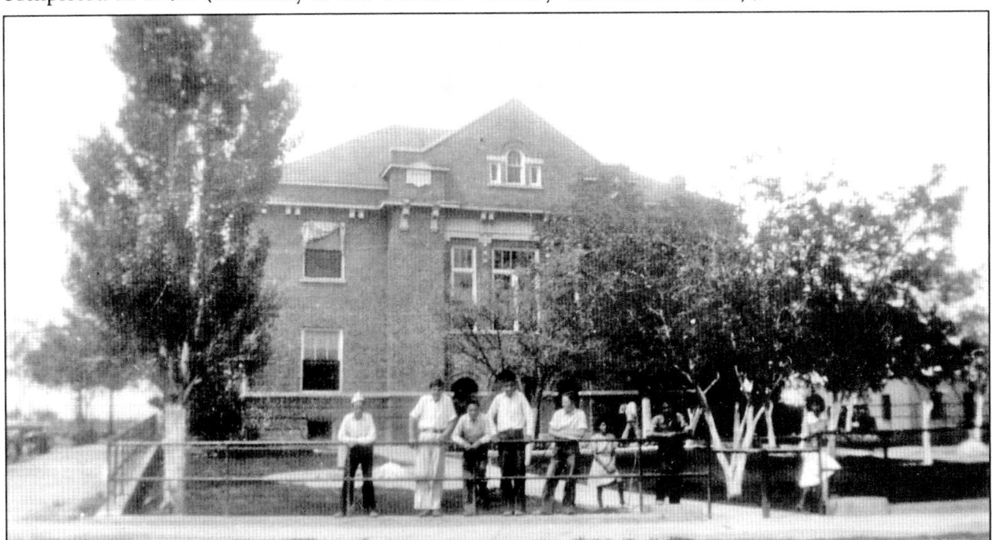

The Valencia County Courthouse was one of the few two-story buildings in Los Lunas. This building served until a new courthouse was constructed in the 1950s. (Courtesy of Los Lunas Museum of Heritage and Arts, Route 66 Project.)

Henry Connelly was born in Kentucky and received a medical degree from Transylvania University in Lexington, Kentucky, in 1828. He moved to New Mexico in 1848 and maintained mercantile operations in Santa Fe. He married Dolores Perea de Cháves, the mother of Col. J. Francisco Cháves. In 1861, Pres. Abraham Lincoln appointed Dr. Connelly territorial governor of New Mexico. (Courtesy of Center for Southwest Research.)

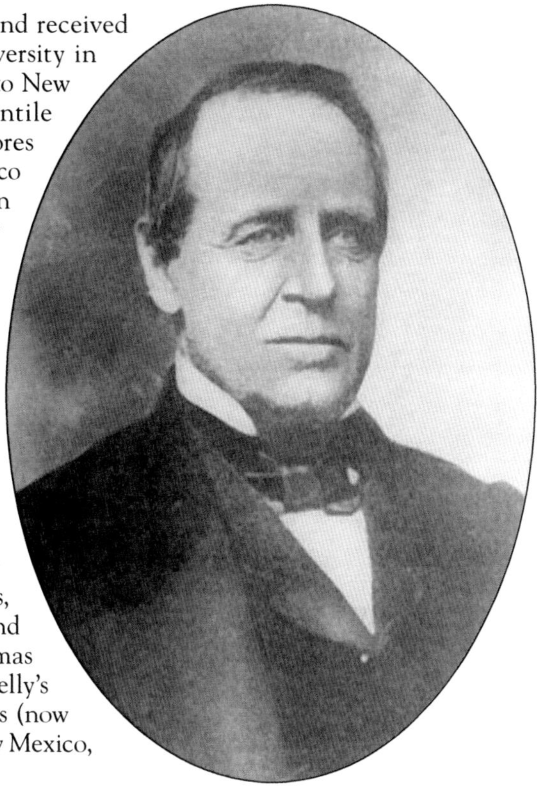

In February of 1862, a band of Confederate soldiers from Texas marched into New Mexico with the intention of capturing New Mexico and southern Colorado and securing an all-weather route to California. Following strategic defeats at Valverde and Glorieta Pass, the Texans abandoned their adventure and retreated south. Confederate colonel Thomas Green commandeered Gov. Henry Connelly's residence just north of Peralta at Los Pinos (now Bosque Farms). (Courtesy of Museum of New Mexico, Negative No. 101938.)

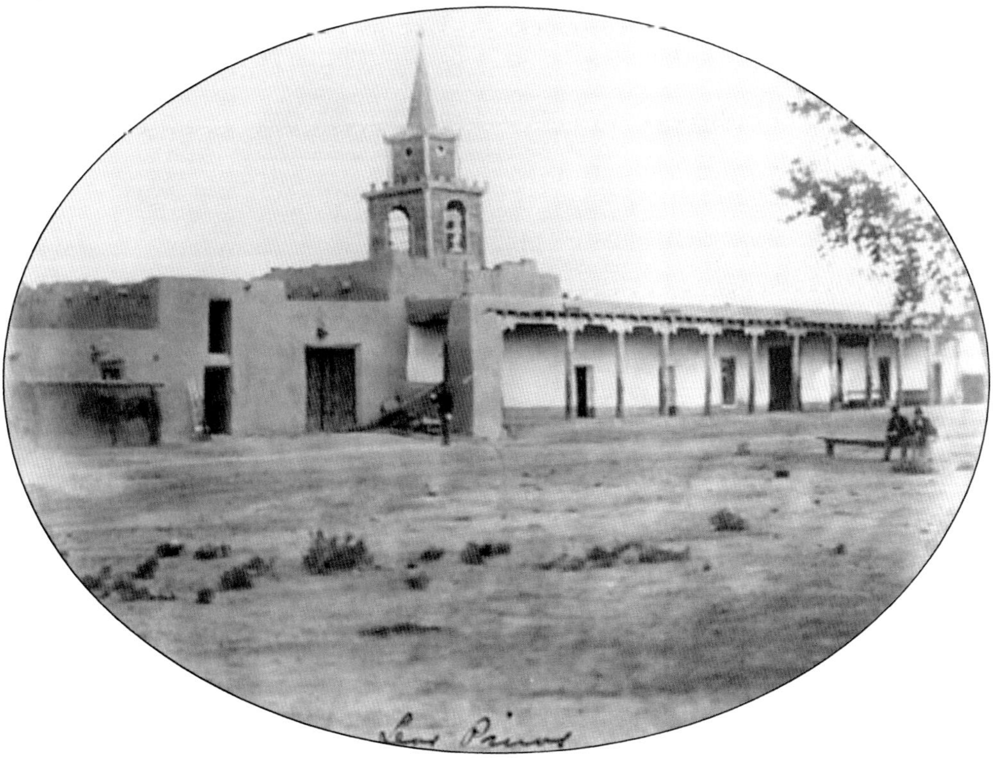

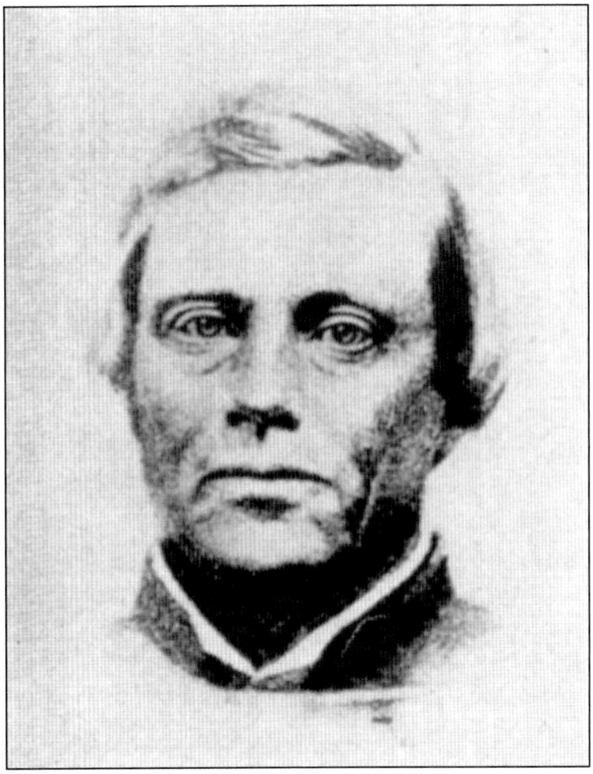

Col. Thomas Green was commander of the 5th Texas Cavalry, a regiment in the command of Gen. Henry H. Sibley. Green led the Confederate troops at the Battle of Valverde and was in command of the Confederates at the Battle of Peralta. (Courtesy of John Taylor.)

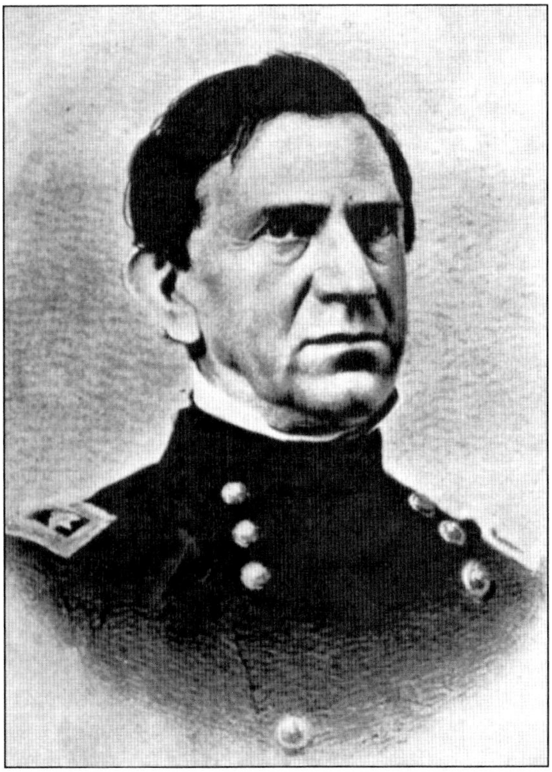

Col. Edward Richard Sprigg Canby commanded the Union troops at the Battle of Peralta. He defeated Confederate brigadier general Henry H. Sibley at the Battle of Glorieta Pass, sometimes called the "Gettysburg of the West." He was promoted to the rank of brigadier general immediately following the battle. (Courtesy of John Taylor.)

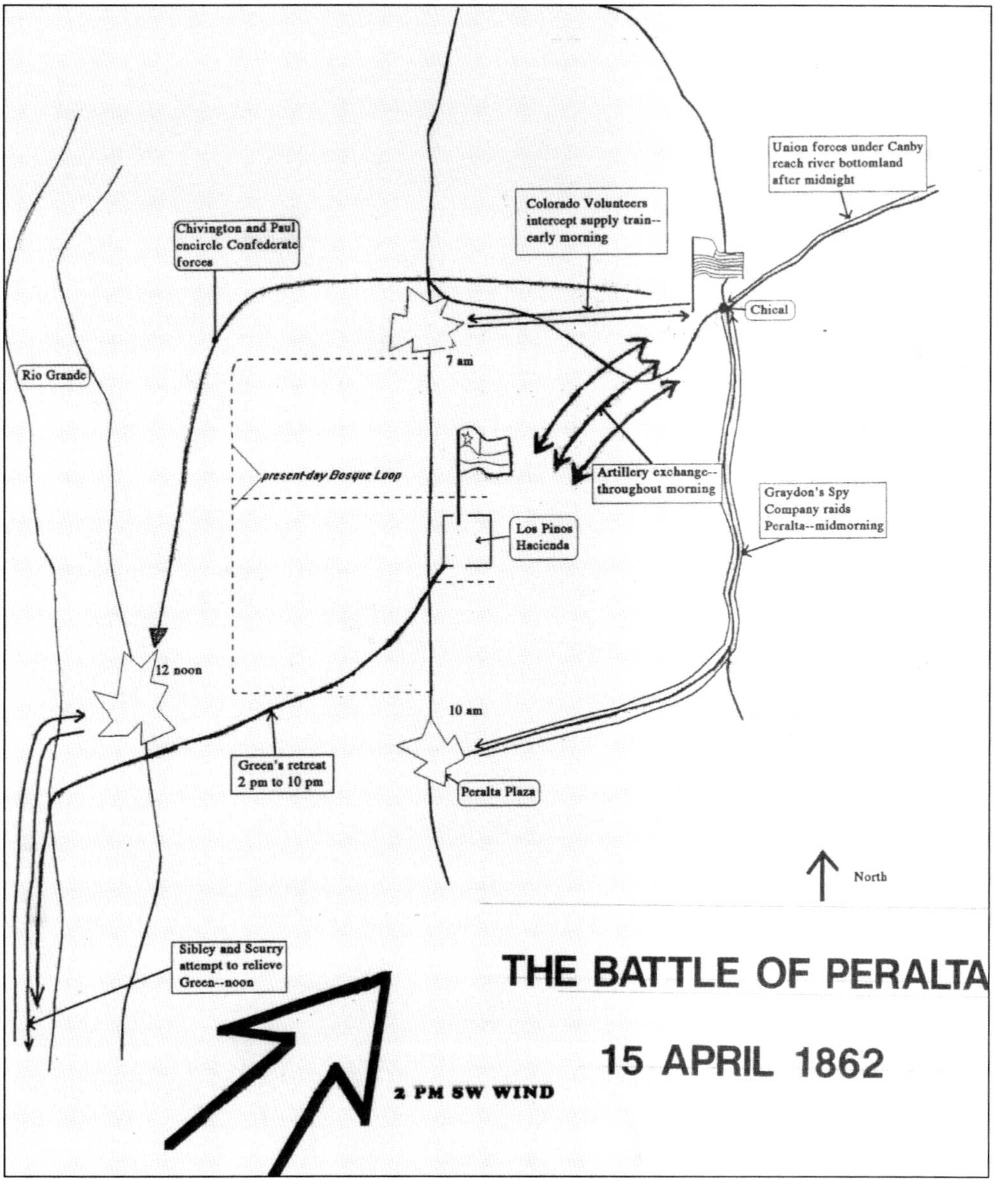

This map shows the activity surrounding the Civil War Battle of Peralta. Bullets, cannonballs, and other Civil War items are still unearthed in the area. (Courtesy of John Taylor.)

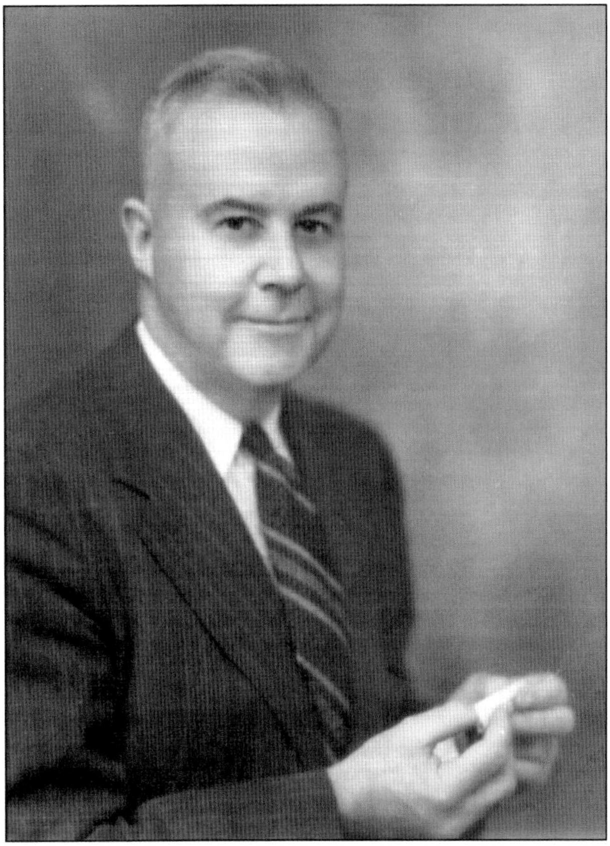

Joseph Tondre was a businessman, county sheriff, US marshal, and school board president in Los Lunas. He was born at Isleta Pueblo on February 26, 1883, but his family soon moved to a farm in Los Lentes. He also served as chairman of the Republican party of Valencia County and ran for both state governor and lieutenant governor. (Courtesy of Los Lunas Museum of Heritage and Arts.)

This cottonwood tree, which once grew on Main Street, was the source of rough justice in Los Lunas. It was known throughout the community as the "Hanging Tree." People have reported feeling something brush against their faces when passing under the tree limb in the dark of night, suggesting that uneasy spirits inhabited the tree. (Courtesy of Los Lunas Museum of Heritage and Arts.)

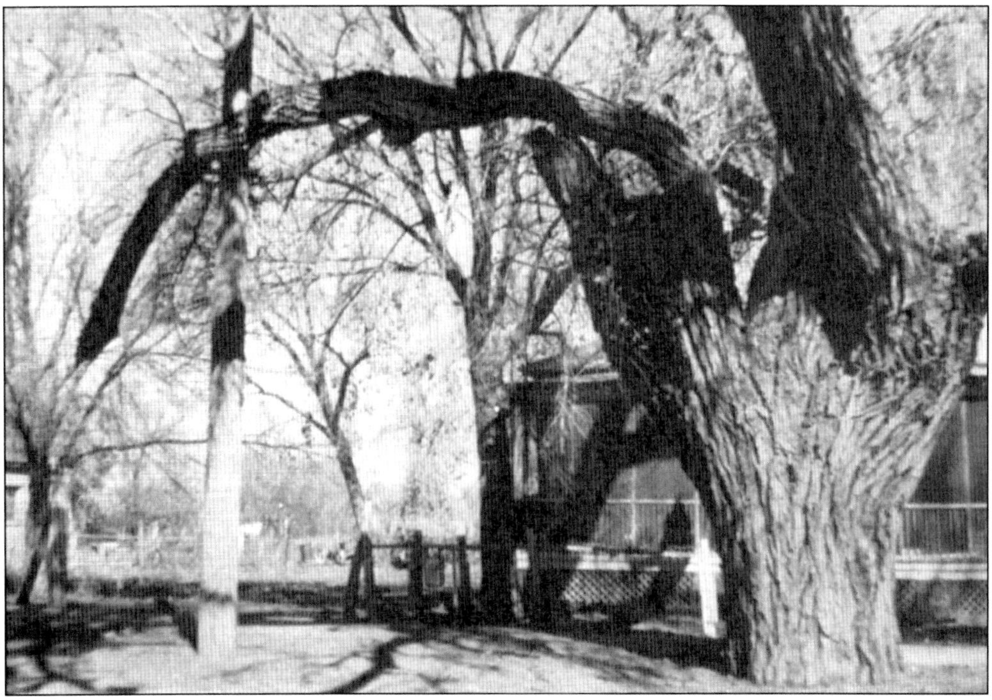

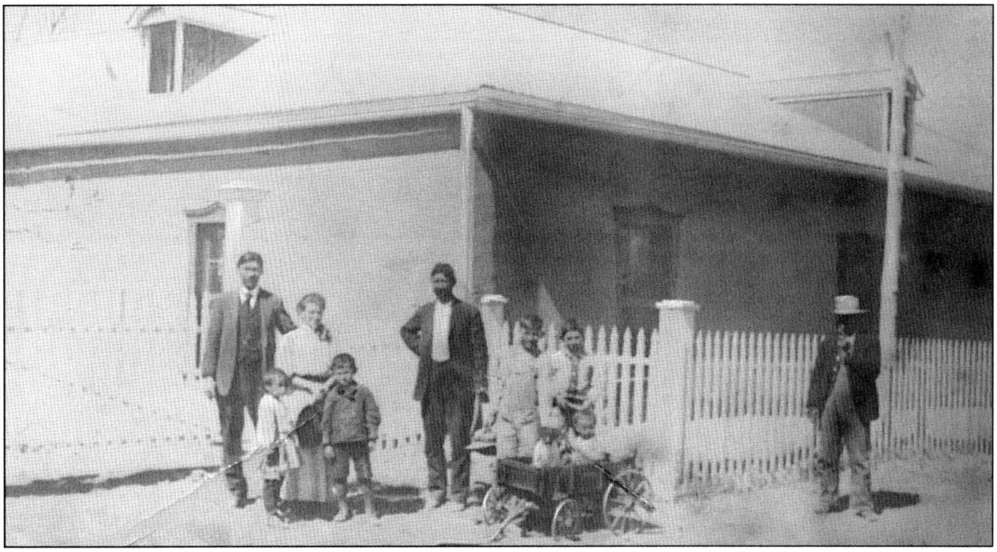

Pictured here in 1911, the Castillo family stands in front of the family home on North Los Lentes Road. The family members are, from left to right, Emiliano Castillo Sr., Anna Castillo, and their children Hattie, Oswald, unidentified, José, Louis, and Fred. Emiliano Castillo Sr. served as the second mayor of the village of Los Lunas. He was the first of four members of the Castillo family to hold that office. (Courtesy of Barbara Arnold.)

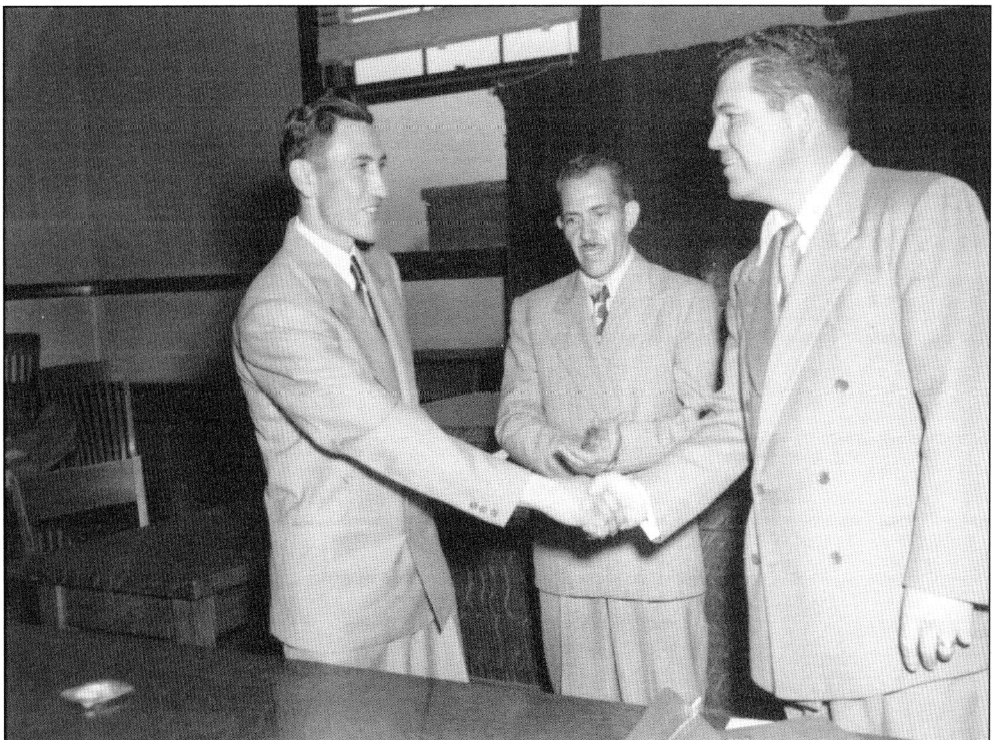

Emiliano Castillo Jr. (left) served as mayor of Los Lunas. He was also elected Valencia County sheriff in 1952. He is shown here being sworn in as sheriff by Madero Romero and Judge Filo M. Sedillo (right). (Courtesy of Barbara Arnold.)

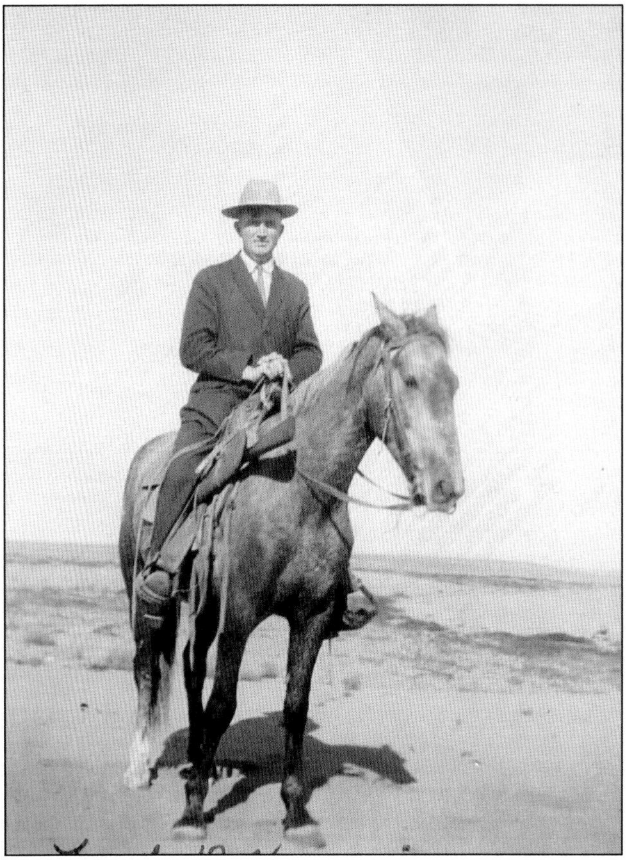

Fred D. Huning Sr. served as mayor of the village of Los Lunas for 20 years. He was on the Board of Regents of the New Mexico School of Mines in Socorro. He served on the Valencia County Commission and was a state highway commissioner. In Valencia County, he was also county treasurer and served on the Middle Rio Grande Conservancy District Board. He was instrumental in building the first paved roads in the state. (Courtesy of the Huning family.)

Louis Huning, in addition to managing the Huning Mercantile business, also served as mayor of the village of Los Lunas from 1982 until 2005—the longest tenure of any municipal leader in the village's history. Louis was the second Huning to serve as mayor. (Author's collection.)

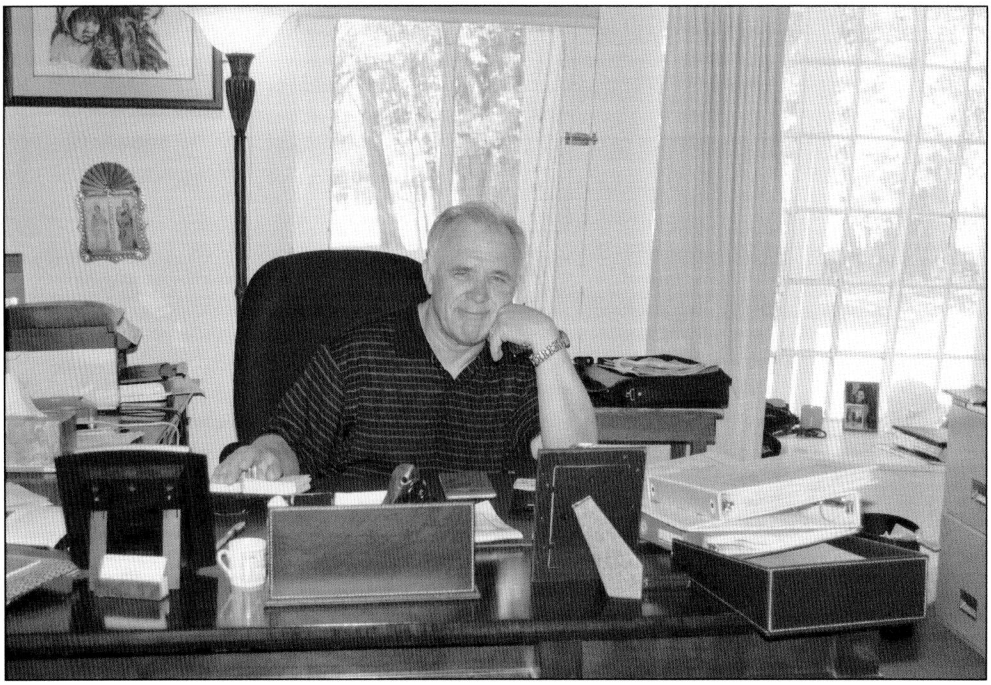

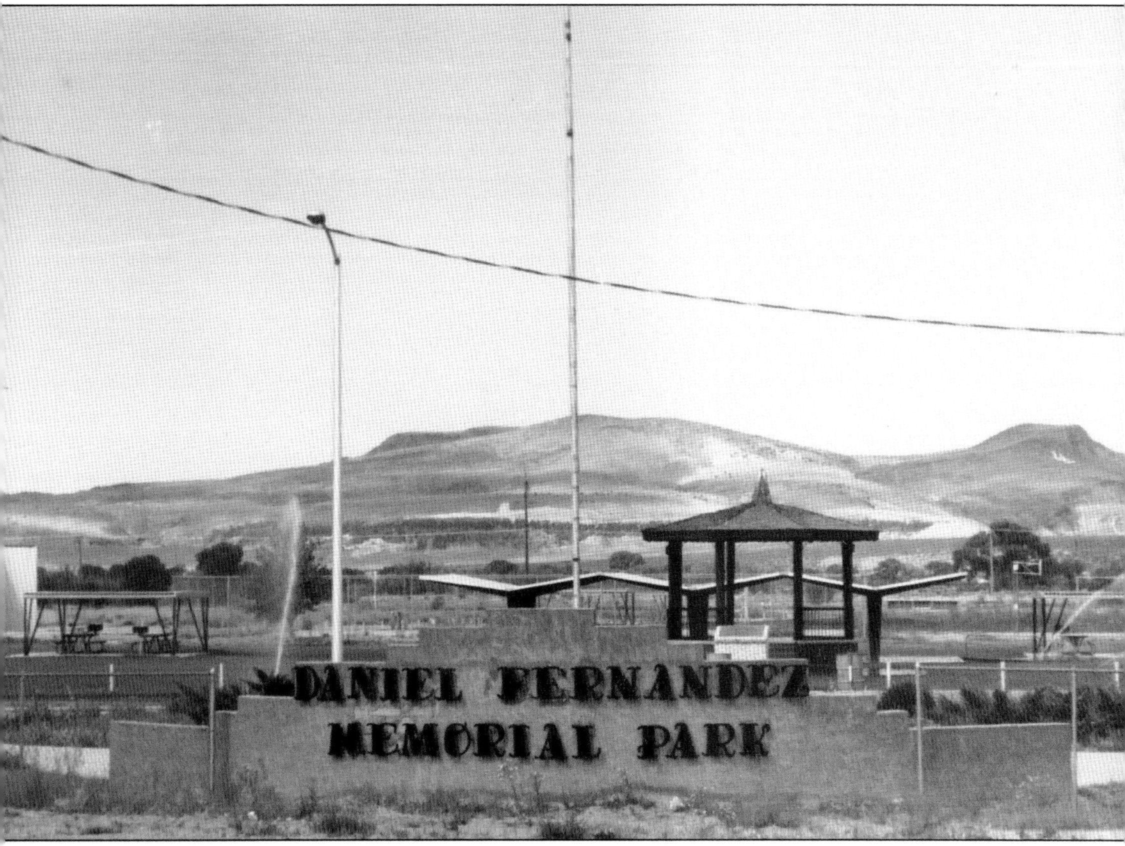

Daniel Fernández Memorial Park was dedicated to the memory of Daniel D. Fernández, son of José and Lorinda Fernández. Daniel was posthumously awarded the Congressional Medal of Honor for bravery during the Vietnam War. (Courtesy of the Valencia County Historical Society.)

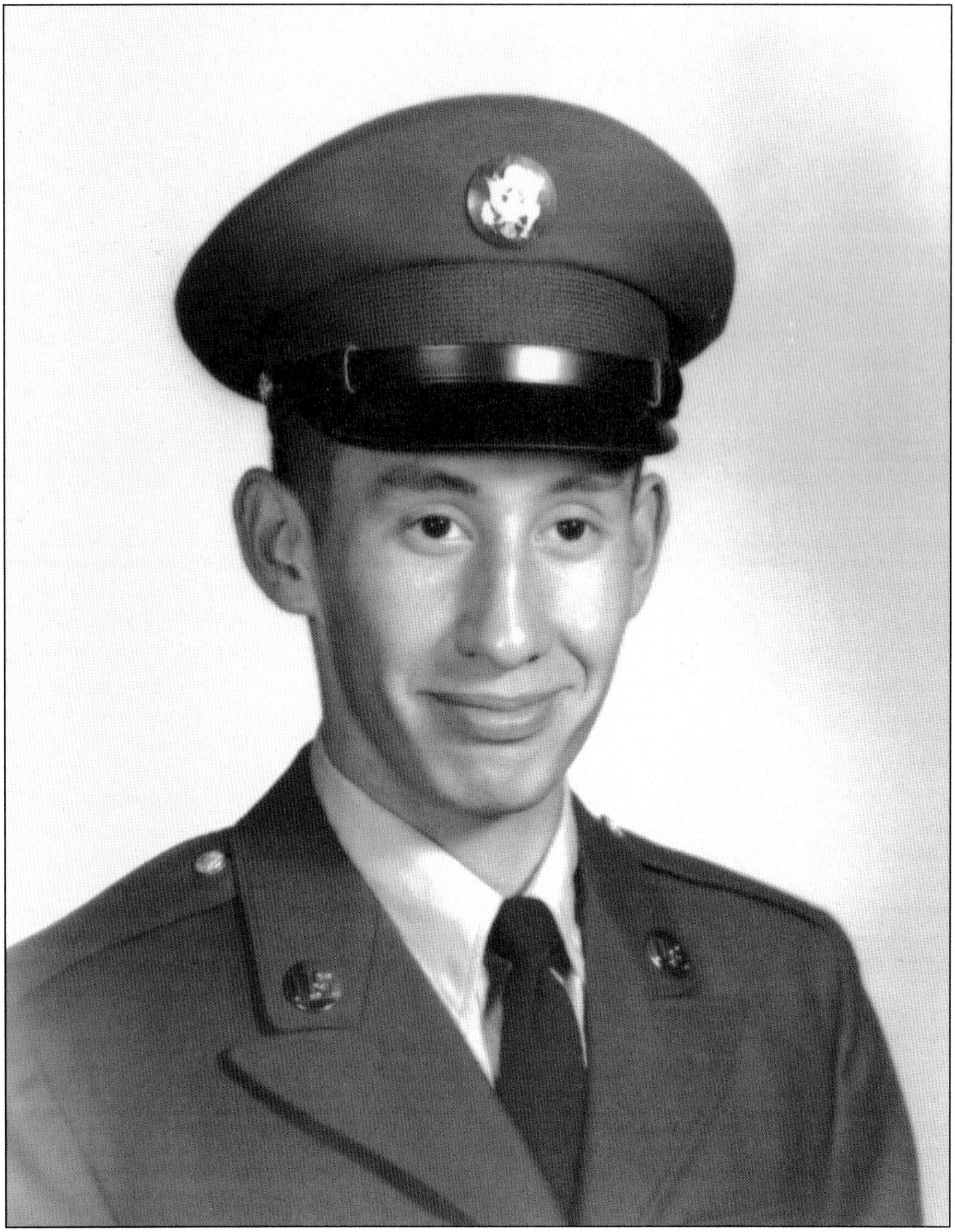

Spc. Daniel D. Fernández was killed at the age of 21 in the Republic of Vietnam on February 18, 1966. Specialist Fernández, who served two tours of duty in Vietnam, threw himself on an enemy hand grenade to save the lives of several of his fellow soldiers. His funeral was so crowded that it had to be held at Los Lunas High School, which he had attended. Pres. Lyndon Johnson honored Daniel Fernández's memory by awarding him the Congressional Medal of Honor, the country's highest military distinction, on April 6, 1967, in a ceremony at the White House. Daniel Fernández is buried at the National Cemetery in Santa Fe. (Courtesy of Los Lunas Museum of Heritage and Arts.)

Seven

Religious Life

Religious practice has been a vital part of life in the village of Los Lunas. The first Catholic church in the area was constructed at Isleta Pueblo in the early part of the 17th century. Other Catholic churches followed, including San Clemente in Los Lunas, Our Lady of Guadalupe in Peralta, San Antonio in Los Lentes, Sangre de Cristo in Valencia, and Immaculate Conception in Tomé.

The Peralta Methodist Mission was established in the 1850s, followed by Lutheran and Episcopal churches and the Church of Jesus Christ of Latter-day Saints.

A Good Friday passion play, staged originally at Immaculate Conception Catholic Church in Tomé, was performed for decades. It has since evolved into a religious pilgrimage for thousands of people, including many from Los Lunas. Worshipers walk to the top of El Cerro de Tomé and participate in services conducted around the three crosses erected there.

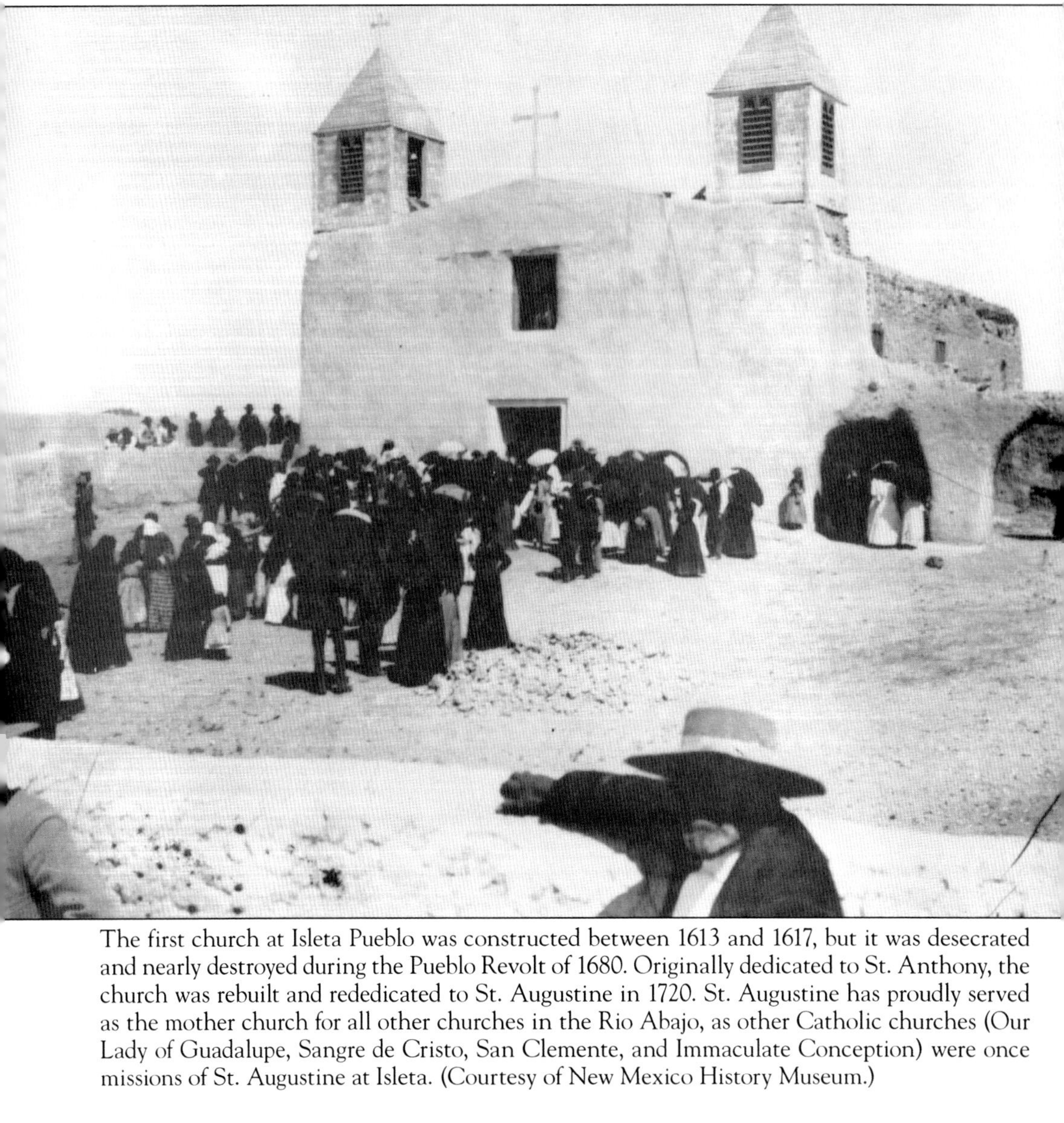

The first church at Isleta Pueblo was constructed between 1613 and 1617, but it was desecrated and nearly destroyed during the Pueblo Revolt of 1680. Originally dedicated to St. Anthony, the church was rebuilt and rededicated to St. Augustine in 1720. St. Augustine has proudly served as the mother church for all other churches in the Rio Abajo, as other Catholic churches (Our Lady of Guadalupe, Sangre de Cristo, San Clemente, and Immaculate Conception) were once missions of St. Augustine at Isleta. (Courtesy of New Mexico History Museum.)

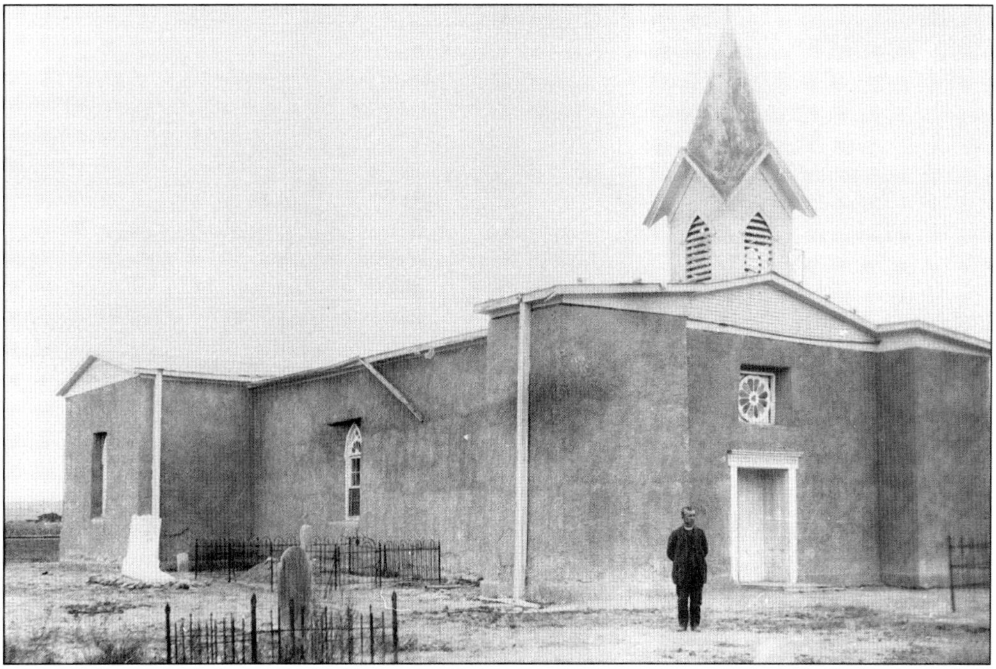

Fr. Albert W. Braun is shown around 1900 in front of San Clemente Catholic Church in Los Lunas. The church was located near the first Luna family hacienda, south of the present site of the Giant gas station on Main Street. Erected in 1894, it served the parish until a new church was built to the northeast across Main Street in 1949. (Courtesy of New Mexico History Museum.)

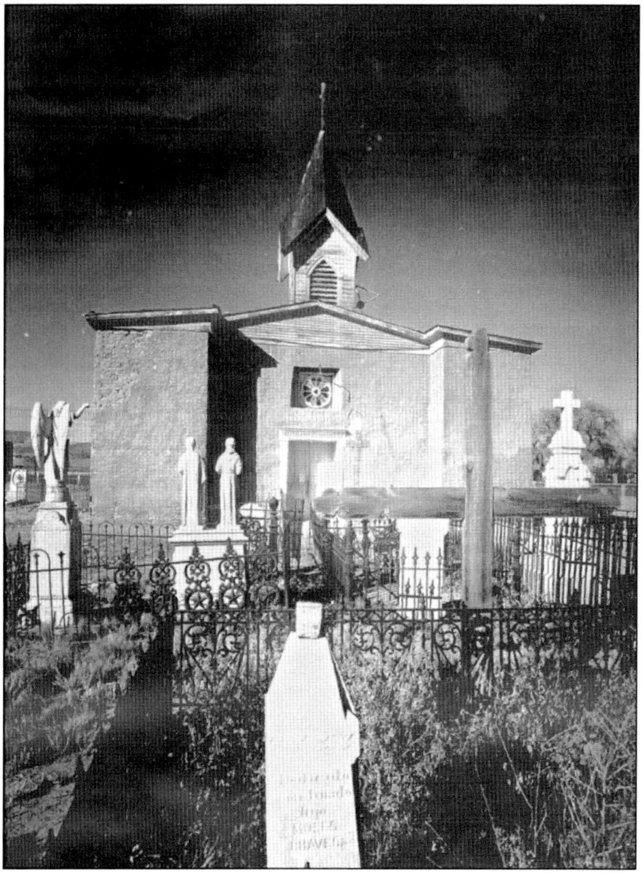

This is an 1894 view of the San Clemente Church. In addition to the round rose window over the entrance, the church also features a *campo santo*, or burial ground, in front. Although the church was torn down when a new church was built in 1949, the campo santo still exists and is tended on a regular basis by church members. (Courtesy of Los Lunas Museum of Heritage and Arts.)

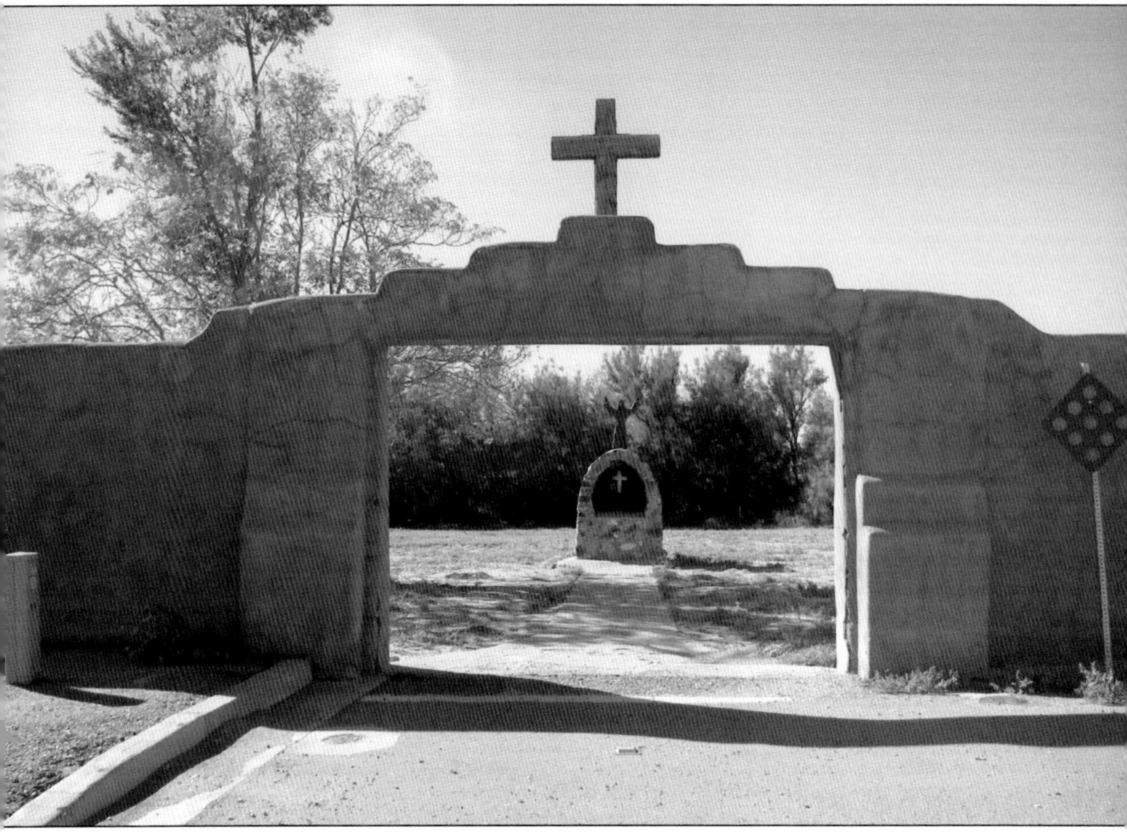

This is what remains of the San Clemente campo santo. The only feature inside the church burial ground is a memorial containing a bronze plaque with the names of those who were buried there. (Author's collection.)

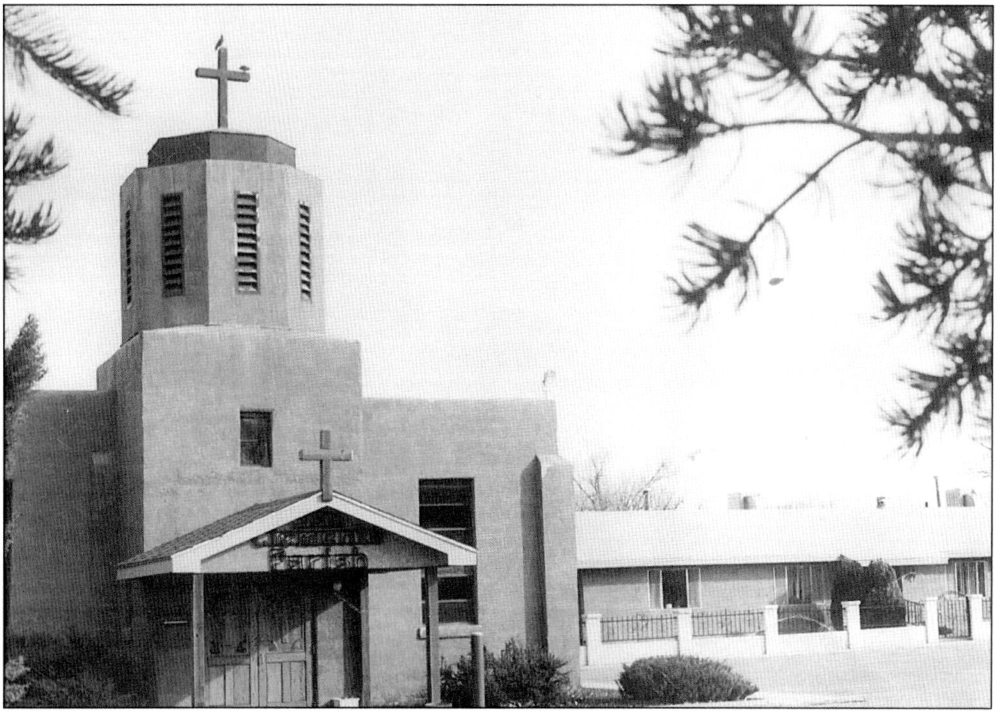

This is the San Clemente Church that was built in 1949 just north of the intersection of Main Street and Luna Avenue. (Courtesy of San Clemente Parish.)

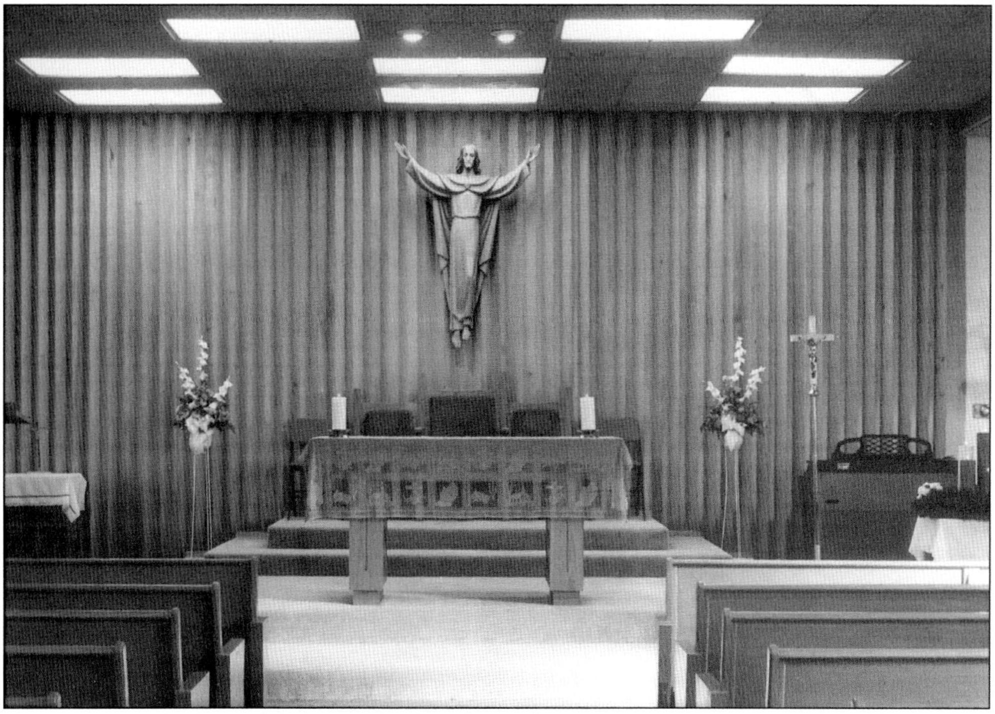

This photograph shows the sanctuary of the San Clemente Church that served members until a new church was built in 2004. (Courtesy of San Clemente Parish.)

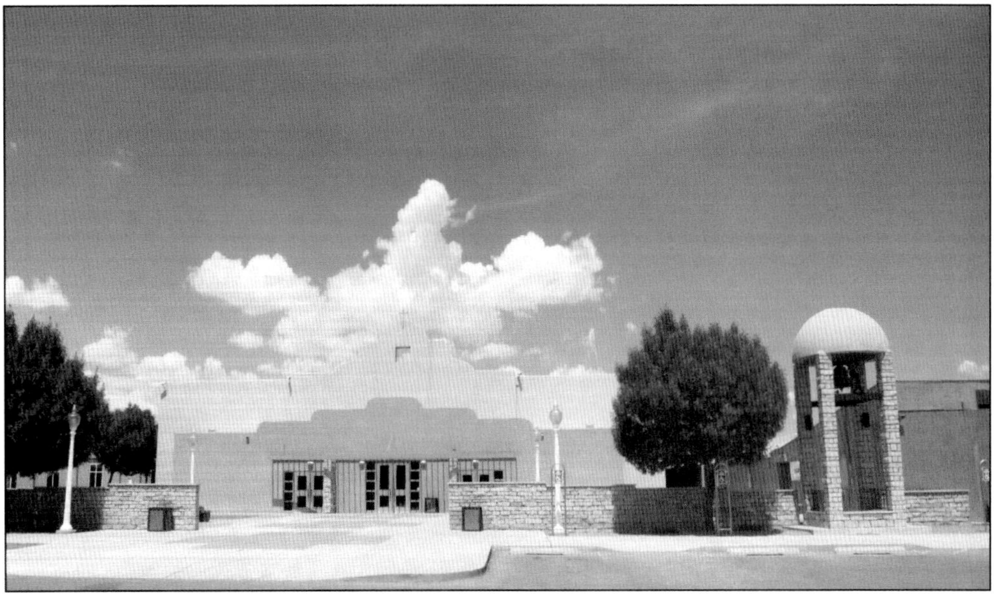

After nearly 50 years of use, the second San Clemente Church, built between 1949 and 1952, was replaced. On the same site as the 1949 church, the new structure featured a separate, freestanding bell tower reminiscent of the cupola on the 1949 church. The tower contains the original bell. The new church, substantially larger than the old one, was dedicated in 2004. (Author's collection.)

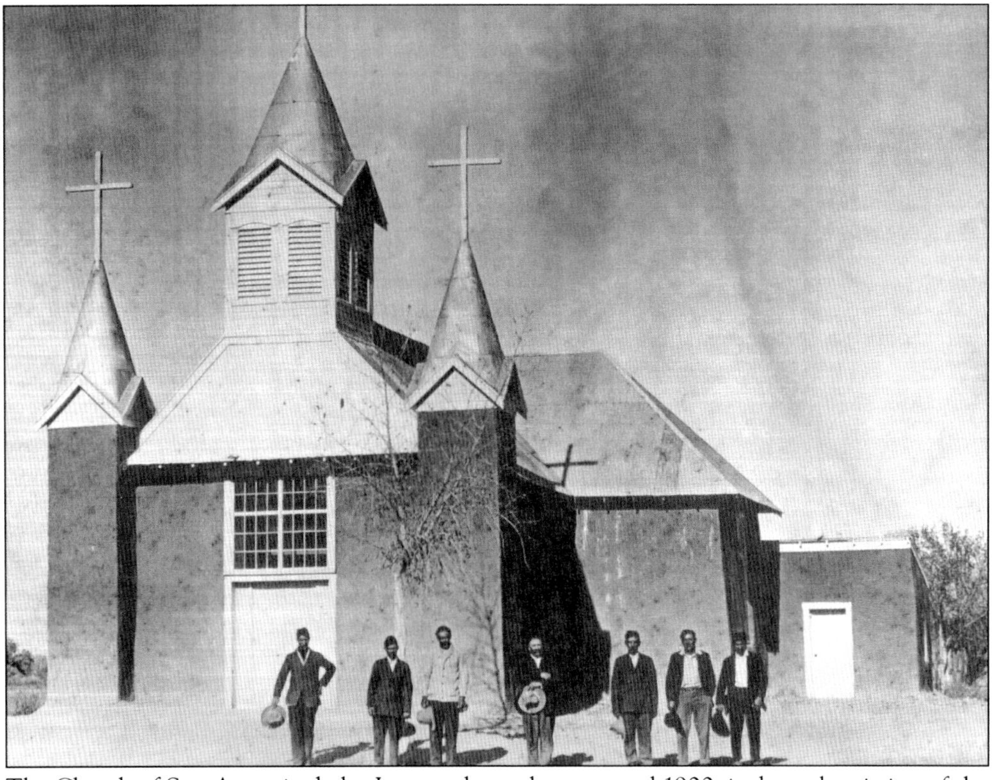

The Church of San Antonio de los Lentes, shown here around 1900, is the only mission of the Parish of San Clemente. (Courtesy of Los Lunas Museum of Heritage and Arts.)

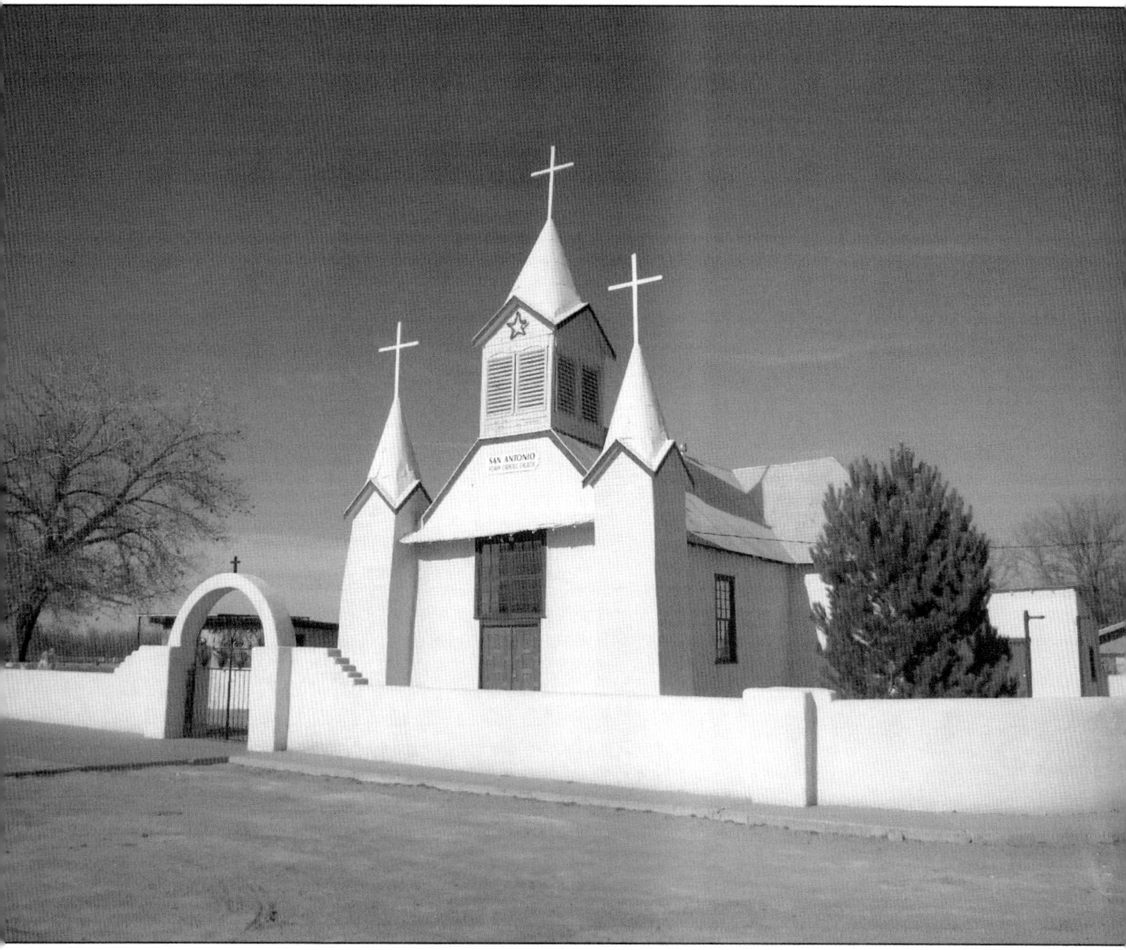

The San Antonio Roman Catholic Church is little changed today. The three Gothic spires were added some time late in the 19th century to the original flat-roofed chapel, built in 1789. The church is located in Los Lentes, between Los Lunas and Isleta Pueblo. (Author's collection.)

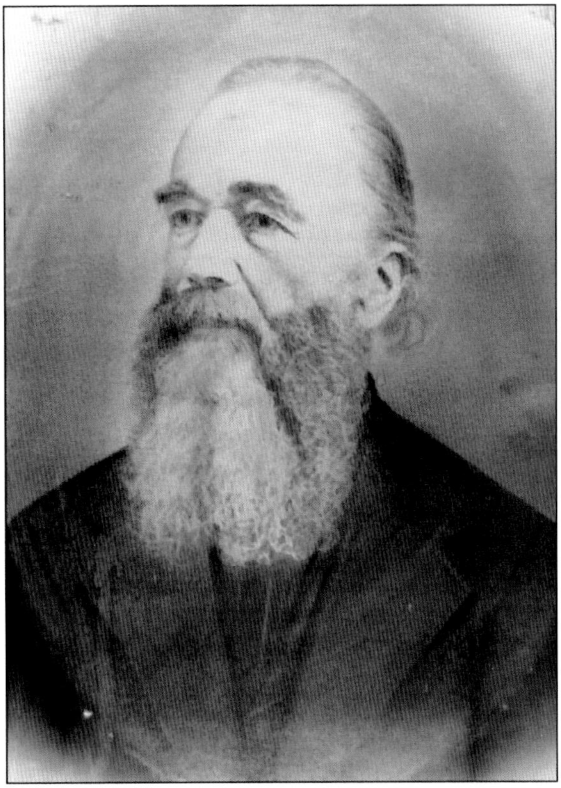

Fr. Jean-Baptiste Ralliere was assigned to the Tomé Parish in 1858 and served until his retirement in 1913. He established a Catholic school soon after his arrival in Tomé. In addition to English, math, history, and religion, he included carpentry and agriculture as subjects in his school. He also taught music and agriculture to locals. Father Ralliere was a champion of education and served as the first Valencia County superintendent of schools in 1887. (Courtesy of the Valencia County Historical Society.)

Fr. Antonin Docher (center) interacted with and advised other parishes in Valencia County. He is shown here with Eduardo Otero and an unidentified Native American at Isleta Pueblo some time in the early 1900s. (Courtesy of Barbara Bergère Nau.)

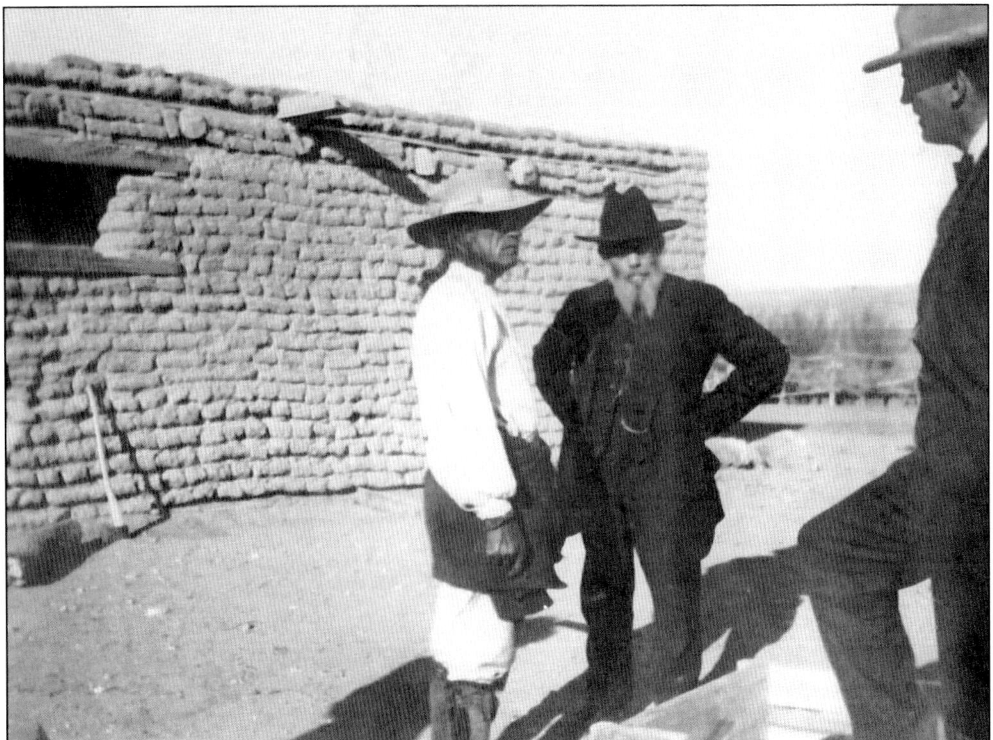

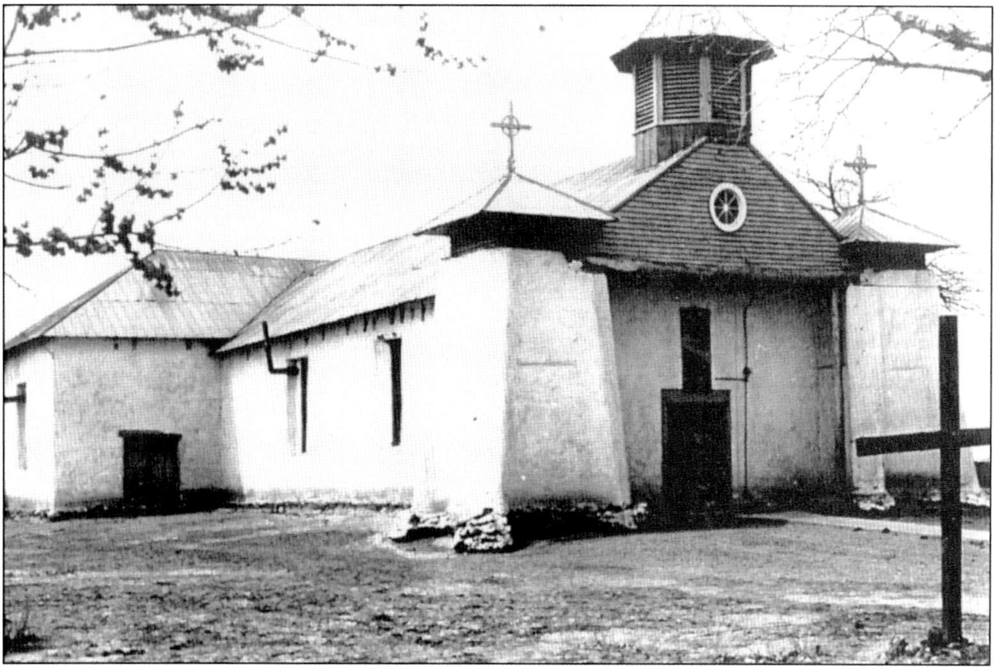

Dedicated in 1892, Our Lady of Guadalupe, the Catholic church in Peralta, was a small chapel built at the home of Don Juan Antonio Otero. A structure located on the southwest side of the church served as the Peralta school until a new school was constructed in 1911. In this 1947 photograph, the church features a pitched roof and steeple configuration that exists to the present day. (Courtesy of Museum of New Mexico, Negative No. 86714.)

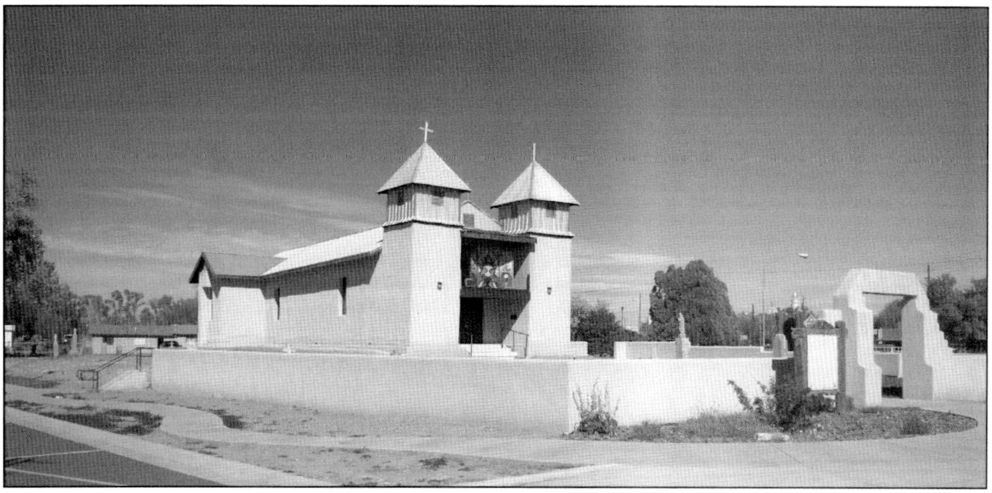

A simple flat-roofed adobe structure, the first Sangre de Cristo Catholic Church was constructed around 1801 in Valencia. Towers designed by Peralta merchant Abraham Kempenich were added in 1902. The north wall of the church collapsed in 1941, and the remaining church structure was razed and rebuilt using the original floor plan. It was rededicated in 1943. (Author's collection.)

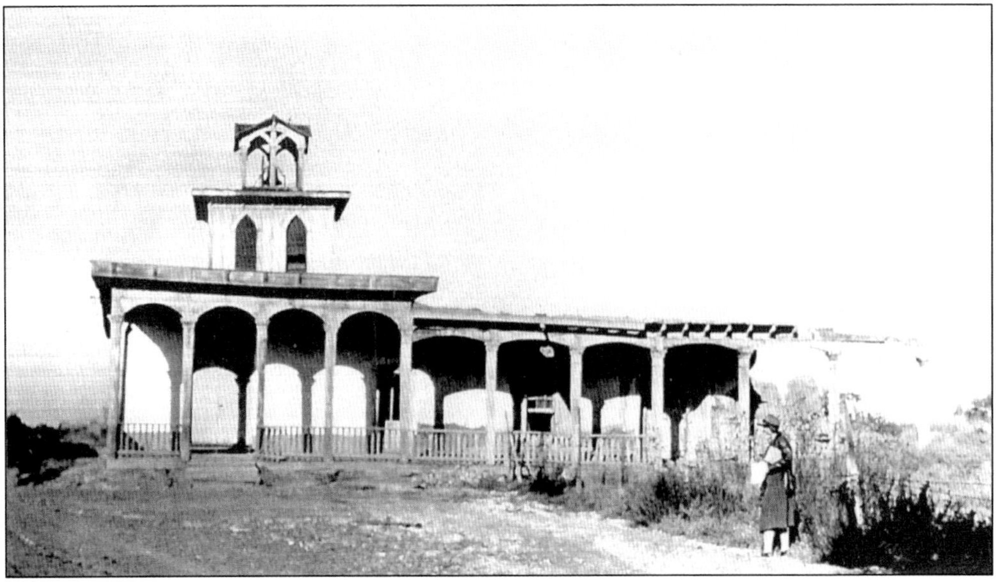

What was to become the Peralta Methodist Mission was established as a Baptist mission on November 17, 1855. Don Ambrosio Gonzales was its first minister. Methodists purchased the mission in 1874. It was located to the south of Our Lady of Guadalupe Catholic Church. The mission's abandonment in 1955 left the area with no Protestant church. (Courtesy of New Mexico Photo Archive.)

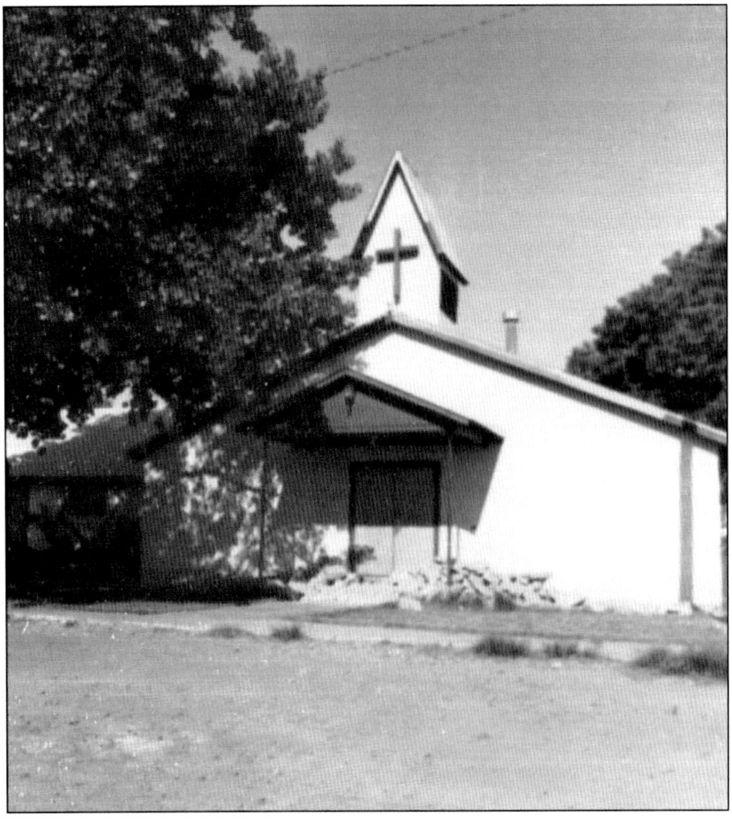

When the Peralta Memorial United Methodist Church was reformed in 1957, the congregation built a new church. That church is shown here in 1981. (Courtesy of the Valencia County Historical Society.)

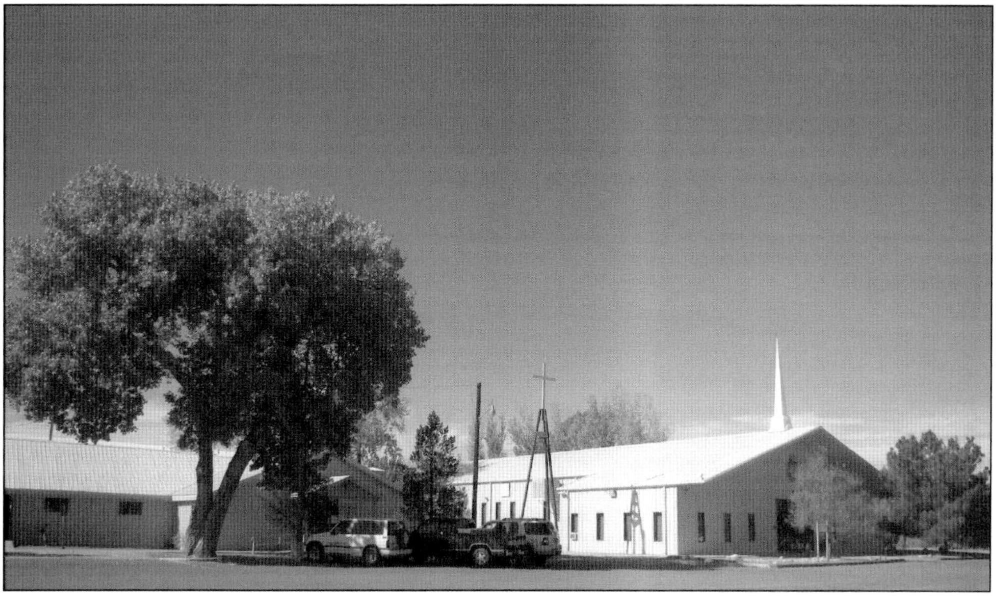

The Peralta Memorial United Methodist Church has moved to its present location on Wesley Road in Peralta. Church facilities were greatly expanded, as can be seen in this photograph. (Author's collection.)

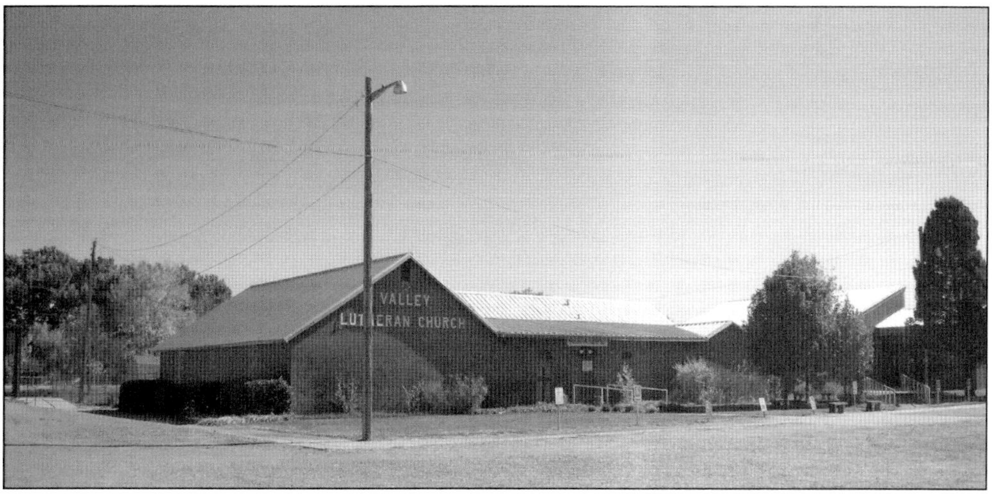

Dedicated on April 9, 1989, the Valley Lutheran Church is located on Highway 47. The original church consisted of two military surplus barracks that were joined together to form a single building. Those structures were later enclosed to form the fellowship hall (left), and a new sanctuary was added. (Author's collection.)

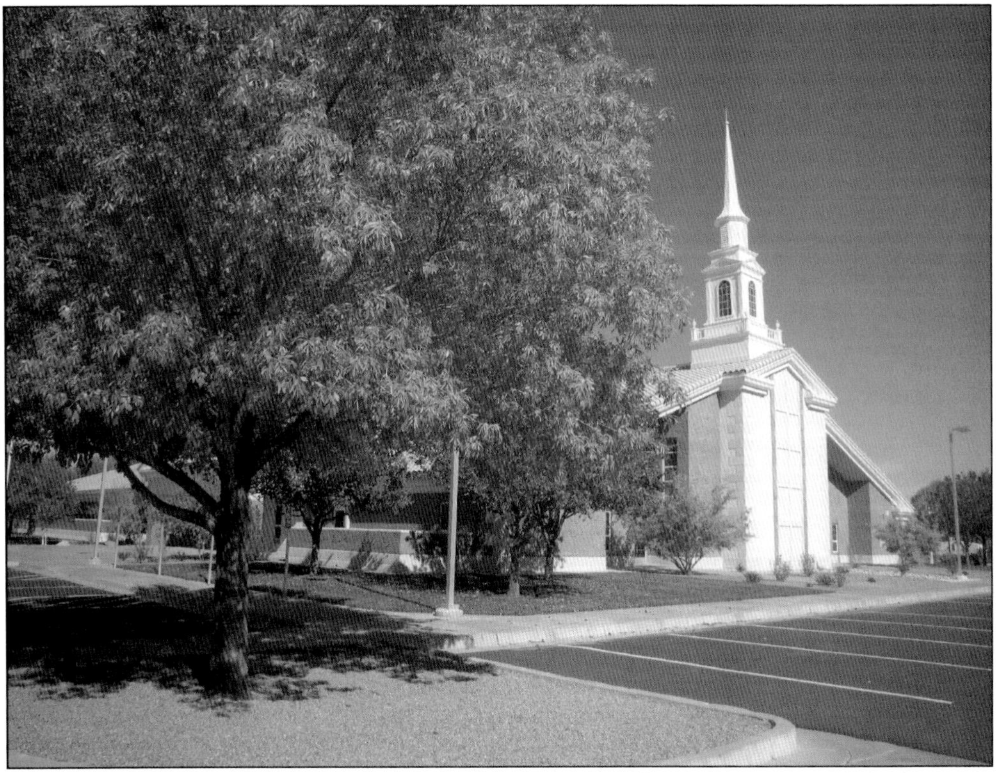

The Los Lunas Stake of the Church of Jesus Christ of Latter-day Saints was established in 1959. The chapel addition was dedicated on October 11, 1970. The church maintains a state-of-the-art genealogy center that is available to the public. (Author's collection.)

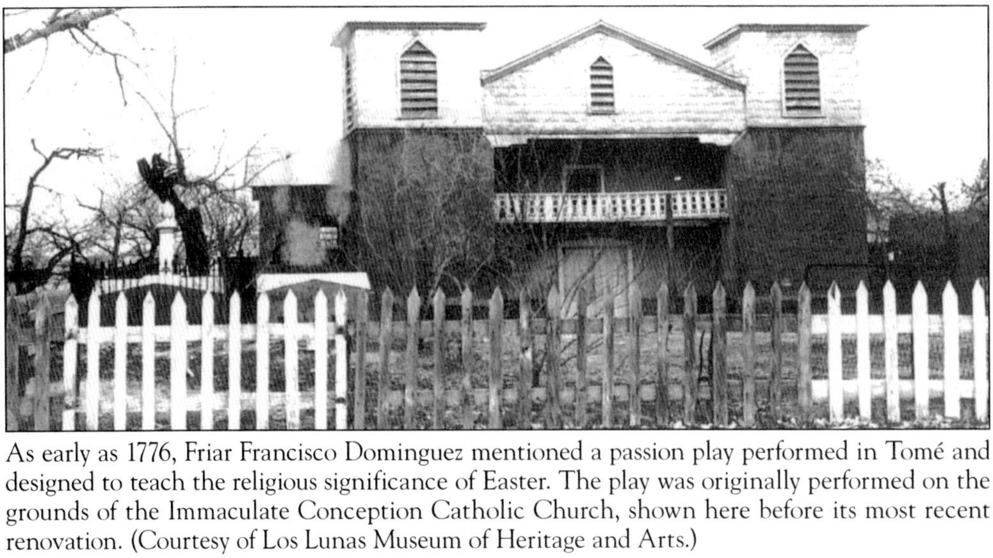

As early as 1776, Friar Francisco Dominguez mentioned a passion play performed in Tomé and designed to teach the religious significance of Easter. The play was originally performed on the grounds of the Immaculate Conception Catholic Church, shown here before its most recent renovation. (Courtesy of Los Lunas Museum of Heritage and Arts.)

Around 1947, Edwin Berry (pictured), Fred Landavazo, Juan Esteban Zamora, and others felt that the pageant should be preserved in a permanent form. They collaborated with Fr. Thomas T. Steele to produce a written script in Spanish with an English translation. The last performance of the passion play was held on church grounds some time between 1947 and 1955. (Courtesy of the Valencia County Historical Society.)

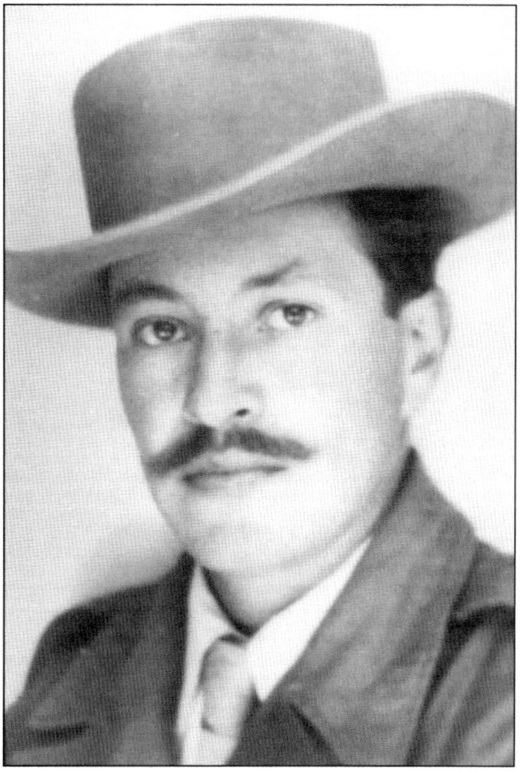

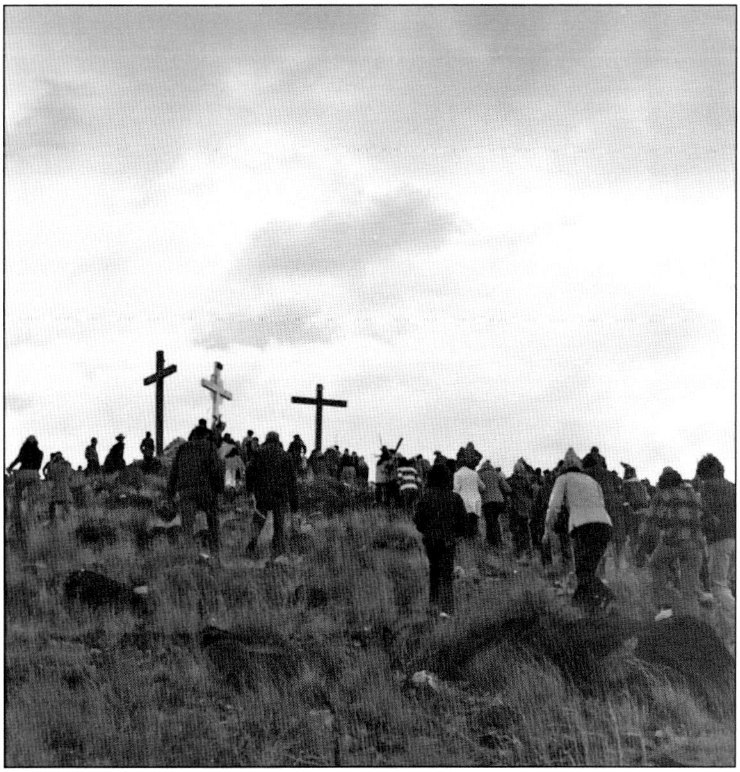

Between 1955 and 1975, some Tomé residents climbed nearby El Cerro de Tomé in observance of Good Friday, but the passion play was not performed. As part of the US Bicentennial Celebration in 1975 and 1976, it was decided to perform the complete passion play again, but instead of the church grounds, the pageant was held at the top of El Cerro de Tomé. (Author's collection.)

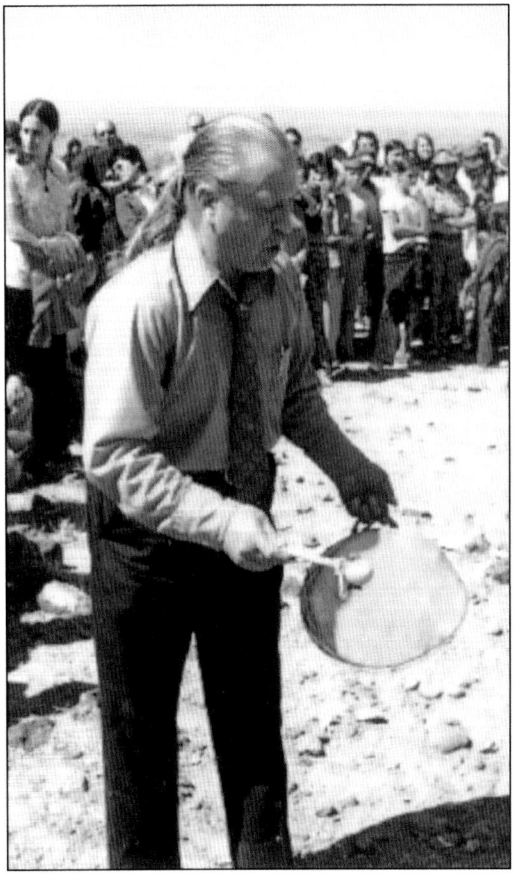

Edwin Berry is shown here more than 30 years after first participating in the pageant himself, leading worshipers in celebration of the Stations of the Cross at the top of El Cerro de Tomé. (Author's collection.)

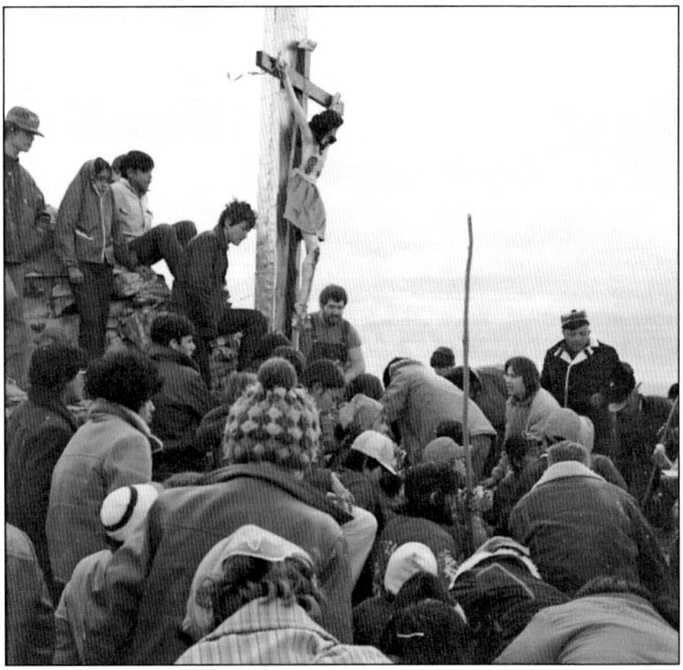

Edwin Berry passed away in 2000, but the El Cerro de Tomé pilgrimage continues with the help of his family and the community. Hundreds of worshipers of all religious faiths participate, traveling for many miles on foot to reach the three crosses at the top of the hill. (Author's collection.)

Eight

Education, Sports, and Recreation

Sports and recreation activities for residents of the village of Los Lunas have largely centered around the schools. Education was important to residents from the earliest Hispanic settlements in the late 1600s to the present day.

The first private classes were taught in the homes of prominent citizens. Later, public education was championed and implemented by representatives of the Catholic Church. When New Mexico became a state in 1912, the state constitution made a provision for publicly funded elementary school and secondary school education.

In Los Lunas, schools within the school district have been named in honor of citizens who made major contributions to the community. Solomon Luna, Raymond Gabaldon, and Katherine Gallegos are among those so honored.

Organized sports, especially baseball, have long been a source of entertainment for residents of both the village of Los Lunas and Valencia County. Each local community had a baseball team, and they competed intensely with each other. Some of the best local baseball teams were from Isleta Pueblo.

Camping, fishing, hunting, and casual outdoor picnics were also popular pastimes. This combination of school activities, sports, and recreation opportunities all contributed to a sense of community that was a part of living in the village of Los Lunas.

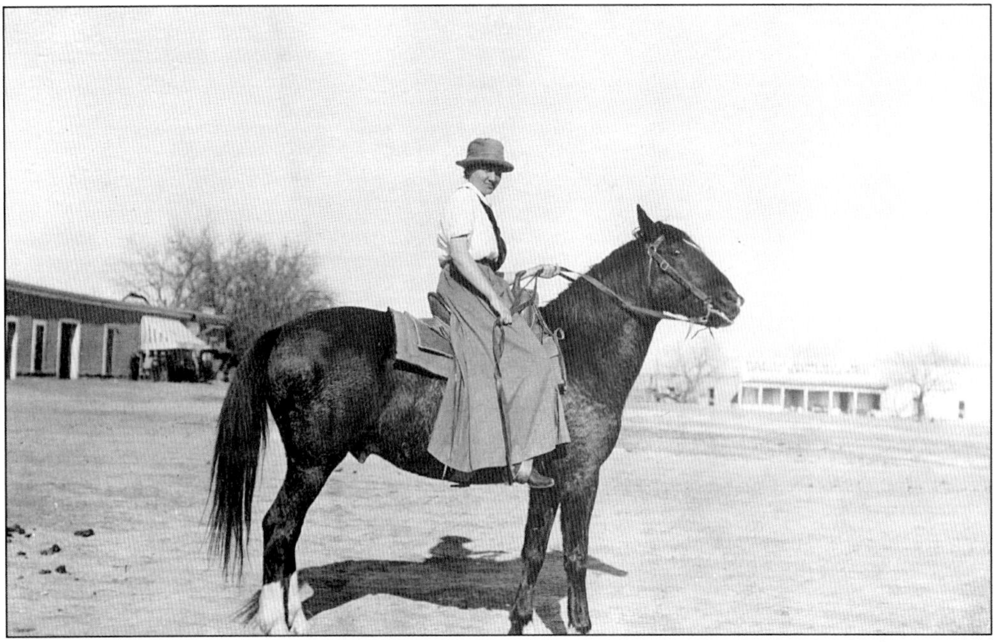

Ethel Tyler was born and raised in Los Angeles, California, but came to Los Lunas by train in the early 1900s. She said that she would not look out of the train window until she reached her destination. Her grandson Louis Huning said that when the train arrived at Los Lunas she looked out the train window "but she stayed anyway." (Courtesy of the Huning family.)

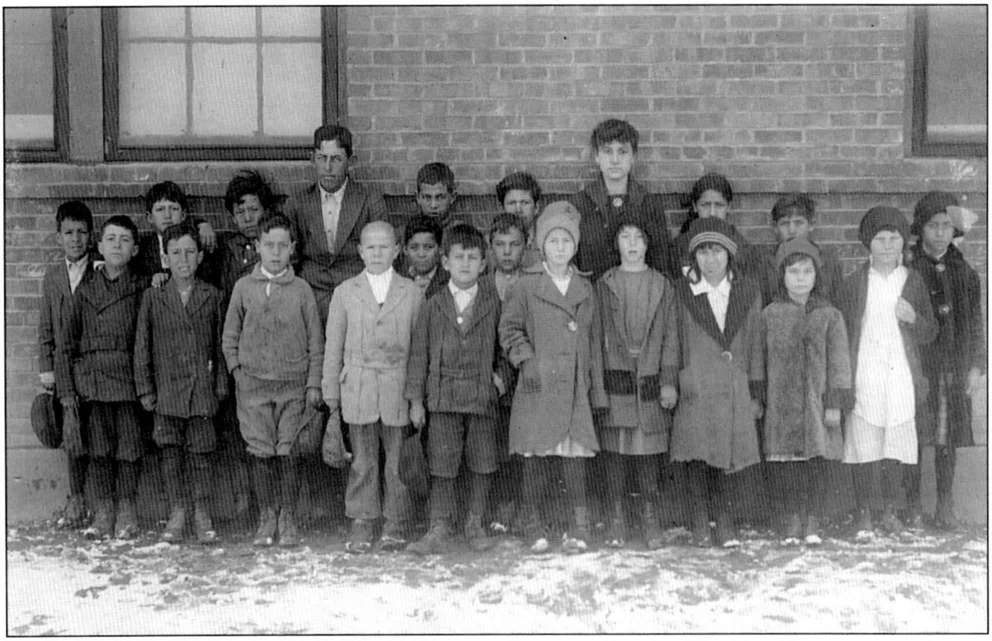

Ethel Tyler came to Los Lunas to teach. She was the second wife of Fred D. Huning, son of Louis Bismark Huning. She graduated from Los Angeles Teachers College and got a teaching position in Los Lunas. She is pictured here with her first-grade class at Los Lunas Elementary School in 1915. (Courtesy of the Huning family.)

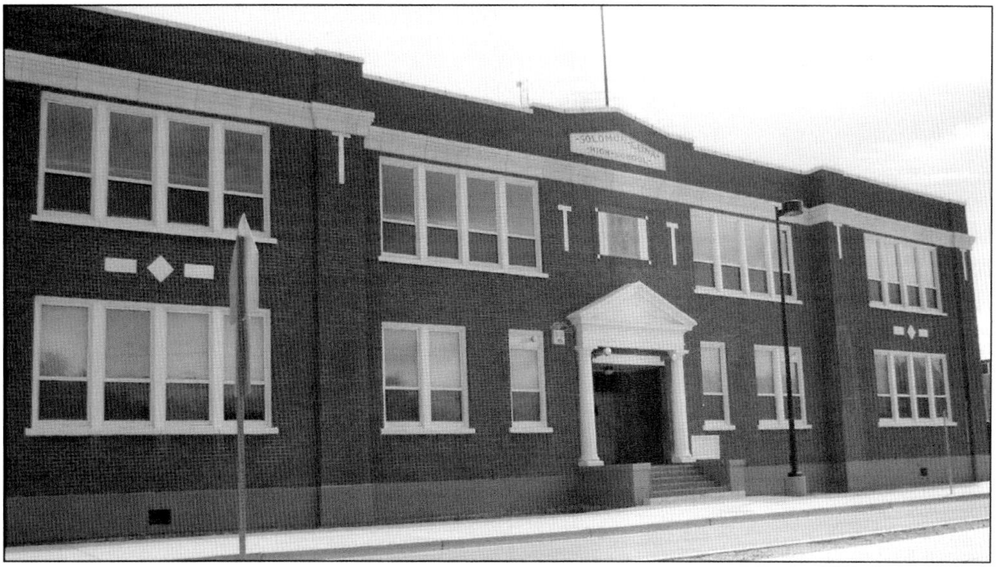

In 1926, a high school named in honor of Solomon Luna was erected in Los Lunas. A dedication ceremony was held on December 26, 1926. Joseph F. Tondre, president of the board of education, opened the proceedings. Former New Mexico governor O.A. Larrazolo gave the keynote address. Native American dancers from Isleta Pueblo provided entertainment. (Author's collection.)

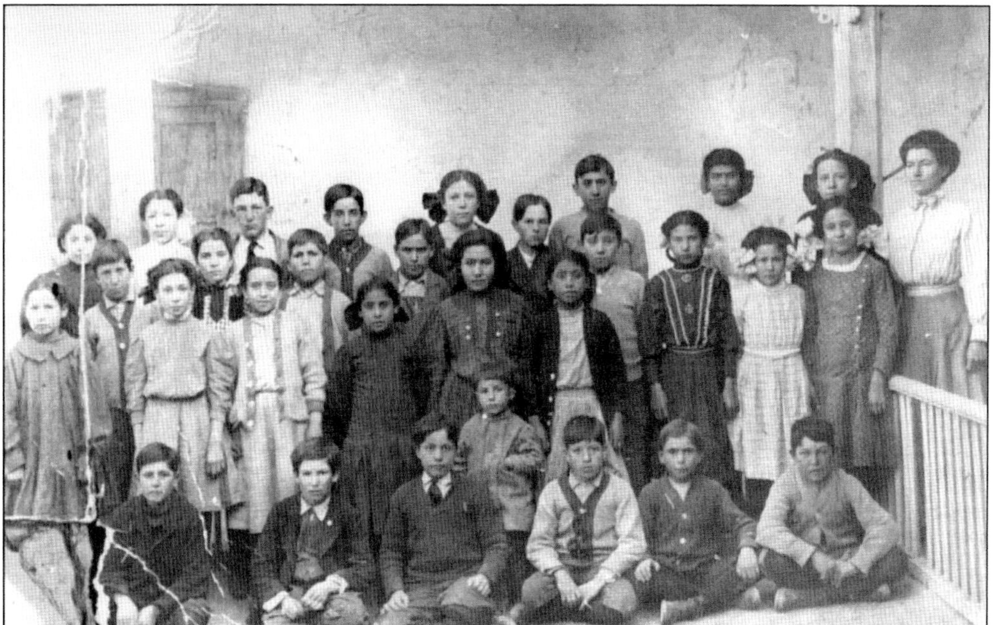

Until 1912, the Los Lunas School (grades one through eight only) was located at the corner of Main Street and Luna Avenue in the adobe home of Doña Rumaldita. Among the students of teacher Emilia Raff shown here are Martin Ryan, Gillie Luna, Salomon Vallejos, Demetrio Jaramillo, Manfor and Alberto Romero, Martin Ryan's sister, Juan Archuleta, Isabel Vallejos, Lucinda Jaramillo, Margarito Otero, Salomon Jaramillo, Eligio Gallegos, Teresa Artiaga, Pancha Romero, Rose Romero, Lupita Aragón, Pabla Aragón, Herman Raff, Blas Vallejos, Emilia (Perla) Romero, Raunfuelle, José Castillo, Mercedes Tafoya, and Reina Romero. (Courtesy of Los Lunas Schools.)

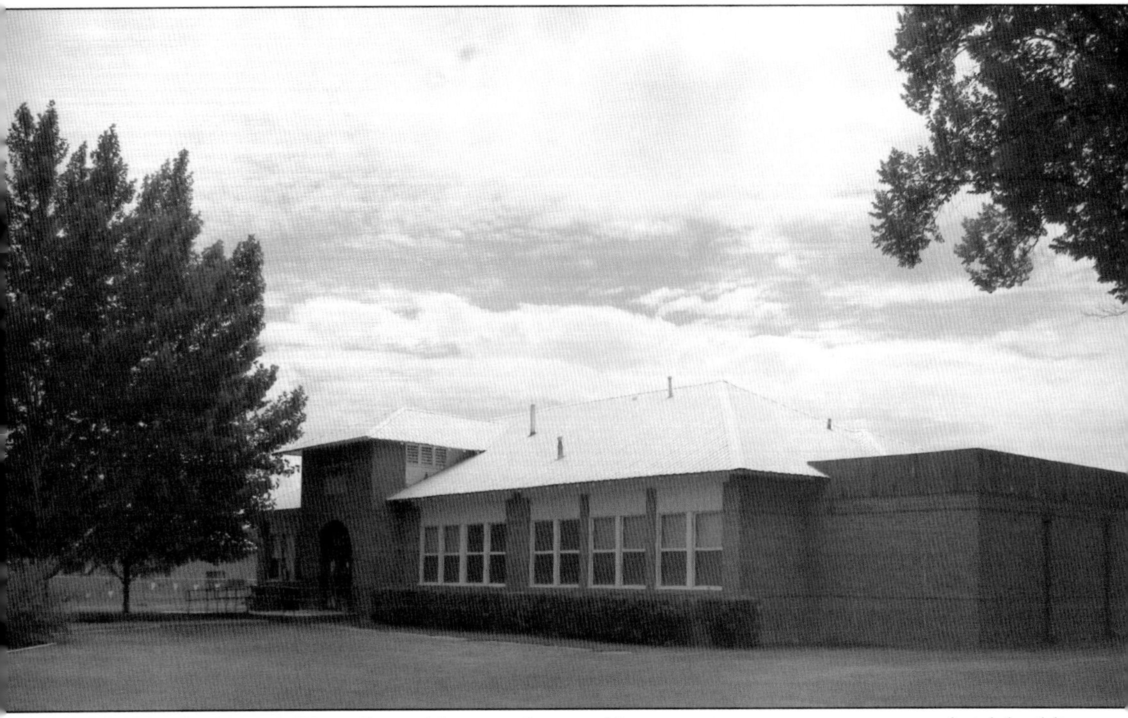

When the home of Doña Rumaldita was damaged by irrigation water, a permanent brick building was constructed in 1912. School board members at the time were Jesús M. Luna, Andrés A. Romero, and Boleslo Romero. The building later served as the administration building for the Los Lunas Schools. It still stands at the corner of Main Street and Luna Avenue and provides offices of the Special Services Department of Los Lunas Schools. (Author's collection.)

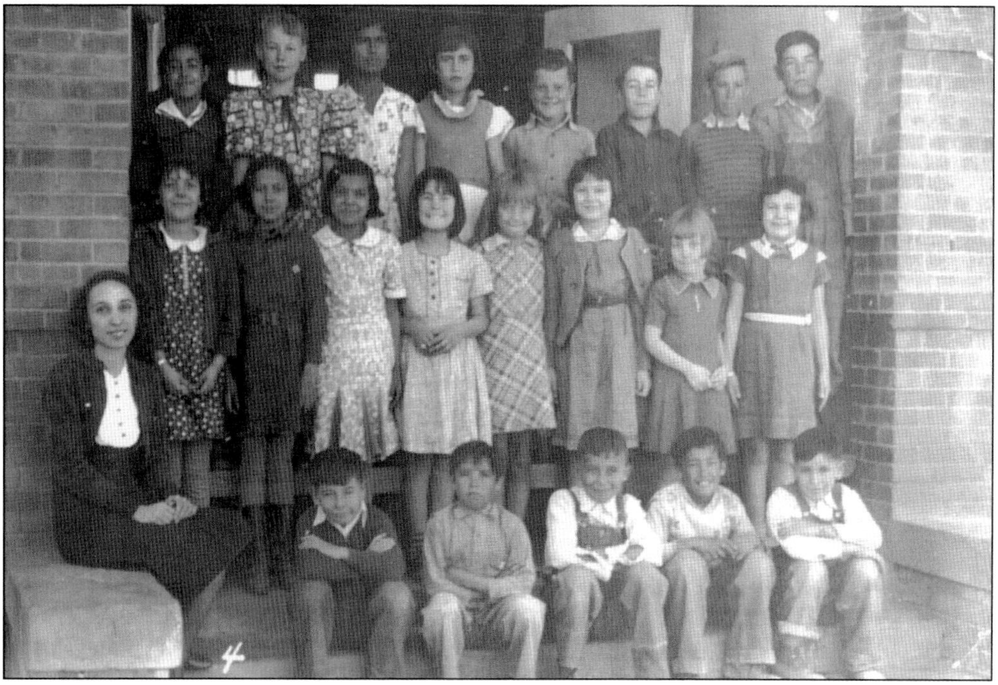

Teacher Lupita Maestas is shown here with her Los Lunas Elementary School class in front of the 1912 elementary school. (Courtesy of Los Lunas Museum of Heritage and Arts.)

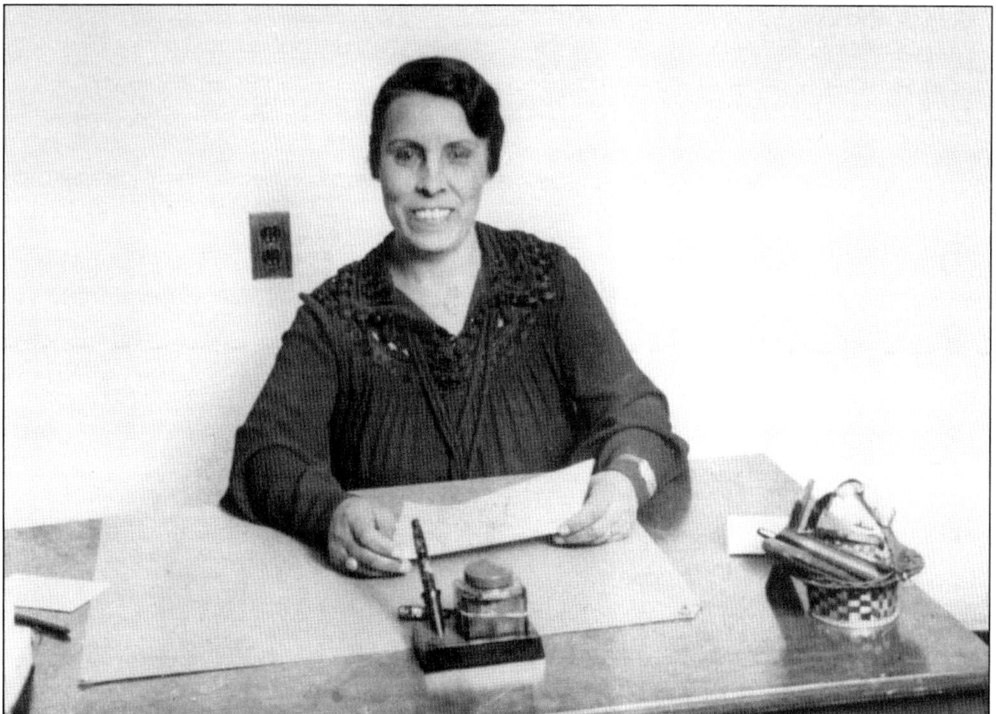

Mrs. C.C. Pacheco (Flora) served as the first Valencia County school supervisor. (Courtesy of Los Lunas Museum of Heritage and Arts.)

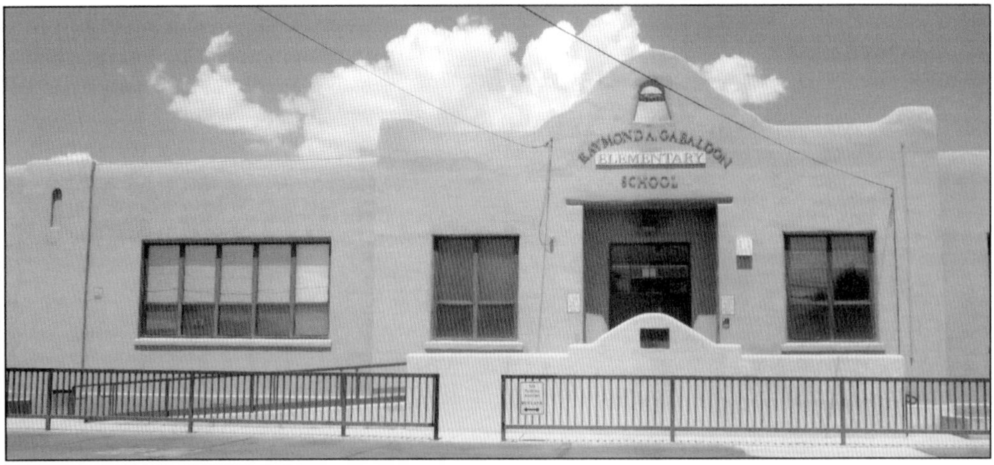

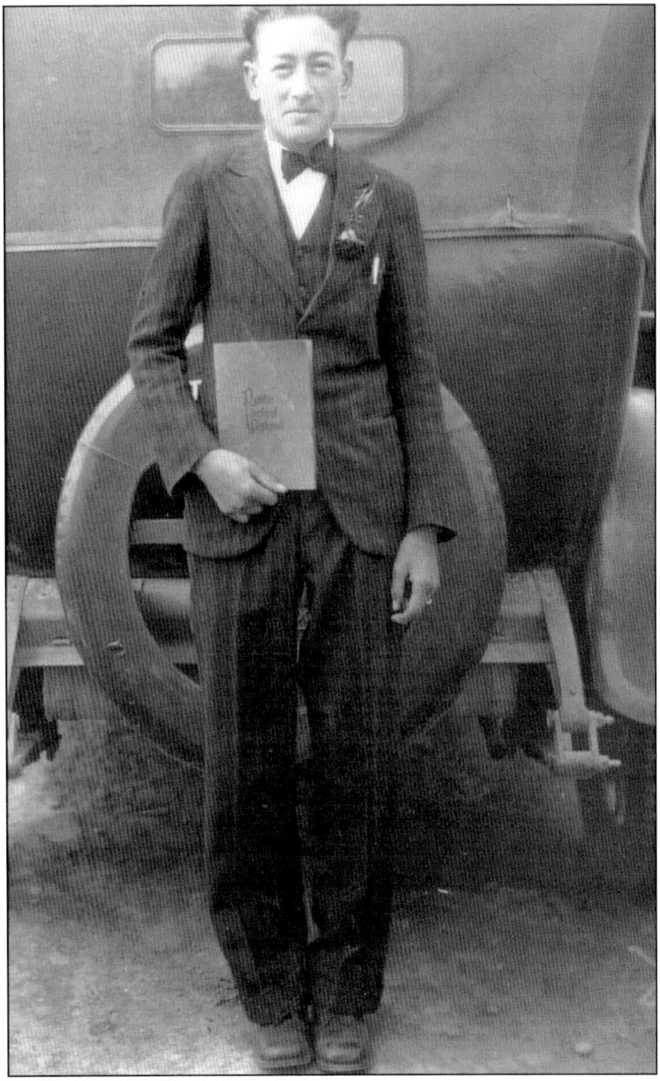

This school, originally named the Los Lunas Elementary School, replaced the brick building on Main Street. It was later renamed in honor of Raymond A. Gabaldon, a dedicated professional educator born on April 10, 1927. In addition to Los Lunas, Raymond Gabaldon also taught in El Rito, La Joya, and Belen. He served as superintendent of Los Lunas Schools. (Author's collection.)

Manuel C. Chávez poses with his diploma on the day he graduated from Los Lunas High School. He shows obvious pride at having obtained his public school diploma, indicating the import of this achievement. To mark the day, he has borrowed a suit from a neighbor. Chávez later became a judge and served two terms as Valencia County treasurer, from 1949 to 1953. (Courtesy of Charles Griego.)

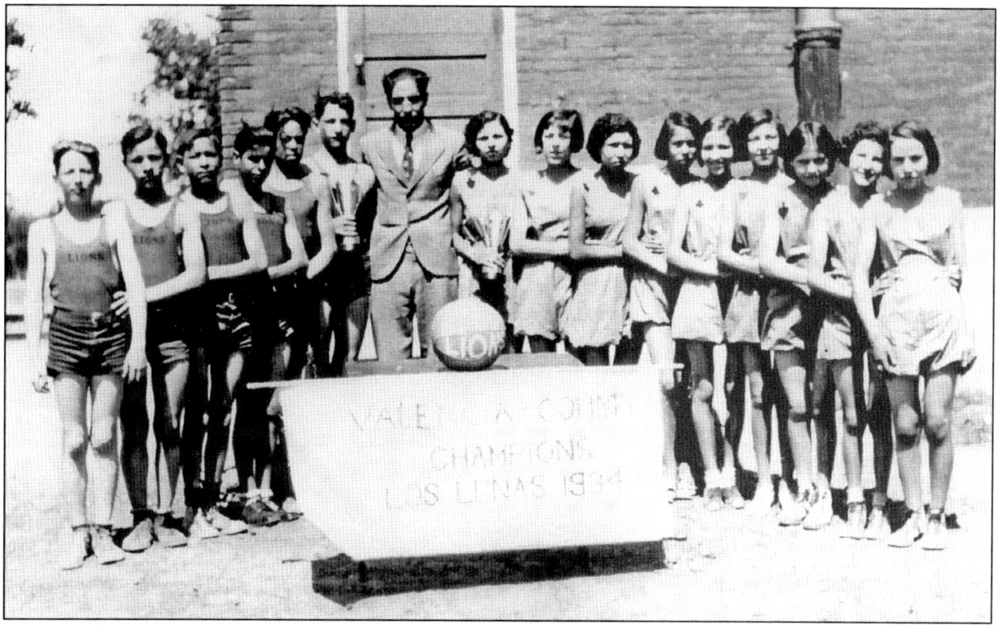

In 1934, the Los Lunas Lions were Valencia County champions in both boys' and girls' basketball. On the boys' team are, from left to right, Dick Young, Ralph Gallegos, Napoleon Artiaga, Augustin Artiaga, Eloy Vialpando, Foch Romero, and coach S.R. Daley. On the girls' team are, from left to right, Celina Gutierrez, Emilia Romero, Mary Stella Daley, Minerva Romero, Lorina Romero, Carmelita Otero, Frances Sandoval, Rosa Baca, and Amanda Otero. (Courtesy of Los Lunas Museum of Heritage and Arts, Route 66 Project.)

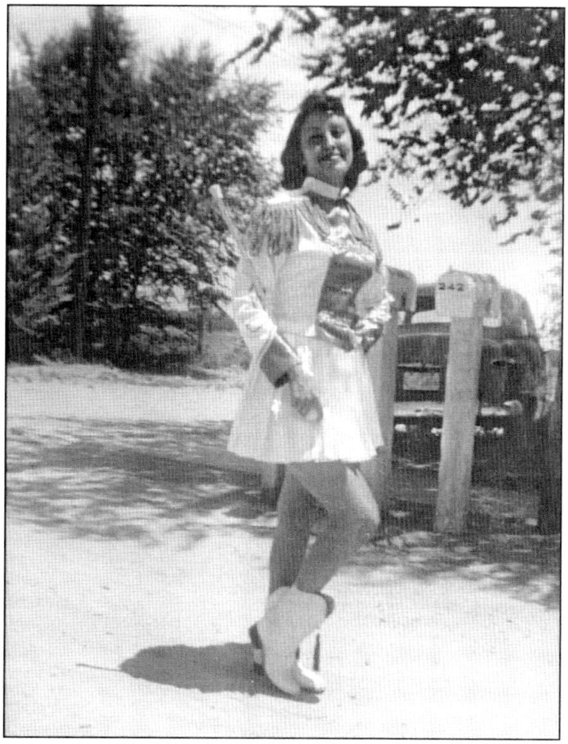

The baton twirlers and dancers for the Los Lunas High School band were called the Tigerettes. Nellie Gomez is shown here in 1961 in her Tigerette uniform. She is proudly posing in front of her family's home at the corner of Los Lentes and Cortez Streets. (Courtesy of Charles Griego.)

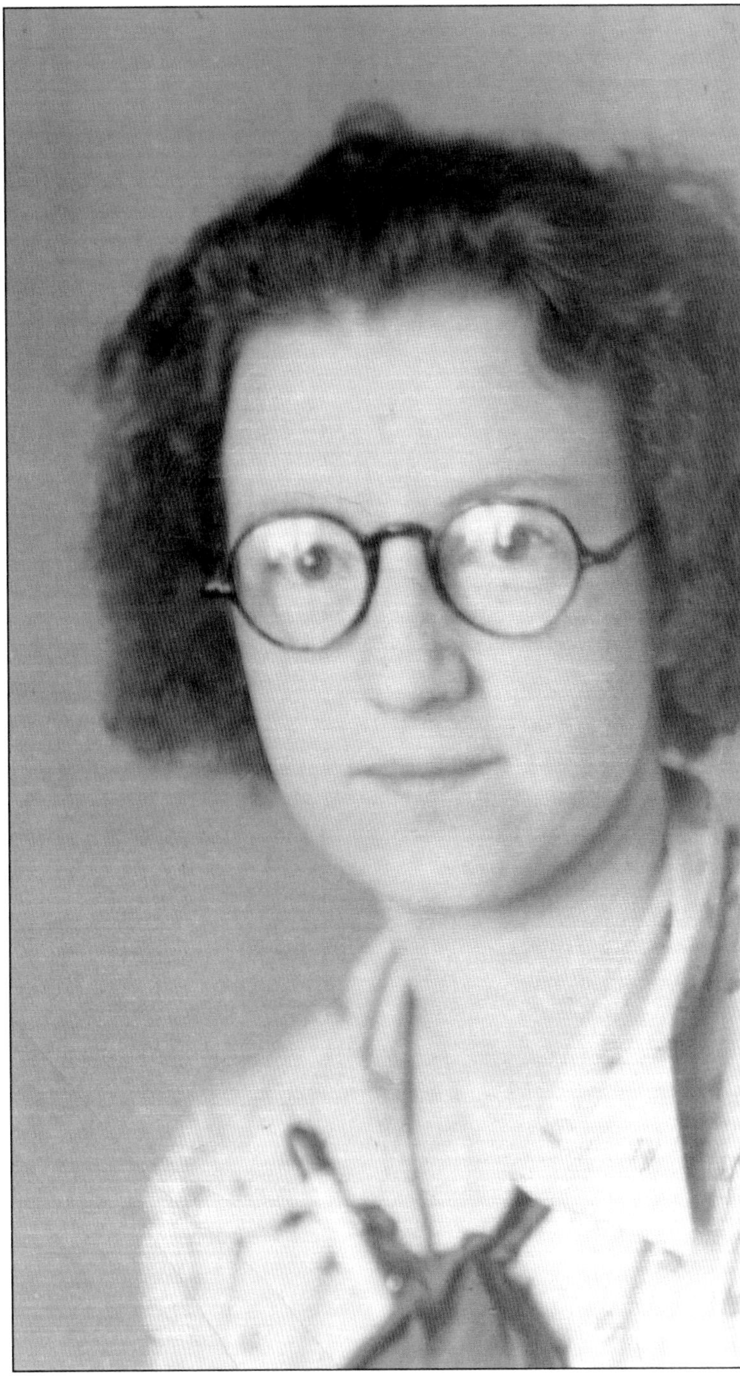

Katherine Powers Gallegos was born in Las Vegas, New Mexico. At the age of 19, she moved to Los Lunas to live with her sister Ruth, who was married to Sheriff Joe Tondre. Katherine began her teaching career at the grade school in Los Lentes. She taught in the Los Lunas schools for 60 years and ended her career as the director of instruction for the school system. Katherine Gallegos often purchased clothing, food, and Christmas gifts for local children using her own funds. (Courtesy of Ruth Perea.)

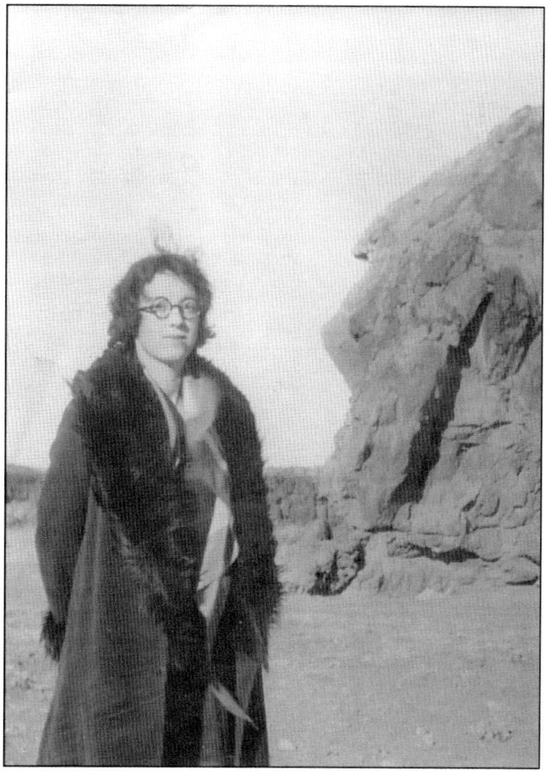

In this 1926 photograph, Katherine Powers stands at Laguna Pueblo. In 1927, Katherine and Eligio Gallegos were married, and they were together for almost 60 years. They had four children: Julie Nesbit, Stephen Gallegos, Rosalie Douglas, and Ruth Perea. (By Eligio Gallegos, courtesy of Ruth Perea.)

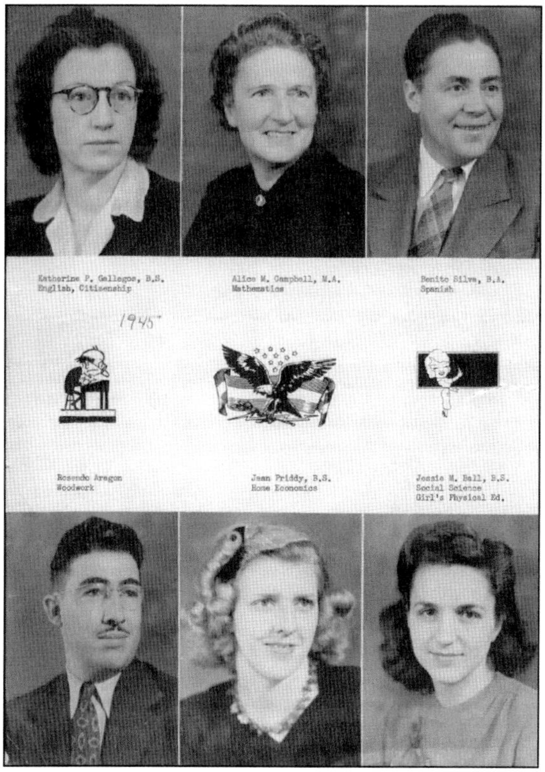

Katherine Gallegos taught English and citizenship at Los Lunas High School. She is shown in the upper left photograph on this page from the 1945 Los Lunas High School yearbook. Fellow faculty members Alice Campbell, Benito Silva, Rosendo Aragón, Jean Priddy, and Jessie Ball are also shown. (Courtesy of Ruth Perea.)

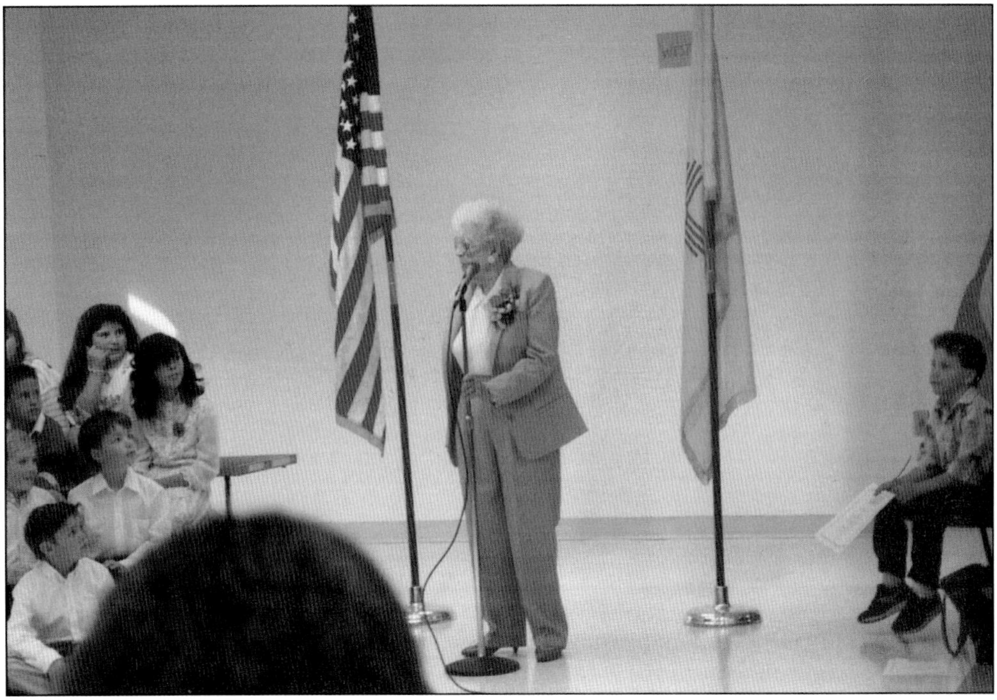

Built in 1990, the new elementary school was named for Katherine Gallegos. A "name the school" petition was circulated among school district staff, students, and parents to choose "the exemplary educator in the Los Lunas Schools." A great majority chose Katherine Gallegos. When she spoke at the dedication ceremony for the school, she joked, "I thought you had to be dead to get such an honor." (Courtesy of Ruth Perea.)

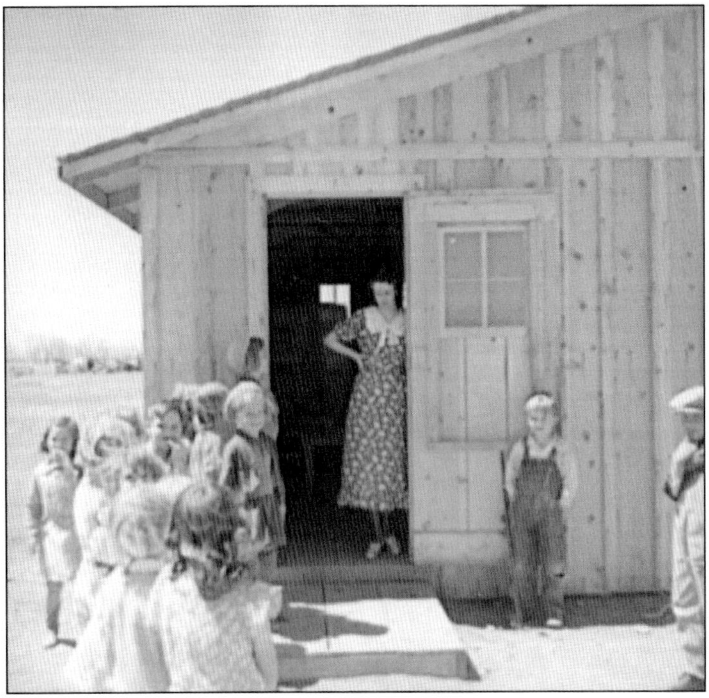

The first school in Bosque Farms was the wood-frame building shown here. It served until a permanent school could be constructed of adobe. (Courtesy of the Library of Congress, Negative No. 8b27438u.)

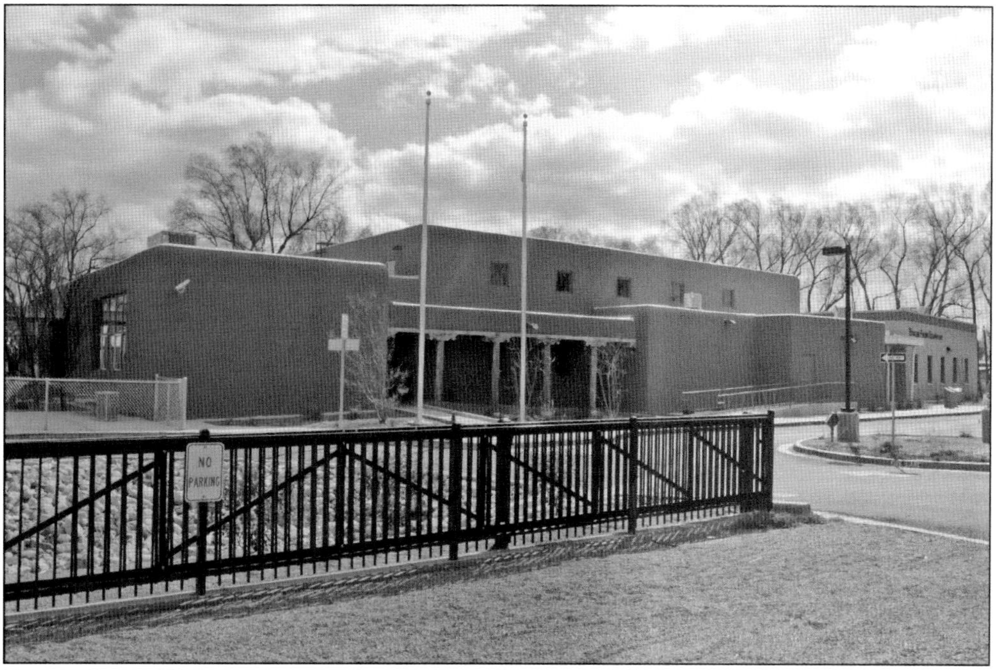

Bosque Farms Elementary School, constructed as part of the Bosque Farms Project in 1936, was extensively remodeled and expanded in 2011. The renovation retained the architectural integrity of the original building while still meeting the needs of a modern educational facility. (Author's collection.)

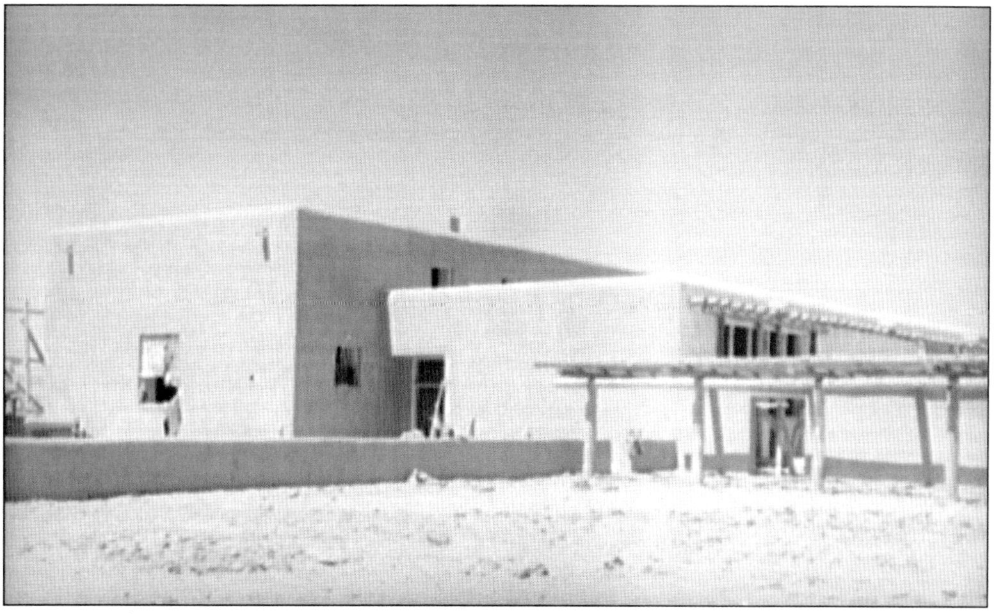

Constructed in 1936 as part of the federal Bosque Farms Resettlement Project, the Bosque Farms Elementary School is shown here nearing completion. This school is still in use today and recently underwent a significant restoration, renovation, and expansion. The new addition to the school honors the Pueblo style of architecture, seen in the original building. (Courtesy of the Library of Congress, Negative No. 8b38339u.)

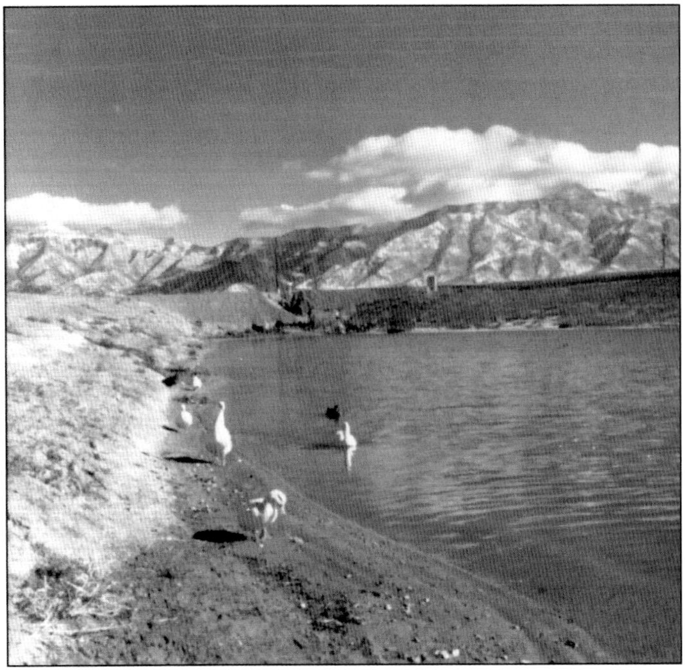

Although it has been dried up and filled in for many years, there was once a man-made lake at Meadow Lake, a small community just east of Los Lunas. This 1972 photograph shows the Manzano Mountains in the background. (Courtesy of the Valencia County Historical Society.)

Meadow Lake was stocked with fish, and fishing contests were held on a regular basis. These anglers are participating in the Meadow Lake Fish-O-Rama in 1971. (Courtesy of the Valencia County Historical Society.)

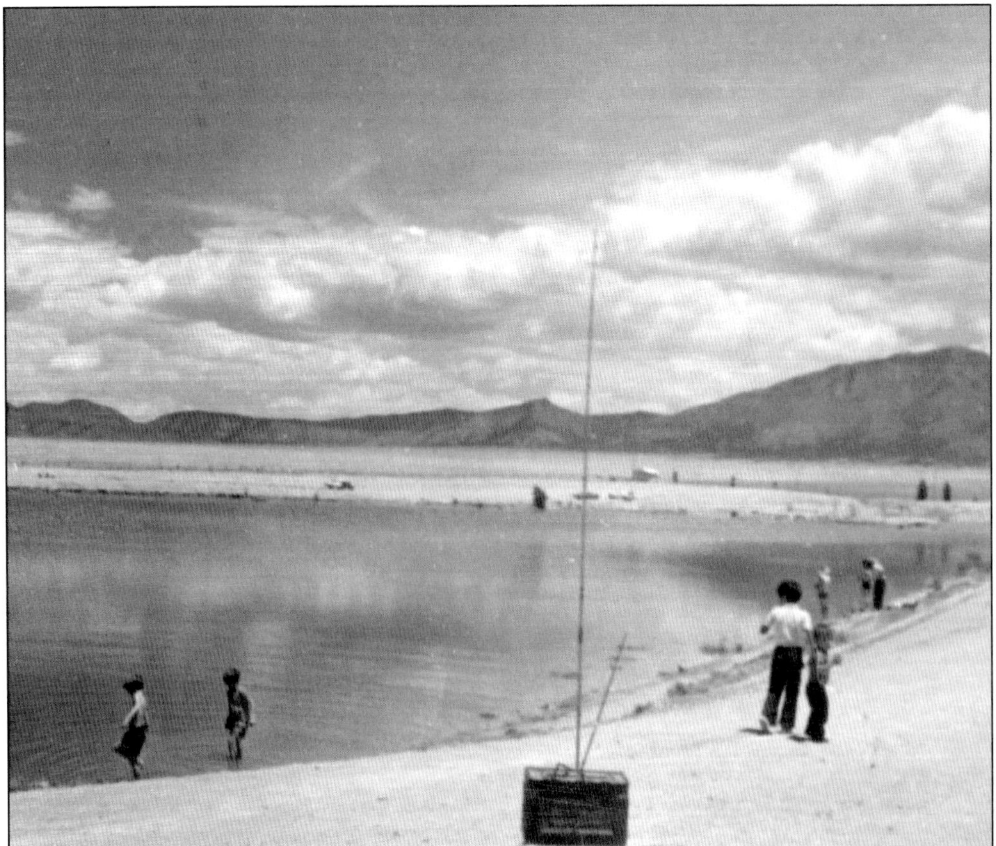

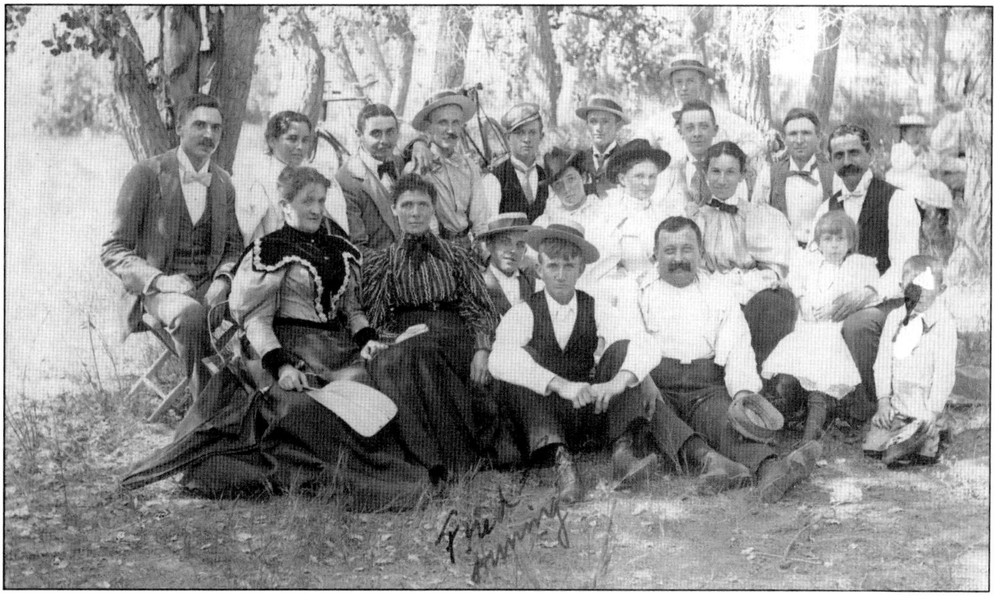

Gathered for an outing around 1890 in the bosque (a forested area along the river) are members of several prominent Valencia County families. From left to right are (first row, seated on the ground) Fred Huning and Louis B. Huning; (second row) Henrika Busch Huning, Mrs. Goebel, two unidentified, Emma Huning, Nina Otero and unidentified; (third row) Charles Reinken, two unidentified, Paul B. Dalies, John Becker Jr., L.C. Becker, Carl Huning, and two unidentified. The person standing behind the seated figures to the right is also unidentified. (Courtesy of the Huning family.)

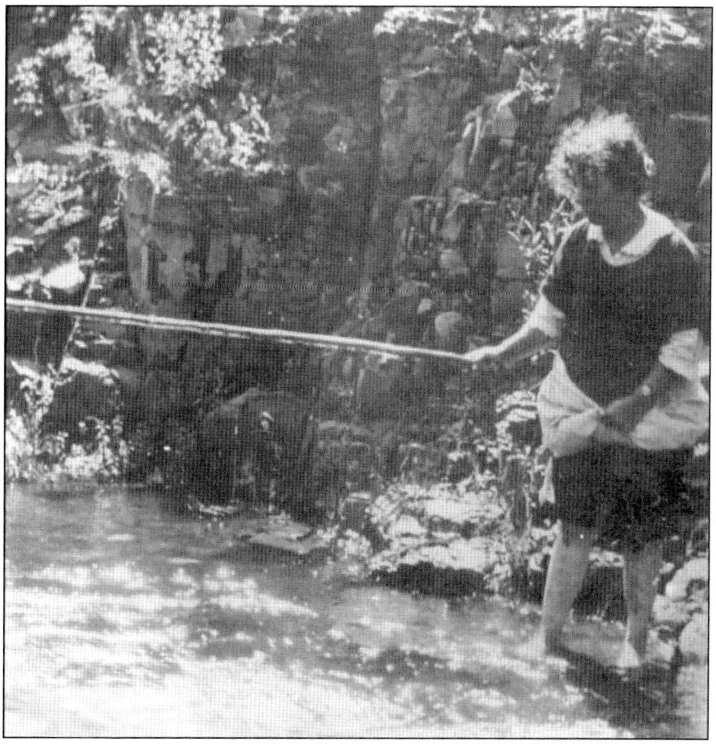

Fishing was a popular pastime for Los Lunas residents. The Rio Grande and the clear ditches maintained by the Middle Rio Grande Conservancy District provided good fishing for catfish and carp. There were also excellent trout-fishing streams in the mountains far north of Los Lunas. This photograph shows Josephita Otero, wife of Eduardo Otero, fishing in the Jémez Mountains. (Courtesy of Barbara Bergère Nau.)

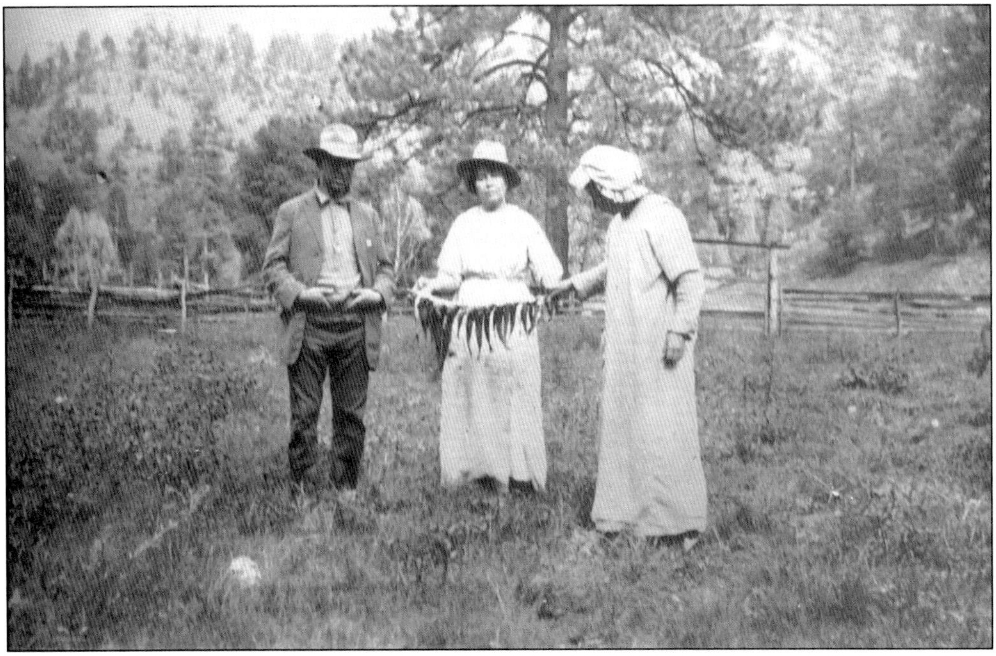

Josephita Otero shows off a string of trout she caught in the Jémez Mountains near one of the Otero sheep camps. On the left is her husband, Eduardo "Lalo" Otero. Nene, the nanny for Josephita's son Teddy Otero, is on the right. (Courtesy of Barbara Bergère Nau.)

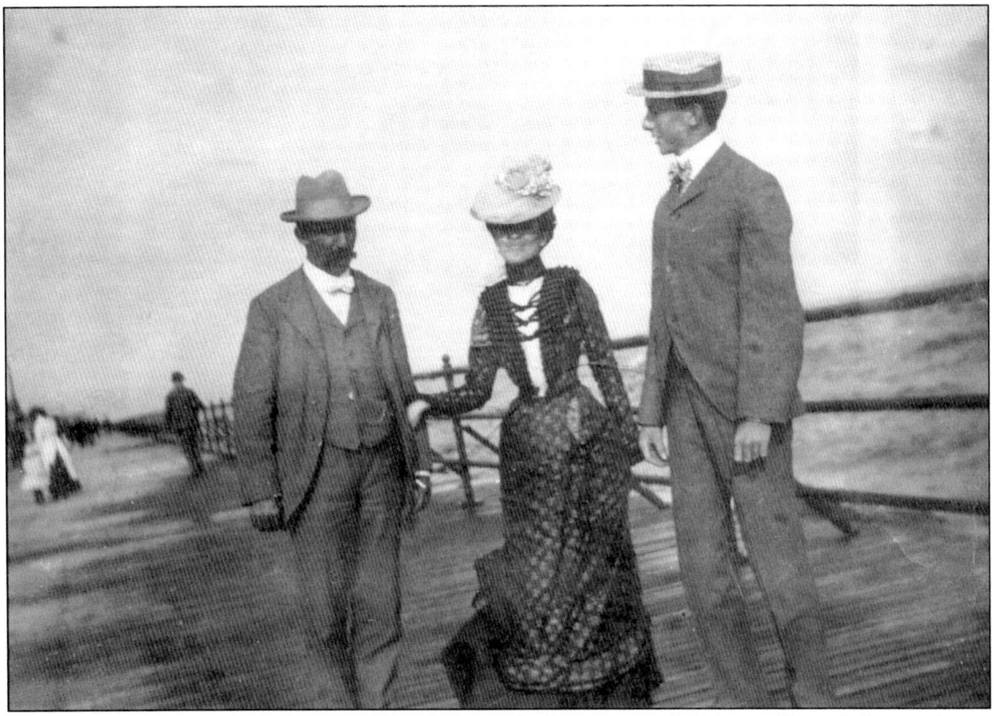

Prominent Los Lunas families often traveled east for business and pleasure. From left to right on the boardwalk in Atlantic City, New Jersey, are Solomon Luna; his wife, Adelaida Otero Luna; and an unidentified gentleman. (Courtesy of Los Lunas Museum of Heritage and Arts.)

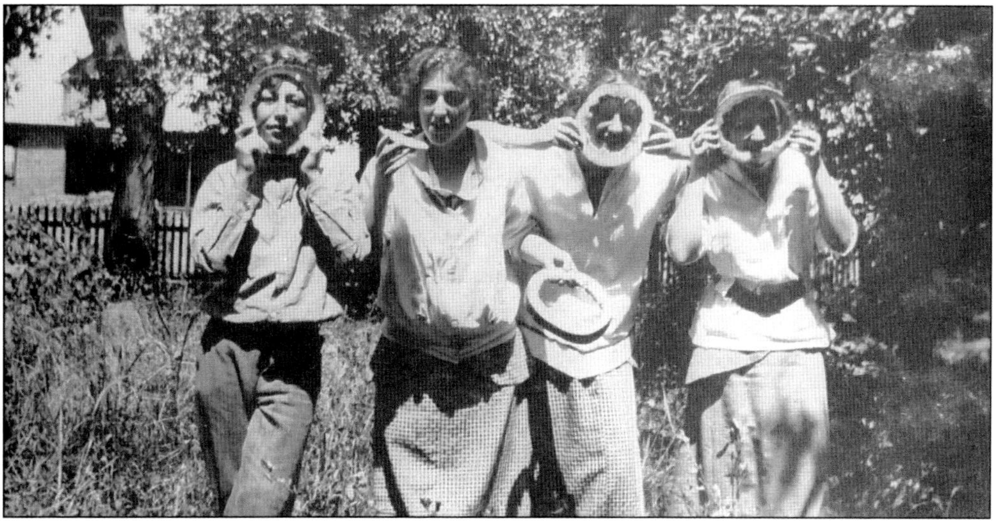

Teddy Otero (left) and three unidentified friends have fun with watermelon rinds. (Courtesy of Barbara Bergère Nau.)

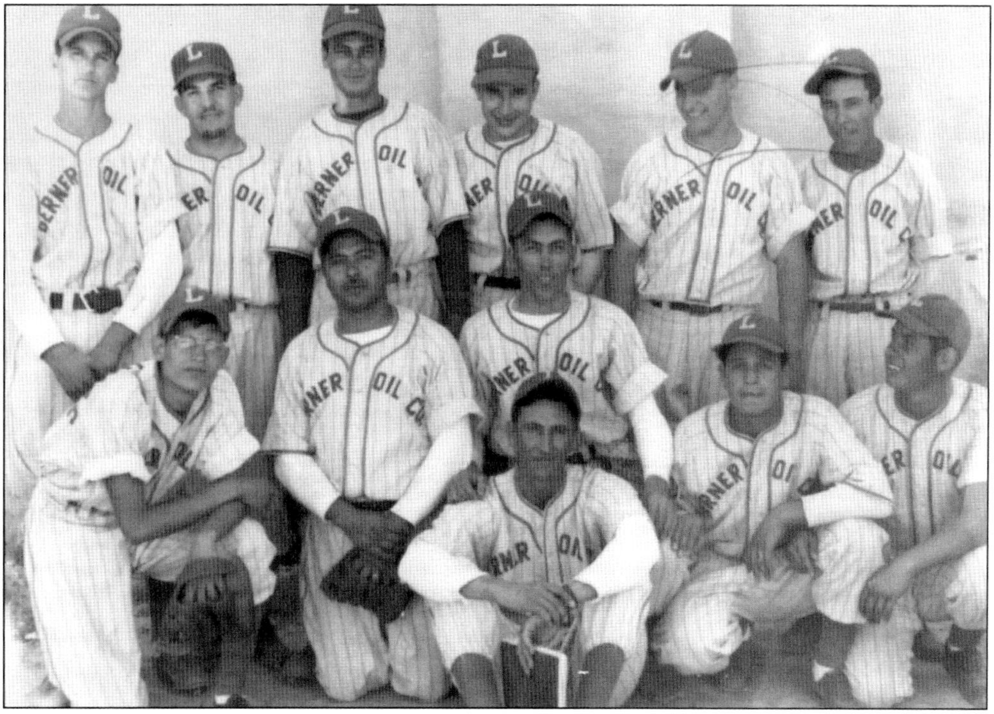

Active in the 1950s, this semiprofessional baseball team was sponsored by Bert Ball Sr., who owned a gas station on Highway 314 where Mountain States Towing Company is located today. The following are from left to right: (first row) Emiliano Castillo Jr.; (second row) Alvarado Romero, Vivian Otero, Tony Vialpando, Eloy Garley, and Joe Aragón; (third row) Fred Romero, C.B. Chávez, Tibo Gallegos, Eloy Romero, D.D. Romero Jr., and Joe "Wedo" Perea. Baseball was hugely popular in Los Lunas, and there was keen competition with surrounding towns, including Tomé and Belen. (Courtesy of Barbara Arnold.)